ABOUT CHURCHILL: The Playwright and the Work

Author and Series Editor: Emeritus Professor Philip Roberts was Professor of Drama and Theatre Studies, and Director of the Workshop Theatre in the University of Leeds from 1998 to 2004. Educated at Oxford and Edinburgh, he held posts in the Universities of Newcastle and Sheffield before arriving in Leeds. His publications include: *Absalom and Achitophel and Other Poems* (Collins, 1973), *The Diary of Sir David Hamilton, 1709–1714* (Clarendon Press, 1975), *Edward Bond: A Companion to the Plays* (Theatre Quarterly Pubs., 1978), *Edward Bond: Theatre Poems and Songs* (Methuen, 1978), *Bond on File* (Methuen, 1985), *The Royal Court Theatre, 1965–1972* (Routledge, 1986), *Plays without Wires* (Sheffield Academic Press, 1989), *The Royal Court Theatre and the Modern Stage* (CUP, 1999), *Taking Stock: The Theatre of Max Stafford-Clark* (with Max Stafford-Clark) (Nick Hern Books, 2007).

Series Editor: Richard Boon is Professor of Drama and Director of Research in the University of Hull. He is the author of a number of studies of modern British political theatre, including *Brenton the Playwright* (Methuen, 1991), and is co-editor of *Theatre Matters: Performance and Culture on the World Stage* (CUP, 1998). He is also author of *About Hare: The Playwright and the Work* (Faber and Faber, 2003) and editor of *The Cambridge Companion to David Hare* (CUP, 2007).

ABOUT CHURCHILL
The Playwright and the Work

Philip Roberts

faber and faber

First published in 2008
by Faber and Faber Limited
3 Queen Square London WC1N 3AU

Typeset by Wordsense Limited
Printed in England by CPI Bookmarque Ltd, Croydon

A CIP record for this book
is available from the British Library

ISBN 978-0-571-229628

2 4 6 8 10 9 7 5 3 1

For Stephen Wall

Contents

Editors' Note

There are few theatre books which allow direct access to the playwright or to those whose business it is to translate the script into performance. These volumes aim to deal directly with the writer and with other theatre workers (directors, actors, designers and similar figures) who realise in performance the words on the page.

The subjects of the series are some of the most important and influential writers from post-war British and Irish theatre. Each volume contains an introduction which sets the work of the writer in the relevant historical, social and political context, followed by a digest of interviews and other material which allows the writer, in his own words, to trace his evolution as a dramatist. Some of this material is new, as is, in large part, the material especially gathered from the writers' collaborators and fellow theatre workers. The volumes conclude with annotated bibliographies. In all, we hope the books will provide a wealth of information in accessible form, and real insight into some of the major dramatists of our day.

Foreword

We must find a balance that doesn't impose form and poetry unrelated to the details of life nor pile up details without finding form and poetry. Form is in itself a means of expression, and a good play is like music in the reappearance of different themes, changes of pace, conflicts and harmonies; and fuller use of form should make plays not less but more true to life. (Caryl Churchill, 1960)

. . . what gets lost is Shakespeare's restlessness, his unusual development as a writer, his daring refusal to stick to what had brought him success. His less successful experiments have as much to tell us about the nature of his accomplishments as his masterpieces do. (James Shapiro, 2005)

So many people who are not creative artists don't understand that art is hard work. (Stephen Sondheim, 2006)

It's as though the play [*Drunk Enough to Say I Love You?*] combines the free 'late manner' of a great artist with the fragmented modernism of Churchill's early work, and there's the sense of abiding preoccupations newly considered. A deep form of originality is to go back with fresh insights to origins. So it's in a manifold sense of the term that one might describe Caryl Churchill as a true original. (Paul Taylor, 2006)

Like Penelope: picking and unpicking. (Audrey Niffenegger, 2005)

Abbreviations

Plays: 1	Caryl Churchill, *Plays: 1* (Methuen, 1996)
Plays: 2	Caryl Churchill, *Plays: Two* (Methuen, 1990)
Plays: 3	Caryl Churchill, *Plays: 3* (Nick Hern Books, 1998)
Shorts	Caryl Churchill, *Shorts* (Nick Hern Books, 1990)
Chambers	C. Chambers, *Peggy: The Life of Margaret Ramsay, Play Agent* (Nick Hern Books, 1997)
Cousin	G. Cousin, *Churchill the Playwright* (Methuen, 1989)
Doty and Harbin	G. A. Doty and B. J. Harbin (eds), *Inside the Royal Court Theatre, 1956–1981: Artists Talk* (Louisiana State University Press, 1990)
Fitzsimmons	L. Fitzsimmons, *File on Churchill* (Methuen, 1989)
Hanna	G. Hanna, *Monstrous Regiment: A Collective Celebration* (Nick Hern Books, 1991)
Itzin	C. Itzin, *Stages in the Revolution* (Eyre Methuen, 1980)

O'Malley   J. F. O'Malley, 'Caryl Churchill, David
                      Mercer and Tom Stoppard: A Study of
                      Contemporary British Dramatists who
                      have written for Radio, Television and
                      Stage' (unpublished Ph.D., Florida State
                      University, 1974)

Ritchie   R. Ritchie, *The Joint Stock Book: The
                      Making of a Theatre Collective* (Methuen,
                      1987)

Roberts/Stafford-Clark   P. Roberts and M. Stafford-Clark,
                      *Taking Stock: The Theatre of Max
                      Stafford-Clark* (Nick Hern Books, 2007)

Chronology

1938   Born in London.

1948   Family living in Montreal, Canada.

1957–60 Read English Language and Literature, Lady Margaret Hall, University of Oxford.

1958   Wrote *Downstairs*, a one-act play, staged (in November) by Oriel College Dramatic Society. The play went forward to the *Sunday Times*/National Union of Students Drama Festival the following year.

1960   *Having a Wonderful Time* staged by the Oxford Players at the amateur Questors' Theatre in August.

1961   *You've No Need to Be Frightened*, radio play, recorded by Exeter College Dramatic Society in the spring. Churchill's first performed radio play won the competition. Peggy Ramsay became Churchill's agent until her death in 1991.

1962   *Easy Death* by the University's Experimental Theatre Club performed at the Oxford Playhouse in March.
          The Ants, her first professional radio production, performed on the Third Programme, directed John Tydeman.

1967   *Lovesick*, Radio 3, April, directed Tydeman.

1968   *The Marriage of Toby's Idea of Angela and Toby's Idea of Angela's Idea of Toby* (unperformed stage play).
          Identical Twins, Radio 3, November, directed Tydeman.

1971   *Abortive*, Radio 3, February, directed Tydeman.
Not . . . Not . . . Not . . . Not Enough Oxygen,
Radio 3, March, directed Tydeman.

1972   *The Hospital at the Time of the Revolution*
(unperformed stage play). *Schreber's Nervous
Illness*, Radio 3, July, directed Tydeman.
The Judge's Wife, BBC 2, October, directed James
Fechman.
Henry's Past, Radio 3, December, directed
Tydeman.
Owners, Royal Court Theatre Upstairs,
December, directed Nicholas Wright. Opened
Mercer–Shaw Theater, New York, May 1973.

1973   *Perfect Happiness*, Radio 3, September, directed
Tydeman. Staged by Soho Poly, lunchtime, March
1975.

1974   *Turkish Delight*, BBC 2, April, directed Herbert
Wise.

1974–5   First non-male Resident Dramatist at the Royal
Court.

1975   *Objections to Sex and Violence*, Royal Court
Downstairs, January, directed Tydeman.
Moving Clocks Go Slow, Royal Court Theatre
Upstairs, June, directed John Ford.
Strange Days with Joan Mills and children from
the William Tyndale School, Islington, July.
Founder member, Theatre Writers' Group, later
Theatre Writers' Union.
Save It for the Minister (with Mary O'Malley and
Cherry Potter), BBC 2, July.

1976   *Light Shining in Buckinghamshire*, Traverse
Theatre, Edinburgh, with Joint Stock Theatre
Group, September, directed Max Stafford-Clark.
Touring, then at the Theatre Upstairs, September.
Vinegar Tom, Humberside Theatre, with
Monstrous Regiment, October, directed Pam

Brighton. Then at the ICA, December, and the
Half Moon Theatre, January 1977.

1977   *Traps*, Theatre Upstairs, January, directed John
Ashford.

1978   *Floorshow* (with Michelene Wandor, Bryony
Lavery and David Bradford), for Monstrous
Regiment, Theatre Royal, Stratford East, January.
The After-Dinner Joke, BBC 1, February, directed
Colin Bucksey.
The Legion Hall Bombing, BBC 1, August, direct-
ed Roland Joffé (both Churchill's and Joffé's
names were removed from the credits at their
request).
Seagulls (unperformed stage play; given a
rehearsed reading, Royal Court, 2002).

1979   *Cloud Nine*, with Joint Stock, February,
Dartington College of Arts, directed Max
Stafford-Clark. Then, after a tour, Royal Court,
March and New York, May 1981, for 971 perfor-
mances.

1980   *Three More Sleepless Nights*, Soho Poly, June,
directed Les Waters. Then Theatre Upstairs,
August.

1982   *Crimes*, BBC 1, April, directed Stuart Burge.
Top Girls, Royal Court Downstairs, August,
directed Max Stafford-Clark. Then Public
Theater, New York, December; returned to Royal
Court, February 1983.
In 1982–3 Obies, Churchill named 'Outstanding
Writer' and both UK and US companies named
'Outstanding Ensemble Performances'.

1983   *Fen*, University of Essex, with Joint Stock,
January, directed Les Waters. Then Almeida,
London, February; Public Theater, New York,
May; Royal Court, July.
Churchill won the Susan Smith Blackburn Prize.

Elected to Council of the English Stage Company, December.

1984 *Softcops*, RSC at the Barbican, January, directed Howard Davies.

Contributed to *Midday Sun*, ICA, May, directed John Ashford.

1986 *A Mouthful of Birds*, with Joint Stock, Birmingham Repertory Theatre, written by Churchill and David Lan, choreographed Ian Spink, directed Ian Spink and Les Waters. Touring, then Royal Court, November.

1987 *Serious Money*, Royal Court, March, directed Max Stafford-Clark. Transferred to Wyndham's Theatre, then Public Theater, New York, November. A second Susan Smith Blackburn Prize. Won a *Time Out* Award; 'Best Play' from *City Limits*; 'Best Comedy', *Evening Standard*; 'Best Play', *Plays and Players*; 'Best Play', Olivier Awards, Obie Award. *Serious Money* first Churchill play on Broadway at Royale Theater.

1988 *Fugue*, June, choreographed and directed Ian Spink, June, Channel 4.

1989 *Icecream*, Royal Court, April, directed Max Stafford-Clark. *Hot Fudge* given a 'performance reading', Theatre Upstairs, May. *Ice Cream with Hot Fudge*, directed Les Waters, Public Theater, New York, April 1990.

Resigned from English Stage Company's Council over issue of commercial sponsorship.

1990 *Mad Forest*, performed by students at the Central School of Speech and Drama, directed Mark Wing-Davey, June at Central; September at the National Theatre of Romania; October at the Royal Court. With American cast, and directed Wing-Davey, it opened at the New York Theater Workshop, November 1991, and won Obies for both direction and design.

1991   *Lives of the Great Poisoners*, Arnolfini, Bristol, February, directed James Macdonald, with Ian Spink and composer Orlando Gough.

1994   *The Skriker*, National Theatre, January, with Second Stride, directed Les Waters. Then Public Theater, New York, April 1996.

Thyestes, Royal Court Upstairs, June, directed James Macdonald.

1997   *Hotel*, for Second Stride, Schauspielhaus, Hannover, April, directed and choreographed Ian Spink. Then The Place, London, April.

This Is a Chair, Royal Court, directed Stephen Daldry.

Blue Heart, for Out of Joint, August, directed Max Stafford-Clark. Touring, then Royal Court, September. Brooklyn Academy of Music, January 1999.

1998   Three plays by Maeterlinck (*The Intruder; Interior; The Death of Tintagiles*) translated Churchill, used in a course on site-specific theatre by Les Waters for the MFA (Master of Fine Arts) programme, University of California, San Diego. Repeated 2002.

1999   Directed Wallace Shawn's *Our Late Night* as a production without décor, October, at the New Ambassadors Theatre, temporarily occupied by the Royal Court.

One of the many signatories in a letter to the *Guardian*, 10 April, deploring British government's imposition of sanctions in the former Yugoslavia.

2000   *Far Away*, Royal Court, November, directed Stephen Daldry. Transferred to the Albany Theatre, January 2001, and to the New York Theater Workshop, November 2002.

2002	*A Number*, Royal Court, September, directed Stephen Daldry. Transferred to the Albery, February 2003, and to the New York Theater Workshop, December 2004.

Accompanied at the Court by a season of 'Caryl Churchill Events', which included productions without décor of *This Is a Chair; Not . . . Not . . . Not . . . Not Enough Oxygen* and *Identical Twins*; and rehearsed readings of *Seagulls, Three More Sleepless Nights* and *Owners*.

A Number given special performance, 4 November, in aid of the Stop the War Coalition. The play won 'Best Play' at the *Evening Standard* Awards.

Plants and Ghosts, September, Siobhan Davies Dance Company.

2003   *Iraq. Doc*, Royal Court, November, part of 'A Royal Welcome' (for the visit of the US president to the UK).

Part of an estimated half million-strong protest march against the attack on Iraq, February.

Joined the Lysistrata Project in Parliament Square as anti-war demonstration. Readings of the play and the action co-ordinated with the same event at 830 venues in 49 countries.

2004   Appended signature in two letters to the *Guardian* of 25 March and 16 April, as part of the Palestine Solidarity Campaign, protesting American-backed Israeli activity in Gaza and the West Bank.

2005   *A Dream Play*, National Theatre, February, directed Katie Mitchell.

Part of a conference, September, University of Oxford, of thirty artists and thirty scientists brought together to discuss a cultural engagement with climate change.

2006   Introduced two leading scientists on climate change at the Royal Court as part of Court events on the subject.
We Turned On the Light, text for composer Orlando Gough, BBC Proms, July.

2007   *Drunk Enough to Say I Love You?*, Royal Court, November, directed James Macdonald. Public Theater, New York, March 2008.

Preface

This book divides into two parts. The first offers an analysis of Caryl Churchill's work from 1959 to the present day; and the second contains a selection of material both by and about Churchill and her work.

The analysis in Part 1 runs roughly decade by decade, although it should not be supposed that this is anything other than a convenient way of dividing up a very large body of work. It would be simplistic in the extreme, given Churchill's habitual and steadily evolving refashioning of form throughout her career, to attempt such a neat categorisation. Of all modern dramatists, she is the most likely to upend conventional expectation.

Chapter 1 – 1958–1972 – includes some account of a number of unpublished plays, and is necessarily more descriptive here about pieces otherwise unavailable. The chapter contains plays that indicate very clearly that the approaches and analyses appearing later are already in train. These works range in their form strikingly, and their experimentation is evidence of a major figure developing. Chapter 2 charts the movement of Churchill steadily into a theatre writer. The radio and television plays to a large extent drop away, and the collaboration with the Joint Stock Theatre Group and Monstrous Regiment open a world of possibilities both for Churchill and for the companies. It is here that her long-standing artistic relationship with Max Stafford-Clark begins. Chapter 3 sees Churchill's trademark of overlapping dialogue beginning to emerge, as she becomes preoccupied in the early eighties with the relationship between words, music and dance. By the mid-eighties, the work includes not only these elements powerfully expressed but also a brilliant account of the financial life of London, written in verse. The nineties (chapter 4) continue the experimentation. A play with students, a collaboration with a choreographer and a composer, and the arrival of what she termed her 'fairy play', *The Skriker*, many years in the making, all appear within the first half of the decade. The second half sees theatre work enquiring what works in theatre. The current decade's work (in chapter 5) is intensely concerned with our relationship to global events, and how to express that relationship: war, the march of technology, the destruction of the planet. As always, though, with Caryl Churchill, swimming close to the surface are matters observable in her earliest plays. They are constantly revisited.

Part 2 of *About Churchill* is called 'Voices and Documents'. A good deal of it is previously unpublished and drawn from interviews, and correspondence between Churchill and myself. Here are comment and analysis from actors, directors, designers, dancers, choreographers and writers – all of whom have worked in some capacity on a Churchill piece. There is also published and unpublished work by Churchill. This part runs from 1975 to 2007.

Note: Any unattributed material is from correspondence or interviews with the writer of this book.

Philip Roberts

Introduction

In November 1960, the periodical *The Twentieth Century* published a piece by a relatively unknown writer called Caryl Churchill. The title was 'Not Ordinary, Not Safe'. Recently an undergraduate at Oxford, she had had two plays – *Downstairs* and *Having a Wonderful Time* – staged, respectively, by Oriel College Dramatic Society and the Oxford Players. Churchill, with characteristic modesty, described how the article came about:

> I was a friend of the editor's daughter and he wanted an edition with the views of young people on various subjects, so I think he just asked her friends. I was asked to do theatre because I'd written a few plays by then. It was after I graduated, which was 1960. It certainly wasn't something I'd have written if not asked to do something. It was still sufficiently soon after university that I probably just sat down and wrote an essay . . .[1]

The piece reviews recent theatre in the wake of the establishment of the English Stage Company at the Royal Court Theatre in 1956. Churchill has said of this period:

> I first knew about the Royal Court in 1956, when I had just come back from Canada, where I had been living for quite a long time. I went to the first production of *Look Back in Anger* when I was about seventeen, and I remember liking that and having no idea that it was anything new. I mean, I didn't know what plays were like . . . I certainly thought of the Court as the only theatre there was to work for. It was very different then from what the situation would be were I

just starting now, because writers have a lot of places to go.[2]

What drives the review is a passionate belief that continual radical change in the way theatre is written and performed is vital for its salvation. As she contemplates work by Lessing, Wesker, Pinter, Beckett and Osborne, her response is:

> Of course we're glad it's been said. When *Look Back in Anger* came out it was exciting, but already the working-class intellectual cracking at his wife's caricatured Daddy is a stock character. We know the English are still snobbish about accents, we're not happy about the British Empire, suburban life is often dull, and many middle-aged men are unfulfilled. We can't communicate with each other, have a lot of illusions and don't know what if anything life is about. All right. Where do we go from here?

Churchill's conviction is that contemporary drama, having 'broken open the conventions of drawing-room comedy, is solidifying too soon into clichés almost equally inadequate to expressing life as we know it'.

The plea is for responsiveness to change: 'Playwrights don't give answers, they ask questions. We need to find new questions, which may help us answer the old ones or make them unimportant, and this means new subjects and new forms'.

In effect, the article sets out the writer's stall. It becomes a kind of manifesto in its assertion of what must be aimed for:

> At the moment everything we have is at the expense of something else: poetry without plots, songs and stylisation without observation, naturalism without imagination, character without action, slice of life without form. We must find a balance that doesn't impose form and poetry unrelated to the details of life nor pile up details without finding form and poetry. Form is in itself a means of expression, and a good play is like music in the reappearance of

different themes, changes of pace, conflicts and harmonies; and fuller use of form should make plays not less but more true to life.

The search for what Churchill calls 'a good balance between life and art in contemporary drama' was to occupy a writing life of, so far, towards fifty years. As I write this, her latest play, *Drunk Enough to Say I Love You?* has been playing on the main stage at the Court. How Caryl Churchill arrived at this moment in 2006 is the story of this book.

Part 1

I

Downstairs to *Henry's Past*: 1958–1972

I do seem to enjoy the form of things. I enjoy finding the form that seems best to fit what I'm thinking about. I don't set out to find a bizarre way of writing. I certainly don't think that you have to force it. But, on the whole, I enjoy plays that are non-naturalistic and don't move at real time. (Caryl Churchill, 1989)

None of us know how we work! (Churchill, 1981)

Note: Some plays discussed in this chapter are unpublished. I am grateful to Caryl Churchill for the loan of: *Downstairs; You've No Need to Be Frightened; Having a Wonderful Time; Easy Death; Identical Twins; The Marriage of Toby's Idea of Angela and Toby's Idea of Angela's Idea of Toby; Henry's Past.* Quotations are reproduced exactly as typed in the original scripts.

Downstairs, Churchill's first performed play, came about because a friend of hers had wanted to direct. She therefore wrote a short play, which was performed on 4 November 1958 by Oriel College, Oxford's Dramatic Society in the inter-college 'Cuppers', a competition to discover acting talent amongst new undergraduates. It was placed third. The play went on to the *Sunday Times*/National Union of Students Drama festival in the following year. According to the *Oxford Mail*, 'Miss Caryl Churchill of Lady Margaret Hall, the authoress of *Downstairs* . . . was honoured by the adjudicator by being called up on the stage'.[1] Elsewhere, Churchill has said that she wrote a lot as a child 'and it settled to writing plays when I was at university'.[2]

The play takes place in a small first-floor flat where Susan and Alfred Johnson live, together with their son, Ted. Susan pines for what she thinks of as a utopian life in the country, and she is deeply suspicious of the family that lives downstairs. Her main animosity is reserved for Joe, the eighteen-year-old brother of Catherine:

> Look how the sky's clearing. The wireless says it's going to be rain tomorrow, but they never know do they. It's clear in the east, there's sun on the factory chimneys.
> It was awful earlier, the rain's so dirty. That boy downstairs sat on the front step all afternoon with water running all over him. He kept holding up his hands to it and singing, and nobody stopped him, his sister didn't stop him. He ought to be put away, he ought really.

When Catherine arrives upstairs with Joe, who is mute throughout, his separateness is apparent, and Susan's prejudice clear. Any sense of the unusual, the remoteness, the non-conformity of individuals is, for Susan, a state of affairs to be dealt with. She successfully stamps on a budding relationship between Ted and Catherine – indeed Ted eventually hits and then kills her – and reserves her full venom for the hapless Joe. Towards the end of the play, Joe cowers in the corner, unseen, except by Susan:

> SUSAN (*notices joe*). You little monster, you foul idiot, you're evil, evil.
> Oh . . . I wanted us all to be happy. I wanted Ted to come away to the country.
> (*joe starts to sob*)
> This is never going to end. There's always going to be that girl downstairs now and your idiot crying.

The play announces what were to become familiar preoccupations: the pain and difficulty of relationships; fear and violence towards the apparently inexplicable; idealism and longing thwarted. In a naturalistic piece, though, there is evidence of other worlds and ways of proceeding. Catherine tells an uncomprehending Susan how she deals with Joe, and how she manages a bleak existence:

Joe, will you leave them alone. He likes to touch things, he likes to feel things in his palm. He won't break them, don't worry. When he breaks things I make up stories to frighten him about dragons and bombs and he cries all day and makes Gran cry and me too. We always make up stories and put people we like in them, and people we don't like, and people we used to know.

No, you know what I used to like to do? There were always a lot of empty bottles around from Dad drinking, and I used to fill them with water, and then put dye in to make them coloured, and stand them in the window so the light shone through.

Catherine meets her violent death at the hands of Ted, who casually describes it all to his mother:

She died so easily. I knew I'd never get rid of her while she sat on the floor in the red light and as real as I am, so I hit her again. I hit her a few times. And there she was, dead. It's funny isn't it, how easy it is to end things if you really try, if you do it properly like that. We'll never be bothered by them any more, we'll be safe forever now.

Downstairs was seen by the writer John McGrath, a fellow undergraduate, and theatre director Anthony Page. McGrath's agent was Peggy Ramsay, who was to become the most important agent for British playwrights of the second half of the twentieth century. McGrath put the two in touch, and, at Ramsay's request, Churchill sent to the agent a copy of *Having a Wonderful Time*, written in 1959, a television play called *A Shout in the Street* and her article for *The Twentieth Century*. The two met up in February 1961. The meeting, according to Churchill, lasted twenty minutes, and the two formed a partnership which was to last until Ramsay's death in 1991.[3]

One of the plays which went to Peggy Ramsay, *Having a Wonderful Time*, was performed by the Oxford Players at the Questors' Theatre in London on 5–6 August 1960. Amongst the cast were the future television personality Esther Rantzen and the playwright John Spurling. A central figure is Paul, who works in Paris, and who saves up his money for fifty weeks of the year in order to holiday in the south of France for the remaining two. He stays in a hotel, run by a couple, their daughter Anne, her cousin Charles, and Jeanine. The piece employs a range of theatrical devices to show its story: from a loose free verse to a single spot on an otherwise dark stage, to direct address to the audience (from Paul). The set consists of the dining room, with the kitchen set in another part of the stage. External scenes are played downstage. In one scene there is jazz in the background. As a stage direction puts it: 'In the following scene some of the words are sung, or said to the music, others spoken across the music.' The variety of exploration apparent in this very early play suggests a trajectory of experiment and no little daring. Paul is a world-weary observer of the scene he sees every year:

> Of course she reminds me.
> God, the monotony.
> Every second of every year
> There's sickly sweet seventeen somewhere,
> and the calm girls of twenty and anxious
> girls of twenty-five
> have all been seventeen
> and charmed to be alive.
> They've the same, almost ingenuous
> turn of the head, and delight
> in their astonishing prettiness
> and dress and decorate
> themselves like their own dolls.
> I mean, why bother?

As the play progresses, it becomes clear that Paul likes to manipulate the lives of others. He decides to liberate Anne from the attentions of John, a local farmer. John's obsession is to acquire more land, and to own Anne. Both are of equal importance to him. Paul 'liberates' Anne, only to see her beg John to have her back, to regain her ordinary life, to Paul's scorn. But it is Paul who loses and Paul whose life is arid. The group he seeks to modify ultimately wishes to live in its own way, with its faults, sillinesses and happiness. Paul has no device powerful enough to combat their reality. Even if their reality consists of dreaming. Cousin Charles, regarded by most as quite useless, is a storyteller and lives in his own world. He tells Anne about a car:

> So everyone thought it was a cadillac,
> and really it was a dragon in disguise,
> big teeth and big headlight eyes.
> And so he parked
> close to the beach, and suddenly
> feel on the brown
> bodies the sun
> was cooking and carried them under the sea . . .
> ANNE: Go on,
> what about the boy with seaweed hair?
> CHARLES: The dragon never found him. He's still looking
> on the edge of the sea.

Against this lyricism is the desperate assertion by Paul of what a wonderful time he has each year:

> People we've hurt frequently,
> frequently meet us, the clumsy town
> is our clumsiness, the grass is green
> and this moves us, inevitably.
> Like the stars. Like some girls.
> Like something you might dream
> And you wake up and just for a moment it seems
> as if something is lost.
> Betrayed, almost.
> Ridiculous,
> then it all falls

7

into place, you wake up
completely, and luckily
you know perfectly well
you've had a wonderful time,
just like you always do.
And next year too. We will. Oh yes, we will.

In the same year as the writing of *Having a Wonderful Time*,
1959, Churchill wrote a short radio play called *You've No
Need to Be Frightened*. It was recorded by Exeter College
Dramatic Society as an entry for the university 'Sound
Cuppers' competition in the spring of 1961, and it won. This is
Churchill's first radio play to receive a production. It is written
essentially for two voices, although a third figure, a boy, has
two lines. There is also an important silent guest, about whom
we are never told, but the centre of the piece is about John and
his unnamed wife. The story of the central relationship is told
to the guest. The wife lives a comfortable domestic existence.
She bakes her own bread, milks her own goats and keeps chickens. Her husband is obsessed with the mountain outside, which
towers above the village. He declares his intention of climbing
it soon. As the play opens, John is outside, hiding behind the
garden shed with the guest, and talking both of the mountain
and of his wife: 'Is she still there? Yes, still washing up, washing up the great blue bowl and the three plates. She does it so
slowly, round and round that bowl in the dirty water and with
such love in her fingers, and she wipes it slowly 'til it's dry. You
can't reach her when she's doing that, she holds that bowl like
a child.'

The minutiae of ordinary living are sufficient for her. John
daydreams about an alternative, but his wife is more pragmat-
ic: 'He's always wanting to go up his hill, and he'll break his
neck if he does. He's got no business walking about on hills. Up
to the stars I think he wants to go, and he won't get there,
mountains aren't all that high'. The play charts the detail of a
relationship with precision and sympathy. At the conclusion,

John goes to the aid of a sick villager or, perhaps, to climb his mountain. The wife has a final speech:

> It may be a week, or two, or three. He may not come back
> at all, it's a big mountain, and if he does get up he's just as
> likely to go down the other side and on and on.
> I'm glad he took his coat. It's cold up there you know in the
> snow at night.
> But you will stay 'til tomorrow. He might come back after
> all, he may not go up the mountain now I've let him, he
> may come back from the village tomorrow with a bag of
> flour for me. I'm baking tomorrow, he'll like the fresh bread
> if he comes back.
> But if he doesn't come tomorrow, you needn't stay. As long
> as he thinks you're here, he can go on up his mountain and
> not worry about leaving me alone.
> Come and look just for a moment out the kitchen window.
> You can see the light of the hut from here at night. Do you
> see? On the edge of the trees. That's where he'll be, that's
> where I've let him go.

An emerging characteristic of Churchill's writing is a reluctance to finalise or close down a particular line of enquiry. This results in deliberate ambivalence about some of her characters. John may climb his mountain; the mute guest may go; the wife without a name may understand the nature of John's daydream or she may be content not to have a name and live life her way. Or not. The play's title comes from the wife's anxiety during a storm and:

> I woke up in the night and the room was suddenly lit up,
> and I reached out to him and I said, John are you there?
> And he said of course I'm here. You're not frightened are
> you? And I said, yes, I am frightened. And he said, You've
> no need to be frightened, with me beside you, so I went
> back to sleep.

9

An ordinary moment of reassurance balanced against a longing for something perhaps unattainable. The complex and contrary nature of human affairs is to run centrally through the work to come.

A year after the radio play, Churchill wrote her most ambitious play to date for the stage. *Easy Death* was staged by Oxford University Experimental Theatre Club in the Oxford Playhouse on 9–10 March 1962. There were three performances, including a Saturday matinee. It has fourteen named parts, together with a 'Crowd, including Women, Boys, Speakers, Hecklers, Policemen, Old Man and Woman, One Man Band'. In her programme note to the production, Churchill describes the play as: 'Two plots at different times at different speeds, uniting in the third act, attempt to combine satire and straight writing by stylised action, songs and verse'. The two plots centre on Steve and Jack. The action involving Steve covers one day; that involving Jack is his whole career. The former wanders restlessly from town to town, looking for meaning, and convinced that there is none:

> Got to be somewhere and the sun's shining
> here, so why not? You wake up,
> before you're even awake your mind's groping
> for something to make it worth another day
> and of course there's nothing. It hangs on the sun,
> there's nothing to grip you into the slippery day
> but a patch of yellow dust. It's a sunny day,
> you think, that's all right, it's a sunny day.
> And the sun shines on streets and trees and cranes
> and red buses and all the bloody rest,
> and people, so you think they're all right
> too, and the sun shines on you too
> so you're all right and you won't kill yourself
> this morning after all.

Steve's encounter with the town he is currently in opens the play. He sits, drunk, as a one man band enters, talks to him briefly, turns to the audience and says: 'That was now. Saturday night 1961. This is forty years again. I'm Jack's dad now, Alf King, one man band. If no other band'll let you play with them you have to be your own.' Jack is seven at this point. His determination not to end up like his dad, but to have a career, is already apparent. Two short scenes later, Jack is a teenager, and ambitious:

> I want a house, I want a car,
> I want an office, I want power.
> Then if I want music I can buy it,
> but not before.

Churchill establishes the two plot lines quickly, and combines verse, chronological shifts and powerful images of solitariness, drifting figures, ambition and sadness to create a picture of everyday life.

The mechanism by which Steve and Jack come together in Act 3 shows in Act 1 with the creation of Dory, the local magnate, in whose factories most of the town's population works. He owns the city. Dory does not appear, but his voice is heard on radio, proposing a cash prize for the best public speech on the theme of world peace. There's also to be £25 cash for the best speaker from the Crowd. All the town meets outside the town hall to hear the speeches, and Steve is determined to win the prize. But he meets a speaker, simply called Fanatic, whose banner reads 'Kill for Peace'. He rants at the Crowd:

> They know I'll blow them up, kill them all
> when my words explode, the whole world waste,
> silent, silent, peace, like wormwood,
> galloping horses, I'll melt the wax
> of the seventh seal when my lips burst, the still
> small . . .

To Steve, the mad anarchy of the oratory is fascinating and will have dire consequences for him at the end. He pushes the Crowd into voting for Fanatic, who in turn gives Steve a gun so that he may 'Kill for Peace'. This account of hysteria and anarchy then gives way to the story of Jack's inexorable rise to executive power in Dory's employment. He works in the division of

> Ezy-eat foods – fruit without stones, fish without bones, potatoes pre-mashed, toast pre-buttered, tea pre-sweetened. Sunday dinner pre-digested for quick energy . . . Bite-size food already cut up in pieces and Sip-ezy bottles that let out just one swallow at a time – comes in three sizes, small, average and late-for-work-Drinka gulpa milka second.

The anticipation of the spread of convenience foods, and the pace of living in the modern world, is acutely observed, as is the rise of Jack with his newly acquired wife, Jennifer. Their lives are displayed as a parody of the daily round of the busy businessman, and the docile wife as domestic provider. Intermittently, the scene reverts to the speechmaking sequence, and the rantings of the Fanatic, but this and the domestic scenes are kept separate, reflecting one on the other. Occasionally, domestic bliss is interrupted by, for example, an onstage laugh from Steve or, to close Act 1, as Jack and Jennifer say goodnight: 'Loud noises of a Crowd, a laughing shout from STEVE'.

Steve begins Act 2, roaming with the gun, looking for a victim, trapped in his own nightmare. The Crowd invades the stage. Steve, apart from the others, then joins in. The stage direction reads:

> . . . he joins different groups, passing quickly from one to another, listening, talking, borrowing a bottle, dancing a few steps with a girl. Talk mimed but not dialogue, only music, which gets faster and louder as STEVE moves more quickly. His movements are unsteady with drink, he lunges, stumbles, jerks. The movements of the groups have the same purposeless unbalanced lunging but he is the only noticeable single person. Black and exeunt, but music con-

tinues. Meanwhile lights up on JACK – throb of music
rhythm continues into beginning of this.

The effect of the choreographed Crowd is strongly to emphasise Steve's separation from nearly everyone. The separation is
ultimately to extend to Jack in Act 3. The long sequence that
follows shows a highly stressed Jack steadily falling apart, as he
begins to contemplate his life, rather than ignore it in his pursuit of ambition. He becomes obsessed with the idea that the
last obstacle in his ultimate triumph is the removal of Phil
Dory, the boss's son, who had inherited the business. As the
obsession consumes him, his wife is uncomprehending, his son
wants to paint and not join the business, and everything is
turning sour. At one point, he and Jennifer receive the headmaster of the local school, to which Jack has donated a schol-
arship. The head, unprompted, produces a melancholy account
of his life, to a resolutely cheerful Jennifer:

> But when I was young I hoped to save
> the world and now I'm fifty-one
> I hope to save enough to live on.
>> No mind can fill the sky.
>> Stars go out and men die.
> JENNIFER: No one can do more than his best.
> Your wife must be very proud of you.
> MICHAEL: When I was young I thought I loved
> my girl so well that time stood still
> and now our days drag by too slowly.
>> No mind can hold love
>> in and out of time forever.
> JENNIFER: You have to make the best of it.
> I'm sure we've always been very happy.
> After all, no one's perfect.
> MICHAEL: When I was young I hoped I'd love
> all mankind and now I doubt
> if men are kind enough to love.
>> Who can hold or understand?

We've only got two hands.
When I was young I thought I'd die
to save the world. Now I'm afraid
of death and pray the world will save me.
No mind can fill the sky,
stars go out and men die.
JENNIFER: Stars go out and men die.
But I'm sure it's all right really.
Will you and your wife come to dinner?
MICHAEL: How very kind of you, we'd love to.

The comic and sad aria, counterpointed by the last two lines, is an indication of the impulse away from naturalism, which hall-marks some of the later work.

In contrast to the picture of respectability shown here, the Crowd begins to separate out into groups. An elderly man, his wife and a small boy are seen. They have moved from the country in order to find work. The man tells the boy a story of shooting crows: 'and that was the day I shot ten, ugly black things they were . . . it was good up by the tarn, stoats and otters'. Steve hovers nearby, on the edge of the story, which then turns into a hymn of fear and loathing for city animals.

MAN: Rats and mice, all the small lurking things that run quickly, tough dirty things with sharp eyes. They haven't got rid of them all yet. And insects, spiders, cockroaches.
WOMAN: There's sparrows thick as gravel, and hoarse star-lings like the voice of smoke, the colour of a wet road with oil spilt on it, and pigeons too.
MAN: The city's alive with them, running and killing and shrieking like a wood in winter.
WOMAN: Swans on the canal too.
MAN: The city's desperate with them.

The corruption of the boy with this litany of hate, of the impo-sition of prejudiced views on others, is characteristic, as is the powerful development of imagery far from the confines of naturalism. The writing becomes liberated and insistent. Animals to be hated, or running amok, and minds to be corrupted are to feature again, notably in *The Ants* and *Far Away*.

As the writing looks to go beyond naturalism, so the structure of *Easy Death* stretches after other than straight narrative. Narrative is used principally in the telling of Jack's story, for his story is of a conventional kind – ambition, rise, self-questioning, despair. Steve's story centres on the speech day, which is returned to throughout as a kind of starting and ending point. Since Steve's life is aimless, the way it is told reflects that lack of centre. Both characters are in fact to come to the same end, but by different means. The chronological shifts in the play embody the complexities of existence, the uncertainties, and the disappointments.

Jack duly confronts Dory on the day before the speeches. He plans to kill Dory after the event. As he goes to finalise his plan, Steve, who has shot a man out of panic, meets the one man band from the first scene. Figures occur and recur, apparently in a random fashion. As Act 2 nears its end, Jack assaults Dory and realises that this does not resolve the dilemma. He echoes Steve's remark much earlier in the play, when Steve had said:

> and if you're lucky you go so fast you break
> right through, oh if you're lucky you break
> right through – to where you started from.

And Jack contemplates his fate, alone:

> . . . I've broken
> through to where I –
> through to where I was before.

The two figures meet for the only time in the final Act. Steve is on the run, desperate for a way out. Jack is calm, also looking for a way out, which he suggests might be by Steve's shooting him. At Jack's home, Steve gets a note to Sheila, a girl he met at the play's beginning, who then jokingly agreed to go away with him. Sheila arrives, as do the police. Jack is shot in the mêlée, but not yet dead. And Steve and Sheila escape out of the back door to the sound of shots. Both men die.

The final scene shows the Crowd again. It includes the one man band and Sheila, 'alone among them, apart. Movement, crowd busy, preoccupied, everyday, except SHEILA'. The final sequence is four alternately rhyming lines:

> The sun comes out and the rain comes down
> We may know how but we don't know why,
> Two men died last night in the town,
> Another day starts and we don't know why.

Peggy Ramsay saw the matinee performance. Her view, in a letter to Churchill in March 1962, was that the production was 'too tenuous and over-lyrical' and that Churchill needed 'strong, anti-feminine interpretation'. Ramsay, celebrated for her directness with her clients, had written to Churchill in December 1961 to say that:

> I think you are very difficult to sell, because your writing is in some respects very slight and poetic (this isn't meant disparagingly in the least) . . . In an odd kind of way you are getting more fey and more esoteric, instead of blunter and sturdier, which is not what I expected! Have you thought of writing a novel, or a children's book? I have the feeling that you would find it much easier.

Ramsay was also instrumental in the fate of *The Ants*, Churchill's first professional broadcast radio play, written initially as a play for television. Writing to Churchill on 7 December 1961, she worried about the play as a television piece: 'The subject matter of *The Ants* is very slender, and on television one would wonder *why* a play of this sort was set in wartime. On television, my dear, if a play is set during the war, it's a *war play*!!! The filming of the ants sequence, too, isn't easy, as it would have to be specially done in order to "match up" with the "live" scenes. Honestly I think this is a subject for SOUND.'[4] Ramsay sent the play to the BBC radio producer

Michael Bakewell, who directed it on the Third Programme on 27 November 1962.

The Ants begins a decade of intensive work, in which Churchill produced pieces for radio, television and the stage. In the ten years to 1972, there are at least seven plays for radio, four television plays and five stage plays. Some are not available, but the following are discussed here. For radio: *The Ants* (written originally, as noted above, for television); *Lovesick; Identical Twins; Abortive; Not ... Not ... Not ... Not ... Not Enough Oxygen (Not/Oxygen); Schreber's Nervous Illness; Henry's Past* (written initially for the stage). For the stage: *The Marriage of Toby's Idea of Angela and Toby's Idea of Angela's Idea of Toby (The Marriage); The Hospital at the Time of the Revolution.* For television: *The Judge's Wife.* It is a remarkable count. The first five of the radio plays are between twenty-five and thirty-five minutes. *Schreber* runs for fifty minutes and *Henry's Past* is an hour long. The television play lasts for thirty minutes. Both the stage plays are full length.

Radio demands conciseness, clarity and a structure which is quite quickly apparent. None of the radio plays has more than six characters. *Abortive* is a two-hander, while *Identical Twins* is preferably performed by one actor. Radio plays loom large because: 'there was a better market for them. It was very different, in the early sixties. There wasn't anywhere near the number of fringe and lunchtime theaters, and the radio was an accessible way of having your plays done.'[5] Radio also allowed Churchill to write while bringing up her three sons, born between 1963 and 1969. Broadly, the plays fall into two categories, though they frequently overlap. One addresses social and political issues, and the politics of intervention – *The Ants, Lovesick, Not/Oxygen, The Hospital at the Time of the Revolution* and *Schreber.* The other category is concerned with the nature of self, of human nature and with relationships – *The Marriage, Identical Twins, Abortive, Henry's Past.*

In *The Ants*, a boy struggles to deal with a world at war, and a family break-up, while absorbing his grandfather's sense of despair and a life wasted. The boy's initial delight in the endless industry of a column of ants moves to his sense of bewilderment and betrayal as his parents bicker over who should have the child. Offsetting this is the mordant and cynical humour of the grandfather, who sees the activity of the human race as analogous to the continuous activity of the ants. The mother's distaste for the state of her father's house gives rise to the early notion of destroying the ants by fire. Her way of seeing reflects the larger war beyond, and the mass slaughter of humans. The child, unable to think coherently, expresses his profound fear by shrieking with laughter as petrol poured on the ants by his grandfather explodes.

The piece shows a startling ability at an early stage of Churchill's writing. It has an unadorned, undecorated simplicity and focus, as it connects a child damaged with a couple severed, a grandfather waiting to die and a world destroying itself. What is done to children recurs throughout the work.

Lovesick plays with the notion of aversion therapy as an analysis of the manipulation of others. Popular in the fifties and sixties, this form of treatment was designed to modify undesirable or antisocial habits or addictions by creating a strong association with an upsetting or painful stimulus. *Lovesick* is an early example of Churchill's appropriating a notion that is current and employing it for her own purposes. Here, Hodge, the psychiatrist, attempts to unravel a complex series of relationships by the use of aversion therapy. He acts as commentator, observer, occasionally joining in the dialogue, but always displaying the arrogance of belief. His assumption of the right to act as he pleases without reference to anyone else anticipates later preoccupations, as for example in *A Number*. The tone of the activity is essentially comic, a quality central to Churchill's work, though often ignored critically. Hodge's smug self-belief enables him to observe the peculiarities of people with some detachment and disdain:

> Just then a nymphomaniac walked by, a seventeen-year-old patient who should have been locked up. She was a plump

girl with mousy hair and glasses, and unsuspecting school-boys, teachers, librarians, doctors, priests, business acquaintances of her father's, perhaps her father himself, had found themselves cornered by this dowdy child, till her parents had sent her to me.

For Hodge, people come in categories, and the categories are changeable. 'And so Kevin, Zolotov, Kevin, age twenty-five, loved by Ellen McNab against probability one might think, considering asthma, bitten nails, constipation perhaps, certainly his breath often smelt. People with commonplace interpretations of appearance would have thought at once that he was homosexual.' Add in incest, bisexuality and transvestism, and the resulting mix asserts the difference in humans. The comedy of the proceedings is an assertion of Hodge's contempt for human beings, even if he finds himself besotted with Ellen, whom he tries to cure of her lesbian orientation. He is forced to concede defeat as the human race, inexplicably, chooses to go its own way. His arrogance is undiminished.

A year later, Churchill sent a new stage play to Peggy Ramsay. This was *The Marriage of Toby's Idea of Angela and Toby's Idea of Angela's Idea of Toby* (*The Marriage*). Peggy Ramsay did not like the play. In a letter to Churchill of 19 December 1968, she wrote:

> I have put off writing to you about your new play for two or three days, because I really don't like it at all . . . I hate all these masks and trickery, and for some reason they make me feel embarrassed . . . I wish I knew what I really mean – I suppose what I am really trying to say is that you wouldn't really have a chance with this kind of play in the professional theatre, but could have a very much stronger chance in the amateur theatre. I wouldn't know which London Management I could show it to, because I think they would feel as I do . . . I am awfully sorry to be such a broken reed about this play, Caryl . . . I am not knocking the talent shown in your play, and I don't think I am saying

that every play should resemble another play. Perhaps it is just that I have a blank spot for what I think is basically amateur theatricals, i.e., what you are asking the actors to do on the stage.

Churchill later in her career glossed Ramsay's response: 'She wasn't keen on the fanciful. She didn't like a play I wrote with puppets and said she didn't like plays about circuses, though it wasn't at all about circuses.'[6]

The subject of Ramsay's dislike is a play of nine scenes, which charts the lives of Toby and Angela from their early twenties to their death in old age. It is occupied with how the two, especially Toby, try to understand each other. This effort takes up most of their lives. What is extraordinary is the stylistic freewheeling of the writing. It is by turns comic, satiric, surreal and shocking. Churchill here shows all the inventive flair and disregard for naturalism which is to hallmark her later plays. The opening stage directions give a hint of what is to come: 'There are four actors in the cast. Two play TOBY and ANGELA, the other two play most of the other parts, for which they wear masks. A few of the characters are played by puppets and dummies.' Thus in Scene 1, Angela and Toby are visited by Angela's parents. The parents are puppets, larger than life-size, with disproportionably large heads. They almost fill the small room. They have very loud voices, which come from microphones. Mr Pettit wears pyjamas and a bowler hat. He is 'redfaced, smiling, toothy; he has only one arm and one leg'. As for Mrs Pettit, she wears an apron and a flowered hat. She has a yellow face and 'her left eye and the left side of her mouth are missing, [as are] her left hand and both feet'. The puppets are upstage, unseen by Angela and Toby, who are busy with a tiff. The Pettits advance and a manic visit of the in-laws proceeds, including their laying down the law as to the treatment of their little girl by her new husband, not that he of course can ever replace them. The situation is entirely familiar. The treatment is not. Toby, faced with his in-laws, develops a nosebleed, can hardly walk, loses his voice, collapses on the bed and has a coughing fit. Periodically, presents from the Pettits arrive: a large baby's dummy on a pink ribbon; a yellow, curly wig; a gun. Angela dresses in the wig and fires the gun. The parents vary from declaring themselves very happy with the state of things to the inevitable lament of a poor marriage. Unlike theirs:

MR PETTIT: Toby, you haven't given Angela a dishwasher.
MRS PETTIT: You haven't given Angela a car.
MR PETTIT: You haven't given Angela an orgasm.
MRS PETTIT: How well I remember my orgasms. I used to be radiant with happiness didn't I Bill?

Toby and Angela talk of living together and what will happen. They kiss and: 'A terrible roar and scream from MR and MRS PETTIT. They sway from side to side.' The in-laws are slowly dismembered, with Angela noting that: 'They're in terrible condition,' and Toby agreeing: 'They're just not made of the right stuff.' Finally, the puppets are in a heap on the ground. Toby then reveals that he has his parents 'in his pocket' literally: 'You want to watch my mother. Here she is. Look, give dad back to me. She won't bite you if you hold her properly. From behind, your finger and thumb at her waist – not too tight, you'll squash her.' Angela manages to drop her mother-in-law and 'steps on mother as on an insect'. Dad is wafted out of the window: 'He's very light, he'll just float on the wind, won't you dad?' And Toby and Angela resume their conversation about being together.

Scene 2 shows a fantasy game between Toby and a masked Dominic. They are discussing their affair when Barbara arrives in a pretty blonde mask and carrying an enormous sack, half full. Barbara tells of her school affair with Toby in some detail, listened to attentively by Dominic. The sack contains small stuffed children, all allegedly Toby's. Barbara fantasises about assorted attempts at suicide, while Toby and Dominic put the dolls back in the sack, together with Barbara, head first. Finally Dominic removes his mask to reveal Angela, whereupon a man in a handsome mask arrives to claim Angela as his wife. Don't look for logic.

Each of the scenes tries something different. For example, in Scene 3, Toby is being tortured by a machine. A nurse attends: 'She wears nurse's uniform, rubber gloves, and her mask is a heavy cruel face with blonde curly hair.' The machine demands information, as the nurse tries to persuade him: 'You've suffered enough to engage liberal sympathies everywhere. Articles are already appearing about you.' Toby resists heroically as a picture of Angela on a screen appears. He has ninety seconds to confess and save her. At the last second, he gives in: 'NURSE: If I was your wife I'd have something to say to you for keeping me in suspense like that.' Toby then feeds the machine with names. The roles are then reversed with Angela wired up to the machine, and Toby threatened with a gun. As the machine counts the seconds down to zero, the gunman falls dead. Toby arrives with a soldier with 'a large handsome tanned face'. The machine is disabled, and the pair end the scene with smug satisfaction:

TOBY: But if he hadn't got here in time you would have let them shoot me.
ANGELA: I was certain someone would get here in time.
TOBY: And all the people I betrayed will be quite safe after all.
ANGELA: So we both did the right thing as it turned out.
TOBY: How lucky we are.

Each of the scenes portrays the relationship in a different light. Scene 4 is the story of Mr and Mrs Rabbit, played by Toby and Angela. It is called 'Bedtime Story', displayed on a screen in the middle of the back wall. The story is narrated by Toby's voice through a microphone: 'It has the over-emphasis of slight baby talk.' The scene is set in Mr Fox's living room, where he tries to convince everyone that he is a reformed fox. He gives a dinner party, to which he invites Mrs Hen and the Rabbits. Mrs Hen is upset for she has lost 'little Chickie'. Fox, a smooth figure in his mid-thirties, tries to suggest that times have changed, and that predators such as him have seen the error of their ways. Only Toby is sceptical and wants to go home: 'We've got perfectly good lettuce at home.' Fox's protestations of reform are not helped when he serves up corn and bread, lettuce and carrots for his guests, and 'a steaming bowl of stew' for himself. Little Chickie is still missing. Fox advises on handling a vicious dog which is harassing the animals: 'You have to learn to look as if you're doing one thing when really you're up to several others.' Fox polishes Mrs Hen and Angela off, but is then outwitted by Toby, who sends Fox out of the wrong door, where the dog is waiting. Fox dies, Toby is a hero, who then advertises for a housekeeper. Mrs Fox arrives to take up the position, feeds Toby up and invites him to her house: 'They go out together. Picture of MRS FOX and cubs eating round table.

NARRATOR: So fat Mr Rabbit went home with Mrs Fox and was never seen in the wood again. Mrs Fox had six baby cubs, and they all enjoyed their dinner.' The cosy bedtime story world of rabbits and chickens is totally undermined by a dose of comic realism, and a deal of glee.

On another occasion, there is a scene conducted entirely in one bed, with an almost endless permutation of Toby, Angela and all their friends. A perfectly naturalistic conversation between Toby and Angela goes to a blackout to be replaced by two friends (Colin and Marlene) in masks, who in turn give way to Toby and Julia/Angela and Marlene/Angela and Colin/Toby and Colin/Angela and Julia/Colin and Julia/ finally Toby and Marlene. It is a deliberately tedious discussion of middle-class *angst*, in the strange setting of an actual and symbolic bed.

By Scene 6, the two are in their forties, with a huge baby: 'he has an enormous padded body and a huge mask over the whole head, a smiling baby face.' He plays with a long rope. The baby is demanding, exhausting and, as the scene develops, begins to tie a knot in the long rope. Toby helps him. Baby puts a chair under a hook, and tries to fix the rope, with its noose, to the hook, helped by Toby. The baby hangs himself 'as ANGELA finishes speaking. ANGELA and TOBY pay no attention.'

Ten years later, the two are in their fifties and convinced that a Gunman is after Toby, who goes to see a psychiatrist. The Gunman follows him. Toby tells the Psychiatrist that he is hallucinating, but someone is definitely out to get him: 'He must know something about me. I don't know what it is. He knows me better than I know myself'. There then ensues a 'pantomime-type chase in and out of doors in trees'. The Psychiatrist sets fire to the building. The Gunman shoots the Psychiatrist. As the flames burn the building, Toby and Angela move up, floor by floor: 'Enter CROWD, both actors with extra heads and cardboard figures fixed on every side.' Finally on the roof they look around:

ANGELA: We're so high.
TOBY: Yes, we are high. There's quite a remarkable view. Angela, it's going to be all right. Will you jump with me?
ANGELA: Yes.
TOBY: Hold tight to my hand.
(As flames cover the building and siren crescendos they jump off and fly away.)

In the penultimate scene they are sixty. Toby has a present for Angela. 'The PRESENT is a middle-aged man in a shabby suit, with a sad grey mask.' It is for her collection. Toby tells how he bundled the man into a taxi in Chancery Lane. Angela much prefers this one to the Spaniard they brought back from Costa Brava: 'He is very beautiful to look at but one can't understand a word he says so he's rather boring I find.' The Present tells them about his life in a 'monotonous chant', then wants to go home because his wife will be wondering where he has got to. The couple listen happily together as the Present repeats on demand the same story 'very softly'. Angela has heart trouble, and in the last scene they are very old, in bed, where they began. Looking after them are a doctor, and a neighbour. He is an hermaphrodite 'who wears jeans and a shirt, the shirt unbuttoned so naked breasts completely exposed, jeans unzipped and penis sticking out; light brown skin, black shoulder length hair and a young very beautiful mask. He must not be camped up in performance; he is direct and very gentle with TOBY and ANGELA'. Meanwhile, reported on a large television, there is a riot going on. An initial peace demonstration in Oxford Street has become 'the greatest scene of civil violence that Western Europe has ever known'. Knightsbridge is aflame. Guerrilla fighters from the Congo, Algeria and communist China have arrived. Buckingham Palace is under siege. Angela worries that she hasn't bought Toby a Christmas present. They are both dying. The hermaphrodite, called Muffy, is looking after them: 'They crave stay oneflesh onebed till death does them, don't they. Very right want.' An ambulance arrives to take them to hospital, just as the *deus ex machina*, Father Christmas, descends, with reindeer. He orders the pair to be left in their beds, for:

> Very soon they'll both be dead.
> For a merry Christmas present
> I will make their deathbed pleasant.
> Not apart and not in pain.
> You won't see death like this again.
> Toby, Angela, close your eyes,
> Here's your last Christmas surprise.
> You love each other. Do not fear,
> Everything will disappear.
> Hand in hand they both have gone,
> Neither of them left alone.
> Now off I go with peals of mirth,
> Bringing joy to all the earth.

Peggy Ramsay may well have been correct to feel that a professional London management would be very wary of the play, but it has exuberant brilliance and an air of theatrical muscle flexing. Moreover, it demonstrates the quality which is not always noticed in the more solemn appraisals of Churchill's work. It is hugely funny and daring in its risk taking. It remains unperformed.

Identical Twins was broadcast in November 1968, with Clive and Teddy, the twins, played by Kenneth Haigh. The producer, John Tydeman, attested to the technical complexity of the production:

> It is a fact that we had to record twin A and then sync twin B, who was played by the same actor. He had to wear head cans to keep in sync with himself because the two twins had different personalities. You could not use the same tape and double it up because one is more forceful than the other, so although they are saying the same thing at times, they have to say it in a slightly similar way but in two different voices.[7]

The play is devised for stereo, as opposed to mono sound, so that the voices can be differentiated. It consists of the retailing of memories by Clive and Teddy, sometimes together, sometimes separately. Churchill's initial direction is that: 'When they are speaking simultaneously and don't say exactly the same thing, the alternatives are written "Margaret/Janet has been . . ." which means Teddy says "Margaret has been . . ." and Clive says "Janet has been . . ." ' This overlap, producing a collage of sound, is a precursor to the overlapping in later plays. Both twins have wives and mistresses. Teddy lives in London and is a landlord. Clive is a farmer. They resent each other and are desperate to be rid of each other. Both are trapped in their barren existence, living on memories, unable to break free. The bones of the story are straightforward. Clive allows his wife to die after an attempted suicide, and then takes an overdose. Teddy inherits the farm and Clive's mistress, and will probably suffer the same fate. The cleverness of the piece is the ironic means it takes to show aspects of sameness and identity:

TEDDY and CLIVE: I knew early on I was quite unique though Mummy and Daddy couldn't tell us apart. Which is which? Which is which? they would say, and I stood waiting for them to decide. As often as not they got it wrong. Then I had to go by his name to avoid embarrassment. As soon as we could we got out of sight and came back for re-identification. Sometimes four times in a row. They had spotted some mark. A missing button? A stain on my trousers? Or a spot on my face, would I have the wrong name all week? Or had they at last seen the essential difference, but the wrong way round forever?

The point of this is the acute sense on the part of the twins that they exist for themselves and for others only as an adjunct of someone else. Their identity is not unequivocally established. Their uniqueness is denied. Towards the end of the play, there is a remarkable sequence as Clive takes some sleeping pills:

TEDDY and CLIVE: If I were in his position what would I do next?

TEDDY: I sit down and watch.	CLIVE: Teddy sits down and watches.
Clive takes more pills.	I take more pills.
This is one of those	This is one of those
stupid things you	stupid things you
regret later. I go	regret later, I take
on watching.	some more pills. And
Then I get up without	some more. Then I lean
a word and go	over the table and hide
straight out for	my face in my arms and
a walk, the night	hope I'll go to sleep
is quite mild as the	quickly and whether it
day has been and I	works or not is out of
feel better for some	my hands now.
fresh air.	

As the lines are spoken simultaneously, only fragments will be heard. The effect of the fragmentation is further to bind the two figures together. The language fuses them. Radio's freedom is to allow the fragments to create the picture of the twins, one dying, the other looking on. Teddy goes for his walk as Clive dies. With him dies his image: 'TEDDY and CLIVE . . . (*Clive whispers*) When I was very small I would stand with him in Mummy's triple mirror. If we stood very close we could almost shut it round us. There were hundreds of reflections, all the same. (*Clive's voice gets fainter*) Then I was terrified to move (*Clive silent now*). TEDDY: not knowing which reflections would move with me.'

The intensity of *Identical Twins* was succeeded three years later by *Abortive*, a two-hander set in the bedroom of Colin and Roz, a well-to-do couple, with a house in a village. It was again directed by John Tydeman. In the course of a stormy night, there emerges a figure not given a voice, called Billy, whom Colin brought home and who stayed for several months. He, in the course of the stay, made Roz pregnant, and the effect of an abortion she had permeates the night's conversation. The two struggle to make sense of their current existence, with things having changed irrevocably. The less privileged Billy, after being thrown out of the house, stayed in the area, a persistent reminder of an event neither Roz nor Colin wants to remember. What they both know is that their rural idyll has vanished. Their relationship, such as it was, is permanently damaged. For whatever reason, they have allowed into their comfortable existence something beyond their control, and it will destroy them. Roz ends the piece with a line, the sentiment of which had been contained in an earlier piece, *You've No Need to Be Frightened*, crops up in *Not/Oxygen* and will recur at the end of *Top Girls* and elsewhere. 'ROZ. I do find I'm afraid to go to sleep. Just as I'm going off I get that feeling like in a nightmare but with no content. I'm frightened something's about to happen.'

If *Abortive* studies the fixity of recent experience in determining the present, *Not . . . Not . . . Not . . . Not . . . Not Enough Oxygen* shows a world where the present is a nightmare which will not go away. Set in the year 2010, it is a vision of ecological disaster, which is frighteningly close to current reality. Produced by Tydeman for Radio 3 a month after *Abortive*, the breathless title of the play reflects a world running out of natural resources. It is an apocalyptic account of human neglect, of pollution, of burning buildings, fired by protesters against an unpopular war. Where parks once were, there's only mud. To see a bird is a major surprise. Very few people venture out because of the stinking atmosphere. Inside Mick's flat, he waits with his mistress, Vivian, for the arrival of his celebrity son, Claude, who, Mick thinks, will buy him a cottage in the country. Mick's dream goes back to Susan in *Downstairs*, who yearns to escape but who is forever trapped where she is. Here, Claude arrives to say that he has given his millions away, is about to join the protesters and will then kill himself. Mick's resentment embodies all the disappointment of those who are responsible for the disaster:

> Do you think no one was starving then? In the sixties, seventies, eighties? Do you think there weren't any wars when I was a young man? You're not the first person to see horrors. We learnt to watch them without feeling a thing. We could see pictures of starving children and still eat our dinner while we watched . . .

The most remarkable sound in the play is the tortured and laboured attempts of Vivian to speak:

> Not enough enough oxygen in this block, why always headache. Spoke caretaker, caretaker says speak manager, manager says local authority local authority won't give us won't give us the money. Said I said what's the no point giving us faster – all be dead corpses in the faster lifts if there's not not not not not enough oxygen . . .

The dislocation linguistically mirrors a drastically dysfunctional world, from which there is little escape. Churchill permits herself the observation that: 'It's slightly unnerving to read *Not . . . Oxygen* twenty years later. It's more obviously relevant now than it was then'.[8] Her remark was made in 1990. Ahead lay the related work of *Far Away* (2000), *A Number* (2002) and *Drunk Enough to Say I Love You?* (2006).

Broadcast in July 1972, on Radio 3, *Schreber's Nervous Illness* was again directed by Tydeman, again with Kenneth Haigh. A bigger piece of work, this took as its mainspring the *Memoirs of My Nervous Illness* by Daniel Paul Schreber, first published in 1903 and translated in 1955. Schreber was appointed President of the Court of Appeal in Dresden in 1893. At the age of fifty-one, he suffered his second schizophrenic breakdown and spent the following nine years in hospital. He wrote his *Memoirs* in Sonnenstein public asylum, both to clarify the nature of his experiences and to effect his release. In 1911, Freud published a paper about Schreber. As a consequence, the *Memoirs* became the most written-about document in all psychiatric literature.

Paul Schreber gives his account of exactly what is happening to him. It is his reality. In the play, his narrative is punctuated by the 'objective' commentary of his psychiatrist, Dr Weber, the superintendent of the asylum. Weber is not in the main body of the original *Memoirs*. He appears in the *Addenda* of the published volume, where he offers the court medical reports as to Schreber's suitability for release from the asylum. Weber, according to O'Malley, was not in the play's first draft, but added at John Tydeman's suggestion: 'I said to her she must have this other perspective, this other man to give you the perspective of sanity and reality . . . You cannot just have a mad man talking'.[9]

Schreber is clear that God is contained in divine nerve rays, continuously pouring into his body against their will. By keeping still for long periods, Schreber believes he becomes the host to impure souls, which he could then destroy, and in so doing accord God greater power. He is, he thinks, the last person alive, and any others, such as doctors and patients, the 'fleeting-improvised-men', dissolve when not with him. He also believes that he is changing into a woman, and that it is God's purpose to use him to recreate the human race. As he feels he is changing physically, he begins to heal, accepts the existence of others, feeds off the diminishing powers of the rays and begins a process of being at peace with himself.

Churchill retains Schreber as her central narrator, with Weber as commentator. The rays are dramatised, rather than, as in the original, simply spoken about. The voices of the rays, described in the *Memoirs* as 'soft lisping voices', are incorporated into the play, as is the 'mighty bass' of the God, Ariman. Paul Schreber exists therefore as an actor in his own drama, interrupted by the voices of the rays and Weber. Each of the seven sections is prefaced by a voice-over announcing the substance of the next piece, a device which frames the content and focuses attention on the process as described by Schreber.

Churchill has used source material before, but this is her first attempt at taking a densely written and substantial work (the translation is more than four hundred pages), to create from it a radio play of some fifty minutes. As a play, it is essentially static, and there is intense pressure on the language to hold the attention. The ability both to select and refashion the discursive prose of the original is very much in evidence. For example, the *Memoirs* describe 'tiny figures in human form' dissolving on Schreber's head before which they frequently identified their origin:

> Especially frequent were the names Cassiopeia, Wega, Capella, also a star 'Gemma' (I do not know if this conforms to an astronomical name); further the Crucians (perhaps the Southern Cross?), the 'Firmament' and many others. On some nights the souls finally dripped down on to my head, in a manner of speaking, in their hundreds if not thousands, as 'little men' . . . Other rays which conducted themselves in the manner described above as if they were God's omnipotence itself, carried names such as 'the Lord of Hosts', 'the Good Shepherd', 'the Almighty' . . . Bad news came in from all sides that even this or that star or that group of stars had to be 'given up'; at one time it was said that even Venus had been 'flooded', at another that the whole solar system would now have to be 'disconnected'.[10]

Churchill's version of this comes in the first section:

RAY. I come from Cassiopeia.

RAY. From Gemma.

RAY. From the Firmament.

RAY. I am the Lord of Hosts

RAY. The Good Shepherd

RAY. The Almighty.

SCHREBER. And they dripped from the sky onto my head as thousands of little men. Bad news came in from all sides.

Music plays through the following:

RAY. Orion has been given up.

RAY. Venus is flooded.

RAY. The solar system will have to be disconnected.

RAY. Only the Pleiades can be saved.

RAY. The human race lasted 14,000 years but now it is lost.

RAY. The earth has only 200 years to go.

RAY. It is all over now.

The music stops.

The impulse of the original is towards expansion, whereas the radio play distributes the words among the Rays, and compresses the passages into powerful images.

Schreber, unsuccessfully at first, applied for his discharge. In 1902, the order to detain him was made permanent. Finally and ironically, he appealed to the Court at Dresden, of which he had once been president. He was judged to be insane, but nevertheless capable of managing his affairs. The committal order was revoked. Judged to be insane but capable is perhaps at the heart of Churchill's interest in Paul Schreber. He himself draws a clear distinction in Part 7 of his *Memoirs*: 'although I have a nervous illness I do not suffer in any way from a mental illness which would allow my detention against my will'. Writing the Introduction to the translation of *Memoirs*, Rosemary Dinnage suggested that:

The complicated, mythic universe that Schreber in his cap-
tivity created – an affair of rays and miracles, upper and
lower gods, souls and soul murder, voices of nerve language, struggles against the 'Order of the World' – concerned itself with issues of realness and unreality, identity
and fusion, power and passivity. His own identity having
been invaded, fragmented, distorted and annihilated, a
story had to be found that made sense of it.

If Schreber hovers between sanity and madness, it is a condition, however bizarrely expressed in the *Memoirs*, which may
have attracted a writer for whom notions of the real, of the per-
ceived world and its patterns, of the complex interactions of
human beings, of known and unknown, have been and still are
central to that writer's way of proceeding. The Judge at
Dresden renders simplistic the most common idea in the play:
'The Court has no doubt that the plaintiff is insane. What to
objective observation is hallucination is for him irrefutable certainty' (Part 7). Churchill remarked that both *Lovesick* and
Schreber 'have that movement between being inside someone's
head and out among extraordinary events that works particularly well on radio'.[11] *Schreber's Nervous Illness* appears, at the
onset of the seventies, to have clarified an emerging sense of
direction for its author.

As does an unperformed play for the stage, *The Hospital at
the Time of the Revolution*, written around the same time as
Schreber and reflecting some of the same concerns. The author's
note to the published text states that the play is 'partly based on
Chapter 5 of *The Wretched of the Earth* . . . by Frantz Fanon,
and also owes a lot to the writings of R. D. Laing. Fanon . . .
was appointed head of the psychiatric department of the
Blida–Joinville Hospital, Algeria, in 1953. He began helping the
rebels [in the Algerian War of National Liberation] . . .'

The flat, unemotional title heralds an apparently dispassionate account of the events at the hospital as seen and witnessed
by Fanon. The setting, too, is deliberately forensic: 'There is no

scenery except bare white walls, minimum of furniture: white upright chairs for most scenes; white beds for patients. Bright light.' Both Fanon and the Young Doctor wear white. The three patients wear white hospital pyjamas. Black and white predominate. As the play opens, Fanon is seeing Françoise, the daughter of an unnamed married couple, who are described as 'middle-aged Europeans'. The parents dominate the conversation as they complain about the seventeen year old, who is 'neatly and prettily dressed in a style rather too young'. Fanon's attempts to speak directly to Françoise yield little as the couple endlessly rehearse their litany of complaints about their own child. Provincial France and its prejudices are regularly aired. On learning that Fanon is from Martinique, Madame exclaims: 'That must be a nice carefree place. You must miss the singing and dancing. I saw a film once. In colour.' Françoise is eventually diagnosed by Fanon as schizophrenic. Her disorder is driven by her father's job. He is in charge of the interrogations in the area. In *The Wretched of the Earth*, Fanon writes of the condition of a young French woman who left home. She says:

> The fact was that every time I went home I spent entire nights awake, for screams used to rise up in my room from down below; in the cellar and in the unused rooms of the house Algerians were being tortured so as to obtain information. You have no idea how terrible it is to hear screaming like that all night. Sometimes I used to wonder how it was that a human being was able to bear hearing those screams of pain.[12]

And Françoise 'can't give you a list of the names but I hear the screams all night'. Her father, Algerian born, says that the interrogations are held: 'Sometimes at the police station, sometimes in the empty wing of our house because numbers have sometimes been a problem. Yes, I bring my work home with me.' The numbing casualness of that last sentence, which otherwise might be the weary admission of a stressed executive to his partner, savagely points to his banality of evil – and is a source of his daughter's distress. An apparently domestic problem is irrevocably hooked into the agony of the country, and the nature of the colonised. Fanon says: 'Because it is a systematic negation of the other person and a furious determination to deny the other person all attributes of humanity, colonialism forces the people it dominates to ask themselves the question constantly: "In reality, who am I?"'[13] For the parents, the daughter has become an irritation, a diversion from the work in hand. Monsieur, as with all state killers, absolutely believes he is in the right, and acting properly for his country.

Fanon betrays little of his thoughts. He observes – as he does in Scene 3, where there are three Algerian patients. Some of the material Churchill uses here is taken from Fanon's fifth chapter, entitled 'Colonial War and Mental Disorders'. The chapter details a number of cases of trauma, from which Churchill picks three. Patient A, according to Fanon, on a certain date each year, suffered insomnia, with anxiety and suicidal obsessions: 'The critical date was that when on instructions from his organisation he had placed a bomb somewhere. Ten people were killed as a result.'[14] Patient B is a torture victim of a European policeman whom he meets awaiting treatment in the same hospital, as a consequence of which he tries to hang himself.[15] And Patient C formed the impression that he was considered to be a coward and a traitor.[16]

The figure transformed by Churchill is Patient C. A casual remark in Fanon:[17] 'His physical appearance (he looked like a European) . . .' becomes the driving obsession of the patient in the play. He moans incessantly about his situation whenever he appears. In contrast, A remains dignified, thoughtful and resigned, while B is deeply traumatised. Patient C in truth belongs nowhere. He is disowned by his own people, and certainly not accepted by the colonisers as European. If the hospital walls, the uniforms and the furniture are white, the other patients black, he stands out in his own mind as cast adrift.

The young woman, Françoise, like Fanon, is silent in Scene 6 while her parents quarrel violently in front of her. Her situation mirrors to a large extent the effect of colonised violence on the population at large. If the Algerian, as the Europeans assert is, under a thin veneer, a savage, then this couple's rancid arguments hardly argue for culture or sophistication. For Madame, her husband is a 'filthy Algerian pig'. For Monsieur, Algeria is 'my country. They'll have to kill me before they drive me out.' He speaks for an occupation lasting a century and a half. In the midst of all this, Fanon listens impassively to the story of the events of Françoise's birthday. Dressed up in a new dress, 'a nice clear blue that she's always liked since she was a little girl', and summoned downstairs to parade in front of the couple's friends, she appears naked, with the dress cut into pieces, and defecated on. The silent girl is led away by Fanon as a patient suffering from schizophrenia. And as a victim.

Fanon speaks more to those he empathises with. In Scene 7, he has to tell Patient A that his wife has been killed. The patient's self-control and resignation are in marked contrast to the outbursts from Patient C. Patient B, on the other hand, lives in mortal terror of his torturers and, on seeing his torturer in the hospital, tries to commit suicide. In fact, his oppressor, a police inspector, wants Fanon to cure him, and resists the conclusion that it is his work which is making him suffer (Scene 8). The oppressors exist in a state of denial in order to continue. At the play's conclusion, Churchill comes back to Françoise. After a silence, she speaks directly to Fanon about the birthday dress. It is a moving and grim final moment, with the girl affirming that she has ceased to exist. Starved and poisoned, she represents the disempowered daughter of the oppression, and of the wrongs done by her people to her and to the occupied country.

The year 1972 also saw the transmission of a play for television, *The Judge's Wife*, on BBC 2. It, for the first time in her writing, overtly melds the personal and political in a direct account of the law, the legal process, the hierarchy of authority, and the role of the state as personified by the Judge. Churchill exploits the ability of television to disrupt linear narrative and chronology. The opening shots move from a picture of a figure – the Judge – lying dead in a wood to two more versions of the same scene with each beginning from an earlier point in the sequence. The killing of the Judge, which each time when shown offers more of the preceding events, recurs insistently throughout the play.

After the initial series of shots, the play shows the Judge in full regalia about to sentence Vernon Warren, a revolutionary. A close-up reveals that Warren is the Judge's killer. Or so it seems. The Judge produces, even for a judge, a ranting attack on all dissidents, and a paean of praise to the power of the state to eliminate all forms of dissent. The language employed by him is extreme, violent and hysterical. Its exaggeration is somewhat suspect in its ferocity, and may give rise to the notion that he has an ulterior motive in speaking thus. On the other hand, his caricatured image may reflect him accurately. His conduct throughout the play does little to eradicate the idea of his having become a gross parody of himself. It is, of course, already known how he meets his end, and all his boasting about the might of the state amounts to little when faced with a gun, held, it transpires, by Vernon's brother Michael. Both of these parts are played by the same actor. This means that early on, when there is a shot of Mrs Warren with her son, it is left deliberately unclear as to quite what is going on. Thus, in effect, a Warren kills the Judge, for what the Judge represents will ultimately founder. Does the Judge realise this?

Most of the play is set in his home, with his wife, Caroline, her sister Barbara and an Irish maid Peg. As the Judge is de-robed by his wife: 'He stands naked, fat, old, defenceless.' Minus his robes, his behaviour is exactly as before. Peg has been dismissed to the kitchen for criticising the sentence passed on Warren. She later quits. Caroline panders to the whims of her husband, and defends him from both the maid and her sister, Barbara, who loathes her brother-in-law. The wife is watchful, acquiescent, attentive. There is one shot of the sisters in the bedroom which shows Barbara without make-up, with 'short untidy hair, and indifferent clothes'. She is 'an old woman'. Caroline, on the other hand, makes up and 'looks far younger, bland, without character'. She assumes the role as wife to the judge: 'She smiles radiantly, holds it for a moment, then lets it go and stares at herself as before.' The part played by Caroline echoes the dutiful behaviour of Jennifer in *Easy Death*. However, Caroline is more complex, occasionally allowing another side of her to emerge: 'He keeps me awake too, I'm not allowed to sleep if he can't sleep.' Within the house, a television 'in a small intense corner of the large, still bedroom' imports pictures of the outside world, including a demonstration over the verdict. The telephone rings insistently at intervals and it becomes clear that the caller is Warren.

The Judge dies. After the repetition of the sequence which opens the play, there is a shot of a newspaper picture of him lying dead. He has responded to the challenge by telephone to confront his accuser face to face. His dutiful wife now takes centre stage on the following day. Importantly, she now has no role to play: 'She wears a dressing-gown. Her hair is unbrushed, her face crumpled. BARBARA is standing. They are two old women.' Caroline defends and explains Lawrence, her husband, to her sceptical sister. He had become, she says, 'a parody of a right-wing bigot', so remote from the people and causes he knew he ought to help that he decided to be the extreme enemy of those people and causes in order to force action against him. He would in effect become a martyr on their behalf: 'He wouldn't kill but he could be killed. He could give his life for the revolution.'

Caroline's is the longest speech in the play. Barbara doesn't believe her. Neither, perhaps, does the viewer. There is no previous suggestion that Caroline had any understanding of her husband other than the brutal nihilistic figure he presents to everyone. Caroline may, though, have rationalised her wifely existence as a means of survival and justified her stance as regards her husband's barbarity. It is not possible, nor is it desirable, to be able to 'solve' the wife. It is possible to read her position as tragic. Or heroic. Or craven. It is possible to accept that in the figure there are a number of truths to do with the situation of the wife, none of which singly will be adequate. It is entirely characteristic of Churchill's work that complexity requires and gets here the gamble of ambiguity.

The final, and longest, radio play of this group, written at about the same time, is *Henry's Past*, broadcast on Radio 3 in December 1972. In some ways, the piece indicates an arrival at a decisive point, a moment of recognition and acceptance. It was originally intended for the stage, and its producer, John Tydeman, noted that the initial version would have lasted 'ninety minutes to two hours'. Churchill then cut the original to one hour. One of the interests of the play has to do with a familiar Churchill notion of living in the past as a way of avoiding the present. Henry evades the here and now as absolutely as he is able by insisting on encapsulating everything into categories, frameworks, headings, stifling any possibility of change. Ten years before the play opens, Henry was released from prison, where he had served three years for hitting his friend Geoffrey with a hammer, because of Geoffrey's affair with Henry's wife, Alice. Geoffrey broke his back in the course of the attack, and is now in a wheelchair. He, Alice and daughter Lydia now live in Canada: 'Alternate summers they holiday in England, visiting Land's End, Windermere, the Tower of London and me.' Henry retells all this to Silvy, a young, pregnant woman, whom he has brought to his home, where he lives with his friend Paulina. His response to the events which left Geoffrey paralysed is to fix them in amber so as not to contemplate a present in which he would be forced to confront the real consequences:

> As I get older the past should get longer. But very few things are added to the past now. Their visits of course. It is hard to believe now will ever be the past and it won't be as far as I'm concerned because I'll forget all about it. It seems to me that nothing is happening . . . You withdraw

completely from the present moment because otherwise you become impaled upon it and all time becomes one eternal insupportable moment . . . Nothing happens to me because I am in effect already dead, and the time to be lived until I physically die is only a fiction.

PAULINA: You exaggerate.

HENRY: I exaggerate a little.

Henry's pompous and manufactured defeatism, couched in precisely articulated melancholy, persists through the visit of Geoffrey, Alice and Lydia. It is a fiction of his own devising, as Paulina understands: 'Henry is always talking about his past. If he likes you you'll be admitted to his past the next time he tells it.' Alice, on the other hand, has a view of the world which she announces with comic precision:

But Geoffrey thinks we'll be absolutely happy if we can be good enough. He thinks there is a perfect system. But why? We don't ask an ant to be more than it is. Or even a dog, though we do ask some strange things of dogs, but essentially we realise that their perceptions of reality are limited . . . We can't begin to speak of reality. And by reality I don't mean anything mystical. Sight isn't supernatural just because some people are blind. And you can't explain sound to the deaf by describing waves in the air. What happens to us is entirely different from what can be said about it. So it seems most unlikely that there are not a great many waves, rays, events, which our systems cannot experience. Time for a start is quite beyond me.

Alice's unfussy certainties about the complete lack of certainties in life and relationships form the central truths of the play. It is accepting this that Henry heretofore has resisted. Yet, at the end, he moves: 'Do you know . . . just then . . . now . . . then . . . is the present moment.' The line closes the play, and there is a sense that a writing episode has also closed. It is as if the work done to date is reviewed, accepted and placed.

The day after *Henry's Past* was broadcast, Churchill's first play to appear at the Royal Court opened at its Theatre Upstairs. It marked an association with the Court which has lasted until now. The play was *Owners*.

2

Owners to *Cloud Nine*: 1972–1979

Churchill herself gives an account of these years in the first volume of her collected plays. Her professional stage debut came with *Owners* at the Royal Court's Theatre Upstairs in 1972. The following year saw a science fiction play, eventually titled *Moving Clocks Go Slow*, which received a single Sunday night performance in 1975, again Upstairs. A year later, Churchill wrote *Objections to Sex and Violence*, which became her first Royal Court main stage production. Three plays were written in 1976: *Traps* was first, and went to the Theatre Upstairs in 1977.

It was in 1975 that a relationship was formed between Churchill and two recently established groups: Monstrous Regiment Theatre Company and Joint Stock Theatre Group, for whom she wrote *Vinegar Tom* and *Light Shining in Buckinghamshire* respectively, both performed in 1976. This period also saw a television play (*Turkish Delight*) and a radio play (*Perfect Happiness*). By now, the stage emerges as her chosen form. In the period 1958–72 there are three stage plays, but at least nine radio. From 1972 to 1979, there are nine stage pieces, three television and only one known radio play. There was a further piece of writing as a contribution to Monstrous Regiment's *Floorshow*, early in 1978, and a television *Play for Today*, called *The After-Dinner Joke*. In the same year, Churchill wrote a dramatised documentary about Northern Ireland's justice system under the Diplock courts. When the BBC replaced Churchill's voice-over at the beginning and end of the play, both Churchill and her director, Roland Joffé, removed their names from the credits as a protest. It was also in 1978 that Churchill wrote *Softcops*, which surfaced at the

Royal Shakespeare Company in 1984, in a revised version. At the same time, Churchill began the notes which would lead to *Cloud Nine* in 1979 and *Top Girls* in 1982.

The seventies were of crucial importance for Churchill's work. The decade began with a commissioned piece appearing at the Royal Court, and thereafter in New York. It ended with a uniquely workshopped piece, which again appeared in New York, where it ran for two years. At the beginning of the decade, she was a writer beginning to attract attention. By the end, there was no doubt about her international status. But throughout this time, one characteristic is apparent and that is a readiness to experiment and to take risks, both in the form of her work and with the theatres and companies she became involved with. One of the hallmarks of any first-rate writer is courage. The seventies see such courage with Monstrous Regiment and Joint Stock. It is, however, apparent well before 1976.

Owners was commissioned by the West End producer Michael Codron, prompted by Churchill's agent, Peggy Ramsay. According to Ramsay's biographer, Codron was unsure what to do with the play, until the Theatre Upstairs offered him what Ramsay described as a 'first-class try out'.[1] At the Court, an internal memo from Anthony Page on 14 August 1972 read: 'I have read *Owners* and I absolutely agree that it should be done Upstairs. I think it's well worth thinking of for downstairs if it were done in a shorter Season . . . I did think the idea of the man repeatedly trying to commit suicide was overworked and wondered if she would rewrite and cut down on this.' The production was duly agreed at a meeting of the Artistic Committee on 31 August.

The run-up to the production was not without incident. John Osborne's then wife, Jill Bennett, due to open in *Owners*, fractured her ankle when Osborne, apparently deliberately, drove their car into the Battersea roundabout, as a result of an argument. Osborne had not noticed the police car behind them. He was breathalysed and lost his licence for a year. Bennett was replaced at preview stage by Stephanie Bidmead.[2] The play's director, Nicholas Wright, noted that 'Stephanie Bidmead did very well, but [the replacement] nonetheless gave an unwelcome feeling of emergency and set-back to the whole thing . . . The play was well reviewed . . . certainly better than my production. It played to full houses. There was something about the play, and about Caryl as a writer and a person, that appealed to the public immediately . . . The cast was excellent. This *mise-en-scène* less so: that was my fault.'

And Peggy Ramsay was her usual direct self in a later letter to Churchill of 1 August 1973: 'I was dreadfully unhappy about the production of your play Upstairs and have still not got over it. I find it difficult to even talk to Nick Wright, because I think it put your career as a playwright back at least a year. He should have acknowledged that he couldn't have made that play work Upstairs . . .'

Owners is the first of the stage plays which begins to focus on issues and preoccupations raised in the radio plays of the sixties. Here, the connections between individual actions and the consequence for society overall are articulated and analysed. The play takes the story of Marion, a property developer, whose husband, Clegg, is a butcher. Marion acquires and sells a house, the top flat of which is occupied by Alec and his family. Alec is Marion's former lover. The transaction is actually driven by Marion's wish to demonstrate her power over Alec. This does not happen and so Marion tricks Alec's wife, Lisa, into signing a document which cedes Lisa's child to her. Lisa eventually regains her child, and, in revenge, Marion gets her right-hand man, Worsley, to set the house on fire. Alec dies, trying to save a neighbour's child.

A bald summary does no justice to the quality of the play, which has two starting points. Firstly, Churchill herself worked with a group in Islington, looking at the housing situation, and was present at an old woman's flat, when 'a young man offering her money to move came round'. Secondly, the writer wanted – as she noted in the Introduction to the play – 'one character with the active, achieving attitude of "Onward Christian Soldiers", the other the "sitting quietly, doing nothing" of the Zen poem. The active one had to be a woman, the passive one a man, for their attitudes to show up clearly as what they believed rather than as conventional male and female behaviour.' The statement clearly links the local and the larger territory, and provides the spine of the narrative. Written in three days, the piece contains: 'a lot of things that had been building up in me over a long time, political attitudes as well as personal ones'.³ Thus the play is shot through with questions of ownership, power, coercion, greed and violence. People owning property, owning other people, attitudes, assumptions; people denying individuality except their own; people acting to maintain position regardless of the cost to others. And people as victims, as dispossessed, powerless. It showcased the natural logic of Western, achieving progress – Marion – as opposed to the quiescent, opting-out Eastern passivity – Alec.

What *Owners* is also shot through with is comedy. Churchill in her Introduction concedes that a reading of Joe Orton's *Entertaining Mr Sloane* (1964) 'may have done something to the style'. Orton's figures are liberated from the complexities of psychology. They are what they do. They are expressed in action. Such an approach may have seemed to a writer like Churchill, who in her radio plays creates some figures forever attentive to the nuances of living and language, a means of working essentially in terms of making things happen, rather than ruminating as to why. Thus an account of her characters is set out in the *dramatis personae*, the detail of which is positively Shavian, given her later work. The principals are described, so as to define them, as far as definition is needed: Clegg is 'dowdy and getting fat . . . Forty'; Marion is 'thin and edgy . . . Thirties'; Worsely is 'tall and thin . . . Early twenties'; Lisa 'has a weak pretty face . . . Late twenties'; and Alec is 'tall, rather plain and ordinary, but attractive, Thirties'.

What then follows, particularly as regards Clegg, Marion and Worsely, are figures capable of a deadpan, comic delivery in consciously sculptured, self-reflexive statements. This is not the product of complexity but of a character defined in the *dramatis personae*. There's no need to account for actions taken, but the need is to show the consequence of those actions. Thus Clegg opens the play selling mince to imaginary ladies (the image of a butcher talking to customers recurs in *Light Shining in Buckinghamshire* four years later) and on the arrival of Worsely, Marion's hatchet man, moves into a sequence about killing Marion for, unforgivably, standing on her own two feet:

CLEGG: One thousand five hundred and seventy-five people die daily in England and Wales.
WORSLEY: Fair number.
CLEGG: It's only a matter of making her one of them.

Clegg's ideal woman is unsurprisingly his mother, who worshipped his father: 'I've seen her on her knees. And he would raise her up, very gracious. She knew how to give a man the right support . . .' Worsely, throughout the play, attempts various forms of suicide without success, and appears increasingly mutilated. In Scene 1, his wrists are bandaged. By Act 2, his neck is bandaged. By Act 2, Scene 6, his wrists, neck and arm are still bandaged, and his left leg is in plaster. It is Worsely who ends the play, firing a gun placed by his temple: 'Missed'. Worsely's view of life as not worth living, something to be endured, contrasts absolutely with the views of his boss, Marion. She erupts into Scene 1 as a strong, brisk force, taking immediate control of the situation. For Clegg, Marion refuses to be a proper woman: 'Comb your hair and take an interest in your husband's work. Find a hobby . . .' Clegg, betrayed, behaves like an old actor-manager: 'If I thought for a moment she had dishonoured me, then without hesitation or a thought of the police— (*He plunges knife into meat.*) And also into the heart of the thief. I am more an Othello than a Hamlet. Out out damned candle! She is legally mine'. Ownership replaces partnership. Clegg's vacuous posturing and Worsely's lugubrious responses create a kind of double act in the play. When Clegg reveals Marion is infertile, Worsely remarks and adds quickly: 'But Marion's on the pill. I daresay.'

The comedy partly derives from the fact that these two live in the world, and are constantly betrayed by it. 'WORSLEY: I saw a poster saying Suicide – ring the Samaritans. So this very pleasant young fellow came round and I told him I want to kill myself and could he help. He said in a very feeling voice he would certainly try. But does he hell. The bastard's always trying to stop me.'

Marion's zest for life and passion for Alec is regularly frustrated through the play. It remains undiminished. As a figure created at the beginning of the seventies, she is a remarkable anticipation of Marlene in *Top Girls* at the beginning of the eighties. In Act 1, Scene 5, she lays out her beliefs:

> . . . be clean, be quick, be top, be best, you may not succeed, Marion, but what matters is to try your hardest . . .
> Marion tries hard. I work like a dog. Most women are fleas but I'm the dog.

The work ethic, drummed into her as a girl, is central to how she acts, as is the chilling belief that 'the animals are ours. The vegetables and minerals. For us to consume. We don't shrink from blood. Or guilt. Guilt is essential to progress.' However, she still loves a barely listening Alec, and stakes out her love in overblown, comic declamation:

> I don't care if you're mad or sane, Alec. I'm yours whether you want me or not. Have all the money and stay here too if that's what you want. Empires have been lost for love. Worlds well lost. We men of destiny get what we're after even if we're destroyed by it. And everyone else with us. We split the atom. Onward. Love me.

At the end of the play, with Alec dead, Marion announces a new beginning: 'I never knew I could do a thing like that. I might be capable of anything. I'm just beginning to find out what's possible.'

After the Royal Court production, *Owners* transferred to New York. It received two performances at the Mercer–Shaw Theater on 14–15 May 1973. It was to be the first of many Churchill plays to be seen in the USA.

In the late seventies, the Court was urgently considering revivals of some modern plays, largely because new writing had become somewhat distanced from its repertoire. *Owners* was one such, and received a report from Danny Boyle, then an assistant director:

> With 7 characters rather expensive for the Theatre
> Upstairs but a very accomplished piece – funny and
> accessible yet rich and bizarre in imagery and theatricality.
> Money, sex, death, money and a character of pure spirit –
> effortless texture.
> Only seems to run plain (comparatively) in Scenes 4 and 5
> of Act 2 – Alec and Lisa resolving to get the baby back as
> the Arlingtons go out, and Clegg's abrupt volte-face over
> the baby as he fucks Lisa – both scenes smell of plotting
> and completing. (With hindsight – crawling with class.)

Owners has fourteen scenes and a number of different locations, as well as nine parts. The next piece, *Objections to Sex and Violence*, has one set ('a sandy beach with rocks behind it'), eight characters, takes place in one June day, and was Churchill's first production on the Court's main stage and as the Court's Resident Dramatist. In her Afterword to the play[4] she may be referring to some of the figures in *Owners*, when she recalls 'being slightly alarmed by the knack it seemed to me I was getting of mocking my characters in the way they talked and defining them too tightly, and I wanted to give them more rope, take them more seriously'. As a consequence of this, Churchill points out that in her new play there is 'a difference in style, with the seaside postcard couple Madge and Arthur at one extreme, and Annie, say, and Terry with more freedom'.

The story line of the play is that Jule, in her twenties, has become part of a small cell of revolutionaries and has rejected her middle-class upbringing. A police raid arrested the members of the group, and then bailed some of them. Jule has come to the coast with Eric, another member of the group, to ponder the future. Her sister, Annie, and her partner, Phil, find her and try to persuade her to leave the group. On the same beach are Arthur and Madge, the former with an unquenchable passion for pornography, the latter sublimating her despair into the outrage of a moral campaigner. To the same beach comes Miss Forbes in search of the beach where her passion, many years ago, remained unrequited. Thus all of the figures, including Jule's former partner, Terry, a hard-line Party member, come to the beach for their own reasons.

Writing about *Objections to Sex and Violence* some ten years later, Churchill indicates her dissatisfaction with the title because: 'The trouble with the title now is that it suggests quite a different set of ideas, developed by feminists, of the links between male sexuality and violence, which wasn't my starting point at all'.[5] More likely as a starting point is the examination of Jule's position, and her attempt to relate herself and her ideas to the political world. The play in part is to do with Jule's coming to political consciousness amidst the pressures brought by others. Her sister, Annie, lost her job as a secretary to a top executive, and found herself in the typing pool. Later, she becomes a charlady to the same executive, has regular sex with him and blackmails him. She learns that his wife knows about the sex. He told her each night. The professional couple exert both a fascination and a misery for Annie. They talk together while Annie cleans 'and never a word to me, not a nod, not good morning, not the glance you'd give a budgerigar . . .' She feels the kind of indifference that in fact provokes Jule, but Annie is incapable of action or even hating: 'I never carry anything right through. I'm always turning off sideways. I can't get into an extreme position.' This despite the violence done her, and the sexual abuse. Her partner, Phil, seems to have the role of a soothing voice to comfort Annie, a person always looking for the best in everyone. Except that he once tried, one

Christmas, to make love to Jule and failed. The frustration is very evident: 'You make me want to hurt you. It's a terrible feeling. I want to break you up on these rocks . . . You're proud of being a slut and a murderer. You – oh, you fucking fucking – oh, I hate you—'

What's being said relates to the ambiguities of behaviour. While Phil is important to Annie, he acts and speaks violently to Jule. Later, he deliberately aims petrol at the beach fire so that it threatens Jule. She has tried to explain to Phil and Annie her hatred for the class represented by Annie's former employees: 'being hurt is all they notice'. In the same way, varieties of hurt occur in the other characters. The 'seaside postcard couple', Arthur and Madge, are rather more than caricature. Arthur reads a pornographic magazine while gazing furtively at Jule in her bathing suit. Madge arrives, having nervously escaped 'a most sinister character'. Their opening sequence in the play is laced with comic remarks, mostly from Madge: 'Enjoying yourself by yourself on the beach . . . I don't believe in self-service', and she knows of Arthur's proclivities. The porn magazine is buried in the sand, as Arthur tells his truth: 'I hate women really, you know that. Young women today want to be whipped.' Madge appropriates the role of public campaigner against the very attitudes she unconsciously embraces.

Yet these vicious and comic figures have another dimension. Arthur encounters the demented Miss Forbes, still on her quest for the same beach and exposes himself, while blaming the elderly lady. When Madge arrives to help, it is Miss Forbes who, on seeing Arthur return, recognises his loneliness and describes for the police a figure the precise opposite of Arthur. The three leave together, supporting each other.

Of the group of would-be revolutionaries, only Jule in the play appears to be clear about her course of action. She will return to answer bail. Eric tidies himself up, and leaves because if he returned he would talk to the police and betray the group. He defects, leaving Jule to go back to join the other two, who are in police custody. At the play's end, Jule's former

51

husband, Terry, the communist, tries to persuade her to return to him and their daughter. Jule refuses, and they come to an uneasy truce.

The play caught the *zeitgeist* of the early to mid-seventies, although it ran for only twenty-seven performances, and 21 per cent capacity. Churchill's Afterword refers to writing the piece in the summer of 1974. The Post Office Tower had been bombed by the Angry Brigade, an anarchist group, in 1972, which launched a string of bomb attacks in the heart of the British Establishment. The American heiress Patty Hearst was kidnapped in February 1974, by the Symbionese Liberation Army. She joined the group and was arrested during a bank robbery. And the campaign of the IRA in the UK mainland had begun in 1972. Anna Calder-Marshall, who played Annie, recalls one such incident: 'We were meant to rehearse at the Irish Club, but because of bomb scares we were diverted to the Welsh Club – and there was a bomb scare. Rehearsals stopped, and I went round asking everyone if they would like a cup of tea – which was my solution to the general panic'.[6] The sense of the times is reflected in the play, and in Churchill's Afterword, which noted her thoughts at the time 'of how immediate and pressing ideas about the anarchism, revolution and violence were'.

After *Objections to Sex and Violence*, Churchill co-wrote *Strange Days* with Joan Mills, Director of the Young People's Theatre Scheme at the Court. This was a play developed in workshops by and for the pupils of William Tyndale Junior School, and performed at the school in July 1975. Churchill commented: 'It's interesting I was doing that before the Monstrous Regiment and *Light Shining* workshops which, because of the sequence of main plays, I've tended to remember as having been the first time I did that kind of thing.'

She also became involved in the emerging Theatre Writers' Group, meeting in October 1975, which became the Theatre Writers' Union (TWU). The trigger for this was a proposed reduction in subsidy by the Arts Council. Most of the important playwrights of the time quickly joined in, and the strength of feeling was such that historic agreements were reached as to the working conditions and pay of playwrights. The TWU acted politically in defence of its colleagues elsewhere in the world, and reached clear positions over, for example, plays and their performance in a South Africa dominated by apartheid. Churchill has always been ready to add her voice, either in support of certain causes or in opposition to positions she repudiates. In the same October as the meeting of the Theatre Writers' Group, she wrote to *Plays and Players* about the closure of the Court's Theatre Upstairs by the Artistic Directors on financial grounds. It was not to re-open until May 1976. Her concern is for those made redundant, and for the exclusion of writers in respect of the theatre's policy. Her letter makes it clear that she proposes to arrange a meeting of writers to debate it all.

At this stage, Churchill's career in the professional theatre consists of *Owners*, *Objections to Sex and Violence* and *Moving Clocks Go Slow* (for one performance). The last appeared Upstairs on 15 June, and seems to reflect the novels of Philip K. Dick, whose work, apart from denying the notion of one reality for all, explores a world dominated by monopolistic corporations and authoritarian governments. An earlier name for the play, *Inside Outward*, gave way to the final title, which summarises part of Einstein's Special Theory of Relativity.

The play is set partly on a space station and partly on a devastated Earth. On the station, Kay processes applicants who want to leave Earth and go 'outwards'. 'Outwards' is populated by humans with extrasensory powers, alien life forms and robots. Kay has done her job for fifteen years, but has aged only three years in that time. Her duty is to 'serve space', and do the bidding of Agent Fox. Fox begins wars and creates disasters on Earth, only to rush aid to the stricken area. There is the constant threat of alien invasion. Two such aliens inhabit the bodies of the robots Apollo and Luna, who travel to Earth with Kay, where she encounters both her mother and grandmother.

53

Earth has destroyed itself. The terrain is as if another act was added to the later play, *Far Away*. Kay's grandmother describes the world as it was: 'You mustn't judge our planet by what it is now. There was flower gardens and animals, friendly little animals, called pets . . . You could come to breakfast when I was three and have a mug of milk and bread with butter on it and egg out of the insides of a hen.'

The worlds of *Not/Oxygen* and *Far Away* combine to make a bleak picture of what the human race is proceeding towards. Here, those left in the world wish to leave it, with few exceptions. Aliens eventually take control, and a voice announces that: 'Aliens have reached saturation level. The planet Earth will be destroyed.' It is, but Kay is propelled by the two aliens back to the Earth before its destruction. They observe from afar:

APOLLO: Back down the tunnel to her universe. Her body reassembles. On earth now. She opens her eyes.
LUNA: Where is she?
APOLLO: On a rubbishy plain. Old tin cans and weeds.
LUNA: What's she doing?
APOLLO: Up on her feet. Walking. Something-what? Losing her now. She's crying.
LUNA: Happy or sad?
(*Music*)
END

Moving Clocks Go Slow ends deliberately inconclusively, but the warning is stark. It is a theme reiterated through Churchill's work, and it becomes more insistent as the work develops.

The year 1976 was to produce a quite remarkable run of work. It began with *Traps*, the first play of the year (although not performed until January 1977, in the Theatre Upstairs). It is one of several of Churchill's plays devoted to an analysis of the mechanics of theatre. The play sees the systematic creation of the dramatic parameters within which the action proceeds in Churchill's world. Her note to the published text compares what happens on stage with the prints of Maurits Escher, celebrated for his so-called impossible structures. An example would be his *Drawing Hands*, in which two hands are shown, each drawing the other. Thus in *Traps*: 'the time, the place, the characters' motives and relationships cannot all be reconciled – they can happen on stage, but there is no other reality for them . . . the characters can be thought of as living many of their possibilities at once. There is no flashback, no fantasy, everything that happens is as real and solid as everything else within the play.'[7]

The play is virtually impossible to describe other than in its own non-narrative terms. Or rather, multiple and simultaneously occurring narrative terms. Act 1 is set in an urban first-floor flat. The room is described:

> Plenty of clutter: large jigsaw half done on the floor, large pot plant, newspapers in various languages, oil lamp, cards, airgun, cake, pile of clothes washed but not ironed, ironing board and iron, towels, broken bowl, guitar, suitcase, picture, carrycot, clock showing real time.

Act 2 is set in the countryside, and the opening stage directions take the elements of the beginning of Act 1, and restore them:

> The floor has been cleaned up; the plant is exactly as it was at the beginning of the play; the bowl of peas is unbroken, as it was when Jack finished shelling them; the cards are on the table. The ironing board is folded and the ironed clothes in a pile. REG's coat is across the back of a chair. The folder of letters is where DEL left it. The newspapers are as they were, so is the cake. The guitar and gun are in different places. There is a different picture on the wall. The jigsaw is as it was at the end of Act 1. The clock still tells real time.

Within this contradictory and puzzling framework, a group of figures act out their idea of being part of a dysfunctional family. They all appear to inhabit their own sense of what matters, which includes 'their possibilities'. Syl, for example, has a child, to which she feeds gripe water in an attempt to quieten her. At another stage, however, she muses on having a child: 'If I haven't had a child in the next five years, I'm not likely to have one at all. That's okay.' One moment she may be pregnant. Another not. One character's possibilities sometimes clash, sometimes merge, with another character's possibilities. One figure's scenario may duplicate another, or contradict it. Nobody's narrative runs consistently in a straight line. It does not need to subscribe to the demands of coherence, except to itself.

Though Churchill asserts that reconciliation of time, place, motives and relationships cannot happen except on stage, many of the sequences in *Traps* make the kind of real life sense, which seems chaotic and without form to others, but remains clear to the character involved. Jack may have mismatched socks. Albert has the same. Albert goes out through an unlocked door. When Reg tries the door, it is locked. Syl may have a badly bruised back. Later, she does not. Del cuts his finger. So does Jack. If they inhabit their unique universe, they occasionally collide or come together. At the end of the play, some of the family bathe in a large tin bath. The last to get in is Reg, who also eats his meal while bathing: 'They are increasingly happy so that gradually, each separately, they start to smile.' The family comes together for that moment.

By the time that *Traps* opened in January 1977, Churchill had written both *Light Shining in Buckinghamshire* and *Vinegar Tom*. As she noted about *Traps* in the Introduction to *Vinegar Tom*: 'it seemed more than a year since I had written it.' *Traps,* in its concerns, belongs to the group which began with *Owners* in 1972. But the two later plays of 1976 represent a profound change in working method which affected all subsequent work.

Two of the most important experimental theatre groups established in the seventies were the Joint Stock Theatre Group and the Monstrous Regiment Theatre Company, founded in 1974 and 1975 respectively. Joint Stock began life when two directors, William Gaskill and Max Stafford-Clark, decided to run a workshop as a way of learning about each other's directorial techniques. Directors seldom watch other directors at work. Gaskill had stepped down as Artistic Director of the Royal Court in July 1972, after seven years. Stafford-Clark had stepped down as Artistic Director of the Traverse Workshop Company, Edinburgh, in August of the same year. They came together to workshop and adapt *The Speakers* by Heathcote Williams, which opened in January 1974. It was out of this collaboration that Joint Stock emerged. What also evolved was a method of work which, with a few exceptions, was at the core of the Group's beliefs. A regular pattern of workshops, a gap for writing the script, and then rehearsals. The workshops could last for four weeks, and rehearsals six weeks. In the workshops, ideas were researched by all concerned. Actors went out to find whatever material was available which was brought back and acted out. The writer was part of this. Stafford-Clark had experimented with this method with the Traverse, and with actors swapping parts from scene to scene. What Gaskill brought, among many other skills, was the central tenet of the Court, which was an absolute fidelity to the text, and the primacy of the writer. It is important to note that the workshop's main function was to offer ideas to the writer, whose autonomy over the script was absolute, even it if was, and it was frequently, modified in rehearsal.

Joint Stock, by the time Churchill became involved, had in a brief period, established itself as one of the most impressive theatre collectives of the period. Part of the reason was the two directors, but the actors were also, on the whole, seasoned mainstream and fringe performers.[8] Despite frequent discussions and arguments – and Joint Stock meetings were notorious for both – the Group never settled on a fixed political stance. While some argued that this weakened the Group, it is probably true that the notion of 'taste', especially as expressed by the directors, weighed more heavily in the decision-making process. The central aim in the Group was to create and maintain a context in which new work could be made at the best artistic level.

Monstrous Regiment began in August 1975, and was conceived of as a performers' collective. Many of the founding members had worked not only in fringe companies but also in mainstream theatre and television. Feminist theatre companies had begun to appear with the Women's Street Theatre Company (1970), The Women's Company (1973) and The Women's Theatre Group (1974). The Monsters, as they were known, were occupied with promoting new writing, especially by women, redressing the economic imbalance for women in theatre and examining the history of women in general. *Vinegar Tom* was the company's second show. The company's submission to the Arts Council for funding referred to 'a show . . . at present untitled, the subject will be "Witchcraft–subversion and madness" ', the research for which began in September 1975.⁹ Chris Bowler, one of the company's founding members, knew Churchill from working as an assistant stage manager at the Court. Bowler was, with other members of the company, taking part in a protest march along Oxford Street to the American Embassy 'and spotted Caryl – who joined us for the rest of the march'.

Churchill had spent the sixties as a somewhat solitary writer, mainly in the world of radio. She described an early encounter with the Monstrous Regiment:

Early in 1976 I met some of the Monstrous Regiment, who were thinking they would like to do a play about witches; so was I, though it's hard now to remember what ideas I was starting from . . . Soon I met the whole company to talk about working with them . . . I left the meeting exhilarated. My previous work had been completely solitary – I never discussed my ideas while I was writing or showed anyone anything earlier than a final polished draft. So this was a new way of working, which was one of its attractions. Also a touring company, with a wider audience; also

a feminist company – I felt briefly shy and daunted, wondering if I would be acceptable, then happy and stimulated
by the discovery of shared ideas and the enormous energy
and feeling of possibilities in the still new company.[10]

By this stage, Churchill had already agreed to work with
Stafford-Clark and Joint Stock from May. She in fact wrote a
first draft of what became *Vinegar Tom* in three days, and
possibly some of the songs. Monstrous Regiment took the
draft and agreed to leave any rewriting until after the Joint
Stock project.

Quite apart from the courage and imaginative leap she made
from solitary writer to company member, another factor may
well have influenced Churchill's attraction to alternative companies. The Royal Court was in the middle of one of its peri-
odic financial crises. The Arts Council refused to increase its
grant. Churchill protested against the closure of the Theatre
Upstairs in a letter of October 1975. She may have felt that,
with the Court ailing, both the energy and the ability lay elsewhere. She gave some of her reasons in 1981:

> It's a matter of having a director and actors with whom you
> can share certain assumptions and not have to feel that you
> are constantly the one to be trying to push things in the
> direction you want them to go.[11]

The work which became *Light Shining in Buckinghamshire*
and marked Churchill's debut with Joint Stock began in May
1976. She was asked by Stafford-Clark if she wanted to do a
show about the Crusades with another writer, Colin Bennett.
Bennett had written *Fourth Day Like Four Long Months of
Absence* for Joint Stock, directed by Stafford-Clark, in
October 1974. Bennett dropped out after a brief time, and
thus began one of the most important partnerships in modern
British theatre.

The project was formed because Max 'had stayed at a house
in the country where there was a crusader's tomb and had

wondered what would make someone uproot himself and set off for Jerusalem'.[12] Stafford-Clark, as always, kept a detailed Diary of the work. He, Churchill and Bennett met on 26 April, and the three resolved to try to prepare a scheme which could be used as a skeleton. On 29 April, the two writers produced a scenario. The Diary records that: 'I'm still a bit struck by the idea of a journey. A journey back from Jerusalem to home but with legends and more complex elements woven in.' By 30 April, elements of the play it became are showing: 'Caryl: The Ranters: speeches in and of the "Pursuit of the Millennium" . . . The worse things got the more it proved that the millennium was on its way.' At the end of week one of the workshop, a number of the play's themes fell into place. By then, Churchill had read Christopher Hill's *The World Turned Upside Down*, which had a chapter about the Crusades, and also a chapter about ecstatic religions and the English Civil War. According to Stafford-Clark: 'Caryl said that this looked even more interesting, so that's how we got to it.'[13]

In addition Churchill read Norman Cohn's *The Pursuit of the Millennium* 'with its appendix of Ranter writings [and] I was seized with enthusiasm for changing to the seventeenth century'.[14] On 28 May, the workshop group debated 'a perfect world. Our idea of Utopia. Quakers. What would they want most? Paradise? Jenny (Cryst, workshop member) reads feminist petitions to Parliament. Women beginning to preach . . . Caryl would like to hear Ranter speeches and get to know them more.' The following day, what was to become the scene 'Margaret Brotherton is tried' is sketched out. There is information being aired in the workshop about immigrants and eccentricity; about going naked and eating only vegetables. As a result of Churchill's going to a Quaker meeting, the group created such a meeting on 8 June. There is a constant activity of research, discussion, improvisation, backtracking, all of which fed the writer.

The writer herself was experiencing a new way of working:

So there was reading and a wall chart; talking about ourselves; and all kinds of things mainly thought up by Max. I'd never seen an exercise or improvisation before and was as thrilled as a child at a pantomime. Each actor had to draw from a lucky dip of bible texts and get up at once and preach . . .[15]

It should be remembered that what is now thought of as standard practice was then quite extraordinary. Roger Lloyd Pack, a member of the original Joint Stock workshop on *The Speakers*, recalled the astonishment:

What? Speak directly to the audience and have them walk round us, wherever they wanted? Who had heard of such a thing? I was used to the audience sitting still, in one place . . . A new approach to acting was needed to suit the context, a certain kind of reality is demanded when you are talking to your audience only a few feet away . . . We were engaged in this new way of working which made us feel particularly vulnerable, uncertain how it would work . . .[16]

And Tony Rohr in *The Speakers* refers to going out to investigate the lives of various fanatics, speakers at Hyde Park Corner, begging in the streets: 'Because everyone found it so valuable and such fun it carried on from there'.[17]

So what was new to Churchill was also new to the actors. And being part of that way of working had a profound effect upon the way Churchill subsequently wrote. The workshop and the rehearsals led to an important decision in early August. The Diary asks: 'Should there be "hat" acting or one cossie for everyone in each separate part? Talked with Caryl and decided to make the parts non-specific, i.e., not have a particular actor identified with a particular part all the way through.' Churchill had written one version of the play which she was not happy with, and wrote another in the ten days before rehearsals began. Though unfinished, it tracked six people through the play's events, with actors playing minor parts in the others' stories.

The move to 'hat' acting meant that everyone did everything, of the experience of the times being shared. What began as a kind of joke between director and writer meant that figures in the play now offered a generalised experience of events.

The play was performed with a table and six chairs. Any Joint Stock touring show, as the designer Peter Hartwell has observed, has to be designed to go into the van and be capable of the configurations needed by different tour venues. Necessity drives and forms the aesthetic. *Light Shining in Buckinghamshire* opened at the Traverse, Edinburgh on 7 September 1976, before finally arriving at the recently re-opened Royal Court Theatre Upstairs on 27 September. The production was extended and ran for nine weeks Upstairs. Its director's reaction as noted in his private Diary was: 'I enjoy it . . . it does have a clean, spare beauty and passion in it. I love watching it. The scrubbed table . . . the figures . . . the actors lit against the black . . . Soon it will be gone forever, but it is beautiful. All that stuff about the Crusades a year ago hasn't surfaced in any direct way at all, but I sense that somehow it was relevant'.

The play's framework is the period at the end of the English Civil War in the middle of the seventeenth century. It portrays a revolutionary belief in the millennium, for which ordinary people fought the king to ensure the coming of Christ and heaven on Earth. As Churchill noted in her Introduction, Christ never came. What did 'was an authoritarian parliament, the massacre of the Irish, the development of capitalism'. In fact, the play's analysis is of revolution – in this case a failed one. The condition of the poor and unremarked, the maintenance of political power, the reinforcement of hierarchies, are all presented starkly and without sentiment. The stripped-out simplicity of the scenes (many of them brief) leaves an abiding impression of lives lived by whole groups, rather than individuals. As an example, Scene 2 sees the vicar sitting at a table on which are oranges and wine. A servant attends. He responds monosyllabically. Each response is followed by a full stop.

There is no variation, no attempt to explain or clarify. It is not needed, for the vicar is hardly listening, occupied as he is with his bishop. Compared with that, the servant's sick child hardly counts. It is therefore almost an insult when the vicar gives the servant an expensive orange for his child. He can afford it. The brief scene indicts without explication.

The same vicar welcomes Star, his new landlord. He's a parliament man, who has bought the land, and he bridles when the vicar calls him the new squire. The label is rejected, as Star expounds the new vision, which is actually the old one, expressed differently. He insists on generosity, fair treatment, and does not react later in the scene when the vicar again refers to him as 'the new squire'. *Plus ça change* . . . As Star steps into his new kingdom, the next scene is of two women, one with a newly born child, the other accompanying her. The child is to be abandoned in a place where, possibly, it might be cared for. The mother is ill and starving. It is a scene designed not for tears as a reaction, but for anger. There are, the scene says, many such women. In order to subdue the revolution, Cromwell and some of his soldiers hold the Putney Debates (a much-reduced but skilfully produced version of the original, still showing the powerful, limpid prose it contains). At the same time the revolutionaries hold their own meeting in the penultimate scene. It is the longest scene in *Light Shining*. They wait for Christ. But as Hoskins says in the last scene: 'I think what happened was, Jesus Christ did come and nobody noticed. It was time but we somehow missed it. I don't see how.'[18]

Critical reception was generally admiring. *Plays and Players* described it as 'magnificent . . . one of the finest pieces of English playwriting for years', while the *Guardian* felt that the play 'has an austere eloquence that precisely matches its subject'.

After writing one of the most powerful plays of the time, Churchill returned to Monstrous Regiment to work on what became *Vinegar Tom*. Working with Joint Stock had all but eliminated Churchill's 'shyness at showing what I wrote . . . by the even greater self-exposure in Joint Stock's method of work'.[19] Many of the ideas explored with *Light Shining* were to show up in *Vinegar Tom*, which is a play 'about witches with no witches in it; a play not about evil, hysteria and possession by the devil but about poverty, humiliation and prejudice, and how the women accused of witchcraft saw themselves'.[20]

Vinegar Tom consists of twenty-one scenes and seven songs. The songs are contemporary and are to be sung by actors in modern dress. Churchill specifies that they are not part of the action and not sung by characters in the scenes before them. It is, she says, 'essential that the actors are not in character when they sing the songs'.[21] Gillian Hanna (Alice in the play) described the play's form as:

> extremely bizarre. You had a series of quite naturalistic scenes punctuated by very modern songs in modern dress . . . If you took out the music you would have something akin to a traditional play. But we knew that we had to have the music to smash that regular and acceptable theatrical form . . .[22]

The songs are graphic, powerful, comic and satiric by turns. In one, the moment of a first menstruation modulates to the despair of old age:

> Oh nobody sings about it,
> but it happens all the time.

In another, a patient screams to be released from a doctor. A third, which anticipates *Cloud Nine's* Victorian family, satirically announces:

> Oh, the country's what it is because
> the family's what it is because
> the wife is what she is
> to her man . . .

In the final scene, 'Evil Women' sarcastically evaluates male longings and fantasies:

Evil Women
Is that what you want?
Is that what you want to see?
In your movie dream
Do they scream and scream?
Evil women
Evil women
Women.

The last line assertively loses the adjective.

The play revolves around Jack, an aspiring tenant farmer, and his wife, Margery, who, as their ambitions turn sour, decide to blame a poor widow Joan. Their butter will not come, and their cattle are diseased. Jack's sexual frustration disrupts their lives, and they decide that Joan and Alice are evil and responsible for their plight. Alice and Joan thus become prime targets for accusations of witchcraft. The notion of women living, forcibly, an independent existence, frequently in poverty and outside the main activity of the village, provides an easy target for accusation. Added to this is an action Alice takes when she brings her friend Susan to a 'cunning woman', Ellen, for a medicine to make her abort her unwanted child. The atmosphere is ripe for intervention by witch finder Packer. Churchill noted carefully in her Production Note that: 'The pricking scene [14] is one of humiliation rather than torture and Packer is an efficient professional, not a sadistic maniac.'

Vinegar Tom proceeds to an inevitable climax, as Joan and Ellen are hanged, Susan is duly admonished by the church and repents in terror. The figure of Betty, bled to purge her and render her fit for a wealthy wedding, neatly demonstrates another form of oppression, that of forced submission. And Margery, the wife, and one of the prime causes of the oppression of her own gender, prays in front of the hanging bodies, to God to 'Bless Jack and keep him safe from evil and let him love me and give us the land, amen'. But Alice expresses nothing but rage at what has been done to her mother, and to all of them. The song 'Lament for the Witches' ends with:

> Look in the mirror tonight.
> Would they have hanged you then?
> Ask how they're stopping you now.

The means of oppression may vary. The fact of oppression never does.

It seems the play is over. But there's another scene. The authors of the *Malleus Maleficarum, The Hammer of Witches*, appear. They are dressed in top hat and tails as music-hall performers. As a double act, they share lines from their volume, Part 1, Question 6: 'Concerning Witches who copulate with Devils. Why is it that Women are chiefly addicted to Evil superstitions?' There is a quite horrifying comedy in the scene as the two grin their way through the appalling catalogue of statements about women, delivered in staccato and knowing fashion. The scene was played by Chris Bowler and Mary McCusker, last seen hanging as Joan and Ellen in Scene 19. This involved rather a fast change. As Chris Bowler says: ' I had some of the Kramer costume on underneath Ellen who wore a big shapeless frock and shawl. I just put on the jacket and changed my bonnet for a top hat. It was a mad rush, though. I think we had to have a bit of extra music lead-in to cover the gap.' The hanging in fact used a wooden frame and climbing harnesses under the clothes, hooked on to trick nooses. They were still taken for dummies.

The Regiment's thoughts on the production included audience reaction:

> Some men in particular were upset by it . . . Some people felt accused by the songs, which in their manner of presentation – as well as in the lyrics and music – were direct and uncompromising. It wasn't our intention to make people feel accused or blamed in a simplistic way, but neither did we want to let them off the hook, or allow them to distance

themselves emotionally from the events of the play because they were distant historically. At the other end of the spectrum we were accused of being too heterosexual, some women found the male/female love-making of the first scene offensive. This was the company's first taste of critical reaction to our politics from other women, and it was very chastening . . . At first (when there were very few feminist/women's groups) it often felt as though we were urgently required to embody every shade of feminist belief, and whenever we represented one person we negated another.[23]

Churchill described 1976 as a watershed. The effect of working with both companies and the experience of encountering actors in the process of research and contribution did not mean that she never again wrote in a solitary manner. But after 1976 it can be assumed that she was influenced by her knowledge of just what actors could do, what they were capable of.

In her Introduction to *Plays: 1*, Churchill found it unsurprising, after the pace of 1976, that she did not write a lot in 1977. She was, however, active in the affairs of the Royal Court, in disarray after the very public resignation of Robert Kidd, the joint Artistic Director, followed by co-director Nicholas Wright. It was widely felt that the Court had capitulated to the demands of the Arts Council. Senior writers expressed their anger at the Court's Council, which belatedly decided on consultations with staff. A meeting of writers took place on 24 February. Caryl Churchill was one of eighteen writers present. The meeting discussed, amongst other matters, changing the name of the English Stage Company (ESC). Churchill 'thought it might be a good idea to change the name, but not to one that linked the company to the Royal Court since it was an extremely expensive theatre to run, especially when the work was not necessarily commercial'. A proposal that: 'the policy of the ESC is to present new plays in the English language by contemporary authors' was passed with the addition of a proposal by Churchill, which read: 'And particularly to encourage the work of brand-new writers'. Most importantly, she then proposed absolute support of the Court's staff belief that:

> The future of the Company shall be in the hands of all those who work or have worked for the Company. The details of this reorganisation is to be subject to wide discussion amongst all interested parties, but the change to be completed within six months of the date of this resolution.

This reads very much like a Joint Stock declaration, but nothing much came of it all. Three staff representatives were added to Council. The matter was to resurface in the eighties. For Churchill and her peers, the situation was partly redeemed when Max Stafford-Clark became Artistic Director. He had been appointed as an associate by the then Artistic Director, Stuart Burge, in 1978, and became director for two years from April 1981. He had, of course, been nurturing relationships with most of the writers excluded from the Court in the seventies. Most of them returned with the exception of Hare, who went to the National Theatre and its director, Richard Eyre.

Churchill was involved in two pieces of writing in 1977. The first was *Floorshow* for Monstrous Regiment; the second was a piece for television, *The After-Dinner Joke*, for BBC 1's *Play for Today*. The former appeared at the Theatre Royal, Stratford East from 18 to 28 January 1978; the latter was broadcast on 14 February 1978.

Floorshow was developed during the early summer of 1977. Churchill was one of four writers. The others were Michelene Wandor, Bryony Lavery and David Bradford. The development of a cabaret run mainly by women at that time was pioneering, and Monstrous Regiment knew it was taking a leap in the dark. The form traditionally was a male preserve, and as Gillian Hanna writes:

> not one of us really knew what was going to work. We didn't even know if women could stand up in front of an

audience, without a character, and be funny. So we wrestled endlessly over the problem of each woman finding her 'voice', and the difference between a performer's relationship to a 'persona' as opposed to a character.[24]

Churchill reflected on the difficulty of the absence of models at the end of 1977: '[Michelene Wandor and I] were trying to write about stand-up comics and the sort of relationship that exists between them. Like Abbott and Costello. Except for husband and wife pairs where that kind of conflict is exploited, there are *no* models of two women being funny to each other.'[25] Theatrical curiosity, as Hanna says, pushed the company into new areas to see, for example, whether there was such a thing as 'women's theatre'. *Spare Rib* for January 1978 termed *Floorshow* 'a slick, highly competent show', where:

Not only sexist ideas around work were attacked by using the revue form; the very *form* of traditionally male-dominated humour was shown up in the spotlights. We saw women acting as comperes and cracking bitterly funny jokes, and men talking about their own sexism; women refusing to act the ventriloquist's dummy, and men singing about stereotypical nursery rhymes and minding the baby.

After *Floorshow*, Churchill wrote *The After-Dinner Joke* for Margaret Matheson's TV series, *Play for Today*. The topic of charities was suggested by Matheson, and the hour-long play satirises the charity industry and the uses to which it is put while masquerading as philanthropy by big business. The notion of funding good causes is reduced to the level of an after-dinner joke book, sold by Oxfam. It's called *Pass the Port*. The 'heroine', Selby, moves from naïve bewilderment and a kind of romantic idealism, to promotion and a rest from charitable work. Big business continues. Amongst other things the play is remarkable for its imagery, which has an immediate impact on television. Selby tells a licensee that five pounds would buy a pig. A customer asks for a bottle of whisky and is given a pig; a woman in a shoe shop asks for a shoe in size 5 and the assistant 'drags out a fishing boat'; a buyer of a car asks about delivery and 'Enter fifty calves'. And a woman with a catalogue tells Selby that she and her husband have adopted a granny: 'We had a catalogue from your company and we chose one. We'll get a grandpa next year to match. SELBY. Which one did you choose?' It is characteristic of Churchill's skill that conventional expectation is disrupted by the apparently irrelevant. The acquisition of people as pets is an idea first found in the 1968 play *The Marriage*.

In her collection of *Shorts*, published in 1990, Churchill included a very brief piece called *Seagulls*, written in 1978. The play 'felt too much as if it was about not being able to write for me to want it done at the time'. The piece has Valery Blair, a middle-aged woman, waiting to demonstrate her unique gift of moving matter with her mind. She is due to go to Harvard to be investigated by scientists. She repines at the burden. Having discovered its existence, she remained quiet about it for five years. An American fan, Cliff, enters to quiz her about her life. She remains evasive and uneasy, gets bored and tired with what she can do, doubts on occasions whether she can do anything. She finds herself explaining her dilemma, and her confusion about something so vague, difficult if not impossible to pin down, an ability hated and loved by turns. As she is invited to perform in public, red with effort, she fails. Her manager, Di, tries to bring her out of her depression, beginning a mock row. Being, as she says, a businesswoman, 'I'm on my way', she tries to persuade Val to try again: 'Why don't you just nudge that teacup and see if it goes?' The young American tries to console her, but at bottom still wonders whether she is a fake.

What emerges is the impossibility of assumptions. A man in a story told by Cliff is surrounded by seagulls. When asked by his sick father to fetch a seagull, not one comes near him. The power to assume can be fatal. At the play's end, Val sits 'Watching things move'. Not by her, but of their own volition. The play reflects a moment of doubt and resentment at the expectation to perform at will, without the demanding actually understanding what is involved in the act itself.

Like *The After-Dinner Joke*, *The Legion Hall Bombing* was a 'Play for Today'. While the former was being made, Churchill acquired the transcript of the trial of Willie Gallagher for the bombing of the British Legion Hall in Strabane in 1975. The trial took place in a Diplock court, that is, one where there is no jury. The rules of evidence were modified to allow a confession as evidence, however obtained. Churchill visited Northern Ireland with her director, Roland Joffé, to talk to people involved in the case. The original transcript was shortened. There were to be voice-overs by Churchill at the beginning and end of the play, explaining the implications. Before the play's transmission in August, the BBC asked for cuts in the opening voice-over, and the removal of the Epilogue. The BBC said that advice from BBC Northern Ireland was that it might raise tempers during the spring marching season. Thus, the BBC Head of Drama, James Cellan-Jones, rewrote the introductory voice-over. The Epilogue was removed. Churchill and Joffé removed their names from the credits. It was eventually transmitted in August, in a later time slot than was usual. The spring slot was filled by Mike Leigh's *Abigail's Party*.

Before linking up again with Stafford-Clark to begin work on what became *Cloud Nine*, Churchill read Foucault's *Surveiller et Punir*, and as a consequence wrote *Softcops*, 'which I then put away and forgot'. It surfaced, in a new version in 1984.

Cloud Nine remains one of the extraordinary achievements of Joint Stock, and it mirrors its processes in an exemplary manner. Yet it goes further than the earlier work in choosing actors both for their sexual orientation and for their acting ability. Joint Stock requires of its actors that they commit to a workshop period, a lengthy gap and a rehearsal period, often without knowing what the end product will be. They also commit to a tour of whatever is produced and not very much money. It is a kind of mad bravery, an act of faith. Not all

actors are able to work in this way. Economic realities sometimes dictate an early departure. *Cloud Nine* asked even more
of its participants. Its workshop period was fundamentally
about the lives and sexuality of all the participants, who made
up the group, which consisted of a straight married couple, a
straight divorced couple, a gay male couple, a lesbian, two
bisexual men and heterosexual men. The workshops, for obvious reasons, were closed and confidential. Churchill has said
that the subject of sexual politics was general and vague, but
timely. She and Stafford-Clark discussed another Joint Stock
show:

> and I remember saying to him if it wasn't Joint Stock what
> I'd want to do a show about would be sexual politics. But
> Joint Stock at that time was such a male company, and no
> one ever seemed to think about issues of that kind at all,
> that it seemed the last company in which you'd think of
> doing a show like that. And of course as soon as I had said
> that we realised that it was a very good reason for in fact
> doing it.[26]

The workshop began on 14 September with improvisations
about the childhood of the group members. Throughout, there
was a steady stream of role reversals as part of the procedure.
What emerges strongly from Stafford-Clark's Diary of the
workshop is how the participants moved from natural wari-
ness to uninhibited readiness to share experiences. A series of
improvisations began which explored sexuality:

> Caryl set up one where women were competing for the
> same man with their attraction to him determined by play-
> ing cards they had selected at random. She then initiated
> some work on dependency. How dependent is one partner
> on the other in a relationship? Again both the amount of
> 'approval' required, and the amount the other partner was
> prepared to give was determined by cards. Julie Covington
> set up a passionate scene of sexual experimentation

between two young kids which was discovered by a horrified uncle. Carole Hayman set up a hilarious improvisation with a casting director, an actor or actress and a director.[27]

At one stage of the workshop, there was work on the ways in which figures had characteristics imposed on them by a partner or a parent:

> Caryl then set up a series of improvisations where various characteristics were 'imposed' on a particular person. In the first one Julie was sent out of the room and an office situation was set up. Everybody was told that Julie was stupid and not up to her job. Within seven or eight minutes these expectations had been fulfilled and she was becoming an office catastrophe. Tony Sher was then excluded and we were all told he had a vicious temper. An improvisation was then set up where he was a newspaper editor. Again, even though Tony had no knowledge of the 'characteristic' we were imposing, he became more and more short-tempered . . . We developed this into a game where we tried to identify sexual characteristics. Each actor drew a card to determine how masculine (black cards) or feminine (red cards) they were to be. They were then questioned by the rest of the group. We became surprisingly accurate.[28]

In the last two weeks of the workshop, the focus was on the lives of the actors' parents, particularly as regards sexual repression. All related their life story, upbringing and sense of their parents' upbringing. It was during this period that the group heard the story of the workshop premises' caretaker. She told of her hard life, a loveless and violent marriage, and her eventual happiness with a new partner, with whom sex became a real pleasure: 'Now we have sex sometimes as much as twice a week and I'm on cloud nine.'[29]

The workshop concluded, and the writing began. Churchill has graphically described the relationship between workshop and play:

What's the difference between an idea for a play and just an idea? I think the only difference is that you want to make them into a play, the point at which they become an idea for a play is when you get some sort of technical or physical way of turning it into a play . . . The idea for a workshop isn't necessarily an idea for a play. It's an idea which could lead to a play. *Cloud Nine* started from doing a workshop on sexual politics, an extremely large and general subject from which any number of plays could have come. By the end of that period of two or three weeks' research, there was no play, nothing I would have called an idea for a play. The point at which it became an idea for a play was when I thought 'Oh, I see: it could be set a hundred years ago, it could be set as if only twenty-five years have passed.' It was a very quick idea as I was walking down a street, I suddenly saw that way of physically getting a handle on that material. Before that it had been a whole mass of ideas and feelings.[30]

Originally, Churchill's idea was to set *Cloud Nine* in the present. That was scrapped:

And then got the idea of setting the first half in colonial times, in Central Africa, and that partly came from something that briefly came up in the workshop and that was the connection between colonialism and male colonialism of women and the way both women and subject peoples in a colony were thought of in much the same way as childish, irresponsible, devious – because you have to be devious if you can't get power by any other means.[31]

The parallel between colonial and sexual oppression was explored through the prism of the plays of Jean Genet. Another workshop moment which appears in the play directly was to do with the history of gay sexuality, particularly in the nineteenth century when male homosexuality caused horror, whereas female homosexuality was ignored. Overall, though, what came out of the workshop were attitudes, values, discoveries.

The delivery of the script for *Cloud Nine*, especially Churchill's decision to place Act 1 in Africa and Act 2 in contemporary London, created a great surprise among the actors. Act 1 found immediate approval. Act 2 less so. There were arguments, too, about the casting. On 17 December, the group met to respond to the script so that Churchill could consider rewrites. Max Stafford-Clark's verdict was that: 'the shorter scenes in the second half make it seem more fragmented, while the first half progresses with longer scenes. In the first half people avoid talking about relationships at all, and in the second half they talk about them all the time.' And Churchill, according to the same part of the director's Diary, felt: 'I haven't caught a real momentum in the second half. It's hard to devise an action that will drive it along. But I will go back and start again.'[32]

One of the driving ideas – that of Betty in Act 1 being played by a male actor, and Edward in Act 1 played by a woman – came about almost by accident. According to Churchill:

> Like so many things that happen in plays, it came about from the solution of a quite practical problem and then fell into a theoretical justification as well. The practical problem was that setting it in a colonial country, I wanted there to be a black character in the play. And the particular group for whom I was writing it didn't have a black actor in it. And I then thought what would it be if a white person was playing a black one and realised that if also the woman was being played by a man it would be in both cases that these characters had no sense of their own identity but were trying to be what the white men wanted them to be.[33]

It is evident from Churchill's notebooks that she made a number of attempts to find the right format for the play. The first was to do with the generations of a family. The opening scene of this idea was at the grandfather's funeral, where the dead man talked to his wife, while the children and grandchildren bickered among themselves. Churchill found this too static, and, early in November, she returned to the idea of the parallel between sexual and colonial oppression. This produced the setting of Act 1 in colonial Africa. Act 2 initially was a series of monologues, but neither the writer nor director was happy with this. In the next version, the setting was Clive and Betty's retirement bungalow on the south coast. Finally, the setting became a park where children play, perhaps to emphasise the learning and changing of the characters.[34]

Act 1 of *Cloud Nine* is brilliantly funny and observant. Clive, a colonial administrator, runs his bit of the empire and his family in precisely the same way. They are his. They are expected to act in accordance with the rules set out by figures like Clive. His wife, Betty, should base her whole existence on her role as mother and wife. His son, Edward, needs to be manly and idolise his father. Neither of them is able to do what is expected, even though they try. Betty played by a male actor, and Edward, played by a female actor, constantly reinforce the divorce between expectation and actuality. Clive's beliefs are constantly undermined. For Betty and Edward, life is to be endured, occasionally enjoyed, but constantly to be scrutinised. That Clive sees no distinction between his moral horror at the revelation of a colleague's homosexuality and his own lustful pursuit of Mrs Sanders is the convenient morality of those who govern. The atmosphere of the unreal repression of desires and hopes parallels the decline of the empire, as Clive's world begins to echo with rebellion.

The deliberate painting of a society caricaturing itself allows the rhetoric of Act 1 constantly and comically to undermine its speakers. It is principally contained in the figure of Clive, as he carries out his duties. After flogging some local natives, he opines that: 'You can tame a wild animal only so far. They revert to their true nature and savage your hand . . . The whole continent is my enemy. I am pitching my whole mind and will and reason and spirit against it to tame it, and I sometimes feel it will break over me and swallow me up.' Or Clive on women reveals a mind rigidly excluding any possible complexity: 'Women can be treacherous and evil. They are darker and more dangerous than men . . . You are not that sort of woman. You are not unfaithful to me, Betty. I can't believe you are . . .' The speech comes again at the end of the play, by which time Betty is not touchable by him. The comedy of Act 1 is possible because of the forced simplicities of the situation. The misery, too, is a function of the stark ignorance of character complexity.

In Act 2, that complexity of character comes into focus. Churchill daringly moves the play on one hundred years, but only twenty-five for the characters. Victoria (the doll of Act 1) and Edward are grown up. Betty has left Clive. Victoria is married to Martin, and has a son, Tommy. Edward is with Gerry, who feels oppressed by him. The act shows characters aware of their insecurities, unsure of which direction to travel, uncomfortable with their uncertainties. No Clive means no simple solutions. A figure such as Martin nicely summarises a male readiness to sympathise with and support feminism, as long as it is not inconvenient. His self-assertion is couched in the language of understanding, which renders it futile. Oppressing his wife is probably a desperate attempt to keep her. Edward is happy to play housewife to Gerry, who feels panic at the idea of a permanent relationship. Lin says openly that she is lesbian (unlike her counterpart in Act 1, Ellen, whose homosexuality is invisible) and takes Victoria as a lover.

The play's setting goes from a winter afternoon to a late summer's day. The past echoes in parts, as figures from Act 1 visit their modern counterparts. But they are echoes. Betty arrives at a kind of liberation. Her long soliloquy about the joys of masturbation is an account of her journey towards a plateau of happiness. If the ghost of Clive repeats from Act 1 – 'You are not that sort of woman, Betty' – he is wrong. She is that sort of woman, and no longer the repressed and unhappy figure she was before. A final, moving curtain sees the former Betty enter and embrace her new self. Act 2 does not confer happiness on its figures. It argues the possibility. It never accepts so simpleminded a notion that all is for the best. It is, rather, an argument for the subtleties and nuances of relationships.

Cloud Nine opened at Dartington College of Arts on 14 February 1979, toured and then arrived at the Royal Court. It was revived at the Court in 1980, and in 1981 it opened in New York, where it ran for 971 performances. Churchill's international career was launched.

Three More Sleepless Nights to *Icecream* and *Hot Fudge*: 1980–1989

Churchill began her fourth decade of writing with *Three More Sleepless Nights*, a fifty-five-minute piece which appeared at the Soho Poly at lunchtime on 9 June 1980. Its director was Les Waters,[1] who recalls that:

> Caryl wrote it and gave it to me and asked me to direct it
> . . . the Soho Poly seemed the perfect venue for it – small,
> dark and claustrophobic. It was short (before the days of
> the acceptability of the short play). I feel the experience of
> it there was more overwhelming and satisfying than it was
> as an evening experience in the Theatre Upstairs [where it
> moved to in August].

Waters's point about length is relevant, given some of Churchill's later work, but it was an issue at the time. There was criticism, appropriate in the early eighties, of the play not 'giving value for money'. Danny Boyle in the Court's executive committee, on 24 April 1982, compared Churchill's play to Trevor Griffith's *Oi for England*, also an hour long. The ticket price for the Griffiths was reduced to £2. Despite the criticism, the play, placed on the Court's grid for reading, received seven As and one B. The Court was at this stage extremely anxious to build, review or create a relationship with certain writers maintaining a distance from its doors. Churchill was one such.

Three More Sleepless Nights has three sequences. It is perhaps the bleakest of all of Churchill's accounts of the impossibility of maintaining relationships. The constant and shared theme of all three scenes is the misery of the participants. In its view of traumatic breakdown, it approaches the world of Samuel Beckett. Churchill, in the introduction to her *Shorts*, wanted 'two kinds of quarrel – the one where you can't speak and the one where you both talk at once'. It is the first sequence, between Margaret and Frank, both endlessly shouting and snarling at each other, which sees the beginning of a Churchill trademark, that of overlapping speech: 'When I was writing *Top Girls* I first wrote a draft of the dinner scene with one speech after another and then realised it would be better if the talk overlapped in a similar way. Having got a taste for it I've gone on overlapping in most things I've written since.' But the overlapping begins in *Three More Sleepless Nights*.

Its deliberate fragmentation of the convention that clarity is all in theatre produces, here devastatingly, the parallel between linguistic distortion and the chaos of lives. Its hyperrealism makes the quarrelling almost unbearable to an audience, whose experience of the performance is a grim mosaic of accusation, taunt, rage, distress, lull, grim silence. It is voyeuristic in its raw intimacy. By contrast, the second section deals with the dreadfulness of silence. Faced with a virtually silent Dawn, Pete, comically to begin with, details the plot of the film *Alien*. He speaks at length in order to avoid the silence, hardly expecting any kind of response from Dawn. They are strangers to each other in a double bed. Pete cannot respond to Dawn, who twice says: 'I'm frightened.' He continues his account of *Alien* as Dawn returns to bed with the bread knife. It's as if what is being shown consists of two monologues, which do not connect with each other. Shockingly, the sequence ends with Dawn's blood seeping through the sheets as she cuts her wrist. Pete, noticing nothing, puts the light out.

In the final story, Margaret from story one is in bed with Pete. They compare their stories. They cannot move on from the misery of their situations. Pete retreats into the story of *Apocalypse Now* (both film titles are apposite), and finishes the play. Potentially comic lines struggle for effect in a loveless climate. The play closes down.

Between *Three More Sleepless Nights* and one of the seminal plays of modern British theatre came a television play, *Crimes*, transmitted on 13 April 1982. The group's umbrella title was 'Crimes to be Committed', and Churchill used the opportunity to continue the investigation apparent in *The Judge's Wife* and a number of subsequent plays into how a particular society forms models for dealing with those it considers criminal types. The piece constructs a definition of a criminal to embrace any figure protesting against the government. Set in the year 2002, it reveals a grim world, without freedom or tolerance, a world created for the benefit of a few, without regard to the fate of the rest. The mechanisms of control and therefore repression are an abiding concern of Churchill's work and find their most direct expression in *Softcops*, in 1984.

Top Girls was commissioned by the Royal Court, and a series of script meetings record its progress. It appears as 'Famous Women' in October 1979; a year later as 'Successful Women'. A draft was delivered in August 1981, and a second draft in March 1982. At one stage, a version of what became Act 1 arrived at the Court with the title 'Marlene's Dinner with the Dead'. Churchill told Mel Gussow that she thought of calling the play 'Heroines': 'but I was afraid that one wouldn't see the irony of the title. Perhaps people don't see the irony of calling it *Top Girls*'.[2]

The idea of a successful contemporary woman sitting at dinner with a group of historical figures appears to have surfaced at the time when Churchill was still engaged with Monstrous Regiment:

> Caryl Churchill was commissioned to write another play.
> She was interested in seeing if there was any way of bringing together women from different historical periods and letting them talk to each other. In the minutes of our first discussion with her 'Dull Gret, Pope Joan, Pocahontas, a Japanese courtesan, Isabella Bird, etc.' are mentioned. None of us had any idea how their meeting might be accomplished, but we hoped we might discover that in workshops. *Ms Dante's Inferno* was floated as a possible title. When we came to do

the workshops with Caryl we also introduced Florence
Nightingale, Ruth Ellis . . . and Jane Anger . . .[3]

While looking at her papers, Churchill found a notebook from
1975:

> when I was beginning to think about what became *Traps*
> and found something I had no recollection of at all, the
> beginning of a play I was calling 'Dull Gret', which I never
> went on with. She seemed to be a character who started
> as a housewife and was moving towards being an Ubu-y
> figure. I'd forgotten she'd had a life of her own before turn-
> ing up in *Top Girls*.[4]

There were other starting points. One was 'around the time
when Thatcher had been elected and there were a lot of people
saying: is it good because she's a woman, or is it bad because
she's a Conservative?' Another was to do with the difference
between an American view of feminism (Churchill at that stage
had recently returned from the USA), which equated the term
with successful businesswomen and the fact that: 'I was used to
feminism being more connected with socialism and with a
more collective way of looking at things.' Yet another was the
idea of a play 'in which a woman would be succeeding within
a society but the values of the society itself would be in question'. And the question of what became Marlene and Joyce was
another beginning, the 'feeling of the two sisters, one of whom
had stayed where she was and the other who had left to try and
change her life'.[5]

The play, in fact, concerns the lives of seventeen women: the
sixteen on the title page, and the mother of Joyce and Marlene.
It has the most extraordinary opening scene of any modern
play. In the original production of 1982, the glass front of the
restaurant formed the set's back wall. The restaurant entrance
was upstage right. The parade of historical figures all entered
upstage left and walked the full width of the stage before enter-
ing. Thus, they could be seen before they entered and spoke.

The effect was equivalent to a 'whodunit' or, rather, a 'who-is-it?' The audience, held in suspense, waited for the figures to arrive. The table is set for six including Marlene, and the audience therefore knows how many figures are still to come. None of these figures is formally introduced to each other, and therefore to the audience until late in the scene. The audience is left to glean the information as the scene proceeds. The theatrical audacity and sheer fun of the anticipation serve to put aside the concerns of naturalism and logic. It is theatre at its arrogant and brilliant best.

As the scene develops, along with the levels of drunkenness, the stories are told to whoever will listen. The speakers are Pope Joan, Isabella Bird, the Victorian traveller, the thirteenth-century courtesan Lady Nijo, turned Buddhist nun, Dull Gret from Brueghel's painting and Patient Griselda from Chaucer's *Canterbury Tales*. The layering and intercutting of what is said produces precisely the effect of a normal dinner party. The surreal is anchored by the real. Thematically, the effect is to link the speeches of the characters together to produce composites, as well as individuals. The composites create a play within a play. Women's experience is formulated, as well as individual lives. All the stories are of hardship and a price paid for any gain. The play's preoccupation is with equality, male oppression, female gain against huge odds, sacrifice, and all these themes announce themselves in the opening scene. The group eventually fractures, as it gets drunker. Marlene wonders why they are all so miserable, as the celebration of the promotion in the Top Girls Employment Agency turns to laughter, tears, vomit. And all the time this goes on, the silent waitress tells her story by being ignored, except when being given orders.

There is a real surprise after the excitements of Act 1, for Act 2 goes to the agency. Since the sixteen characters in the play are created by seven actors, it means that the exotic figures of Act 1 never leave the stage. They are represented by their creators in another guise. In Act 2, two scenes are set in the agency, and a third in Joyce's back yard. The agency fixes precisely the world of women's work. Initially, Marlene is interviewing Jeanine, who aspires to a career in advertising. She is offered a job in knitwear or lampshades. She is the first of the interviewees, and her six 'O' Levels will not take her very far. Marlene's tone becomes brisker as she has already placed the interviewee according to her sense of what level she is at. Not everyone will run an agency.

It is in Scene 2 that we encounter another part of Marlene's life, although it is not apparent until later in the play. In Joyce's back yard, Angie, sixteen, and Kit, twelve, play together. The glamour of Act 1 is now far behind, as the two girls hide from Joyce. They inhabit their own world, but Kit tells Angie that there is something strange about a sixteen year old playing with a twelve year old. It emerges that Angie has special needs, and was in a remedial class until she left school. Kit, on the other hand, is bright and, it is implied, ordinary. Theatrically, the link between this world and the agency is deliberately tenuous, hinted at briefly when Angie says she is going to London to see her aunt. This she does on her own initiative, and Marlene is faced with a powerful example of a young woman whose prospects are non-existent.

The casual and efficient world of the agency is displayed in Act 2, Scene 3, as Win interviews Louise, a forty-six year old stuck in middle management, unhappy, ignored and desperate to change. She is sensitive to her age and the fact that the world has moved on without her. Angie finds her way to the agency, and views the action with wide eyes, especially when Mrs Kidd, the wife of the man Marlene has beaten to the top job, comes to plead for him. She displays the attitude of someone with a settled view on gender, and her world has been invaded by someone she eventually calls a 'ballbreaker'. When Marlene asks why Mrs Kidd came to see her, she replies: 'I had to do something.' A figure unable to deal with the change to her assumptions. Louise is unhappy in her job. Rosemary Kidd cannot bear the change in her circumstances. A third interviewee, Shona, has a fantasy of her own, which is all make-believe. It involves a Porsche, the M1, hotels, expense accounts and lavish dinners. Yet her sense of what life could be like is one entirely to do with materialism and being seen. When she's exposed, as twenty-one with no job, she replies to the questions 'And what jobs have you done? Have you done any?' with the defiant: 'I could though, I bet you.'

The eighties were increasingly to suggest to the Shonas that such a definition of success was entirely admirable. Win realises that the interview is a waste of time, but her account of herself to a fascinated Angie reveals a tale of pressure and discrimination. Unpopular with male colleagues because successful, the story involves drink, depression and a failed marriage. A sleeping Angie is looked at by Marlene at the close of Act 2:

WIN. She wants to work here.
MARLENE. Packer in Tesco more like.
WIN. She's a nice kid. Isn't she?
MARLENE. She's a bit thick. She's a bit funny.
WIN. She thinks you're wonderful.
MARLENE. She's not going to make it.

Win's line about Angie thinking Marlene is 'wonderful' constitutes a rebuke to Marlene's apparently dispassionate judgement. When it emerges in the next act that they are mother and daughter, Marlene's view of Angie here is recalled, and Marlene herself is judged.

Act 3 takes place 'a year earlier'. The writer's daring is to reverse the chronological sequence, begin with a celebration which goes wrong, and track the movement towards dinner with the dead back to Marlene's origins. Here, Marlene is making a rare visit to her sister's house, with presents for her and for Angie. Angie's first present is the dress she wore in Act 2, Scene 2, where it is described as 'an old best dress, slightly small for her'. Churchill puts it in this way:

I think in the last scene I wanted to really quite clearly confront two different political views in Marlene and her sister
Joyce . . . I did want people to feel that Marlene was
wrong, I suppose, in rejecting Angie and being prepared to
write her off . . . because she wouldn't be someone who is
able to achieve things. But I think it's complicated and pre-
vented from being just a simple black and white thing by
the fact that Marlene has all the attractive qualities of
wanting adventure and change even though it's actually . . .
a goal that ultimately I suspect, I hope, the audience
wouldn't agree with. And equally that Joyce, though having
other views that I would share is also in some ways rather
limited and bad tempered so that it wasn't a case of just
pitching a good person and a bad person.[6]

The row ends in laughter and tears. As Marlene recovers, she
trumpets her enthusiasm for what she believes the eighties
hold: 'I think the eighties are going to be stupendous . . . Get
the economy back on its feet and whoosh. She's a tough lady,
Maggie. I'd give her a job . . .' Joyce's politics are diametrical-
ly opposed, and the arguments begin again between them. In
the same context as the opposing sisters are the victims.
Angie, and Joyce and Marlene's mother, are the ones without
hope. If their mother had a rotten life because she had nothing, then Angie will waste away as well, given that material
success in the world is the criterion. The sisters are implacably
at odds as to their views about what matters. Aunty Marlene
remains just that, and Angie's last line to close the play –
'Frightening' – prefigures the events of the eighties and
beyond. Marlene ends Act 1 drunk. And Act 3. If Act 1
enthrals an audience with its showmanship, Act 3 appals an
audience with its predictions.

Top Girls has lost little of its relevance a quarter of a century later. This is partly because of its author's insistence that
labels are a form of reductiveness, and an attempt to limit creative freedoms. Labels such as 'feminist writer', 'woman writ-

er', 'left-wing writer' produce different reactions from her depending on who's using them and why:

> I mean, I think it would certainly be true to say of my work, certainly at certain times, that I was a left-wing writer, a feminist writer . . . I think I only mind it in any sense at all, and mostly I would embrace it as being a reasonably accurate description but I suppose you mind it if you think that in the other person's mind that conveys something very narrow or specific which doesn't really cover the breadth of your work or that it conveys with it a stereotype of the kind of things that they expect you'll be writing.[7]

The very form of the above reflects Churchill's refusal to be appropriated by any one ideology or school of thought, and her insistence on her right to go where she will in creative terms. It is an unfortunate failing of some critical thought that a writer of Churchill's quality is thought to be able to be subsumed under any one particular banner. *Top Girls* states unequivocally that success in a system which ignores humanity must necessitate an analysis of motive and achievement. The price may be altogether too high. In Act 1, Marlene's line 'Yes, success is very—' was altered in rehearsal to 'Yes, success is very alarming'. Churchill subsequently changed it back because: 'It seems more appropriate that Marlene doesn't quite manage to find what she thinks about success.'[8]

Top Girls opened at the Court in August 1982, a week late because Lynn Dearth, playing Marlene, left the cast and was replaced by Gwen Taylor. It eventually played to 65 per cent audiences. The production then became the first in an arrangement with Joseph Papp's Public Theater, New York, to exchange productions with the Court. It opened in December 1982, played to capacity business with the original company, and re-opened in New York in March 1983, with an American cast. In the 1982–3 Obie Awards, Churchill was named 'Outstanding Writer', and both casts won in the category of 'Outstanding Ensemble Performances'. *Top Girls* returned to the Court for a further run in 1983. Stafford-Clark revived the play at the Court in 1991. Though it did not transfer to the West End at the time – there were, astonishingly, no commercial backers to take it up – it did reach the West End in 2002 in a production from the Oxford Stage Company, directed by Thea Sharrock. The reviews noted its contemporary relevance.

If *Top Girls* was a script conceived and written by Churchill alone, her next play, *Fen*, was researched and developed as a Joint Stock production. Max Stafford-Clark noted in his Diary for 13 December 1981 a decision at a Joint Stock project meeting:

> Caryl Churchill and Les Waters. Source material is book by Mary Chamberlain [*Fenwomen: A Portrait of Women in an English Village*, Virago, 1975]. Prison records for last 150 years. 4 women and 2 men. Workshop – Peterborough. Caryl much tougher [now] as a thinker and I'm sure it won't get nostalgic.

Les Waters was director on the project:

> I was the originator of the project. My mother's family were land workers in the villages and fens of north Lincolnshire (not the fens we visited but the ones further north). I had wanted to work on a project about rural life for some time as I thought it was misrepresented – people who work on the land were either country bumpkins or more in tune with the earth. It's more prosaic than that. It's back breaking. I think of the play as being my mother's life (she was very moved by it and very offended by it when she saw a performance in Lincoln) although as far as I know she never had a lover and she certainly wasn't killed by an axe, but she was 'a deferential worker' with ambitions that she never realised (hence the last line of the play).

The company (Linda Bassett, Amelda Brown, Cecily Hobbs, Tricia Kelly, Jennie Stoller and Bernard Strother) spent two weeks living in a cottage in Upwell, close to the Fens. Writer, director and sometimes designer were also there and involved in the process. Churchill felt that *Fen* became the most documentary-based work of hers up to that date. Les Waters recalled the process:

> . . . we roamed the village and knocked on people's doors or stopped people in the street, or people waved at us from windows and we just went in and talked to them . . . what we did was that nobody was allowed to record anything that was said or write it down at the time it was happening, and then the actors for the main part would come back and present the person they'd met to us and just talk and say things that the person they'd met had actually said.

And Churchill was struck by:

> . . . the pride that a lot of the women land workers had in their physical strength and endurance, and the ambivalence that we felt about that between admiring what they did and feeling that they were actually exploiting themselves, or letting themselves be exploited by doing it . . . And . . . there seemed to be quite a lot of violence within the society . . . within the people we talked to. There was also a history of violence in the Fens, not just a personal domestic violence, but longer ago, of food riots.[9]

After this period, there was another week in London trying to process some of the material. Ten weeks after that, the group returned to a script and rehearsals. Annie Smart's set had come about when the group noticed that in a stone cottage on the main street, behind lace curtains, someone was using the front parlour as a hay store. The integration of work and the domestic was central to the whole project – a field inside a room.

Some of the elements which make up the play are listed at the beginning of Churchill's *Fen* notebook:

> . . . picking down the field, candles – letter, lonely woman at door . . . green mist, old man/woman telling stories,

many kinds of housework, suicide, child scaring birds, mutilating animals, baptism, yearning, people of different times in field, evacuees, arson, wanting to retire to 'country', prams round field, women told lover to murder her, tied cottage, skating, stilts, blind girl, morphrodite . . .[10]

Churchill's Production Note specifies no interval, almost continuous action, all props and furniture on stage throughout and one set. Everything is thus inclusive, immovable, part of one landscape. Work is a continuous reminder, as the earth invades the house. The field is enclosed on three sides by the walls of a house. The women collect potatoes and stones in the same area which functions as a living area. At the beginning and the end of the first performance, fog crept over the stage, which appeared to become green mist. The world of the fen women is constant, unchanging. The boy who opens the play, and appears at the end, is a remnant a century old. The land is owned, but not by its workers. Once the farmer landowners let it. Now large corporations have it. Down the centuries, violence attached to possession has always been near the surface. But for those who work the land, nothing has changed, and prospects of betterment are virtually non-existent. A Japanese businessman politely informs the audience that what they are looking at is one of the company's twenty-five farms. Up there with Esso and Equitable Life.

Women such as Val, Angela, Shirley and Nell make a sort of living potato-picking for a local farmer. They are overseen by Mrs Hassett, the gangmaster. The banter is mock fierce. They all have a living to make. Except Val dreams of something better. She tries to leave for London with her two children. When that fails, she leaves her children to live with Frank, but returns to her kids; then back to Frank who, in a moment of despair, kills her. The network of family, of what should be a support system, only serves to reinforce the despair of no one ever leaving, of people settling for what they have, but retaining a brooding hatred of the system which so oppresses them. Often, figures do something which they can't help. Angela effectively tortures her stepdaughter, who is fifteen, and she knows she should not: 'You shouldn't let me treat you like this.' She forces Becky to drink very hot water, and derides her for giving in to threats from her. The desperation of both, unable to escape, is numbing. The world of the fens is inhabited by children who, although they sing of being a nurse or a hairdresser, also sing of never leaving the village when they grow up. Meanwhile, the farmer sells his land to the City in the person of Miss Cade, land owned by his great-great-grandfather. But as he tells the ghost of a fieldworker, 'everything will go on the same', to which the ghost replies: 'That's why I'm angry'. As with Star becoming the new squire in *Light Shining in Buckinghamshire*, nothing changes except the owner.

From the endless cycle of work comes a grim comfort and relief from other troubles. Shirley rebukes Val who is upset that she is apart from her children:

> You've too much time on your hands. You start thinking. Can't think when you're working in the field can you? It's work, work, work, then you think, 'I wonder what the time is', and it's dinnertime. Then you work again and you think, 'I wonder if it's time to go home', and it is. Mind you, if I didn't need the money I wouldn't do any bugger out of a job.

Work, time, money, an endless round which inexorably breeds huge, dulled resentment. Shirley's husband, Geoffrey, simmers with rage at virtually everything: strikes, militants, Russians, declining church attendance. His is a generalised rage, where that of Nell aims directly at the bosses: 'Best hope if they all top themselves. Start with the queen and work down and I'll tell them when to stop.' Some take consolation in religion. For Val: 'I'd rather take valium.' And Ivy, aged ninety, puts it all in context in Scene 16, as she recalls schooldays and working in the fields. Her grandchildren, at her birthday, are the latest generation of workers.

Frank kills Val, his love, in the final scene of *Fen*. She reappears at the other side of the stage and links the world of the dead with the current one. Rather than joining the ghosts of all who have gone, she stays with Frank. The worlds unite for a moment as live figures mix with dead. Becky arrives, pursued by Angela, who hurts Becky with her own pain in order to feel real. Nell crosses on stilts and exits. Shirley, in a stage direction, *is ironing the field* and she tells of mutilation: 'My grandmother told me her grandmother said when times were bad they'd mutilate the cattle . . . They felt quieter after that.' The sequence weaves together past, present and future in a choreographed series amidst the green mist. It is a moment of intense outpouring as, finally, May 'sings', that is, as Churchill puts it in her Production Note: 'May sings, i.e. she stands as if singing and we hear what she would have liked to sing. So something amazing and beautiful.' But May doesn't sing it. The play ends with an assertion of strength, but the sheer grind of existence has not gone away.

Fen was a success both in the UK, at the Almeida Theatre and the USA, where it opened at the Public Theater, New York in May 1983, with the original cast. It subsequently re-opened with an American cast in March 1984. There were in total 102 performances, and Churchill won the Susan Smith Blackburn Prize. Back in the UK, the play moved to the Royal Court in the autumn of 1983.

In the Introduction to her *Lives of the Great Poisoners*, Churchill signalled an important development in her work at the end of the seventies and the beginning of the eighties:

In 1979 I saw *The Seven Deadly Sins* at the Coliseum, with Julie Covington singing one Anna and Siobhan Davies dancing the other, and thought of working with three performers, one of whom would speak, one dance and one sing. But it was ten years before I worked on that kind of piece.

Meanwhile, I saw Trisha Brown talking while she danced, the Pina Bausch shows at Sadlers Wells in 1982

and work by Second Stride, and gradually got nearer to
working with dancers. Les Waters and I asked Ian Spink
and Siobhan Davies to work with us on the project that
became *Fen*, but neither of them was free.[11]

This growing interest in forms of expression other than the
spoken word found its real starting point in *A Mouthful of
Birds* (1986), but Les Waters remembered the period as:

A time in London when people in various disciplines in the
arts felt a need to change the form – dancers using text,
actors moving. I think groups such as Hesitate and
Demonstrate, the People Show, were a strong influence . . .
Annie [Smart, designer of *Fen*], Caryl and I would return
from the Fens at weekends during the workshop to see Pina
Bausch at Sadlers Wells. We were very influenced by that.

And Annie Smart commented that: 'Caryl was very interested
in being more design/image conscious. And she, Les and I were
influenced by a lot of image – rather than literary-based theatre
around at the time. Groups like Hesitate and Demonstrate,
Welfare State, IOU etc. affected us.' Tricia Kelly, a member of
the *Fen* group, thought Churchill and Waters:

were interested in looking at how you could tell stories
using multimedia and dance. I remember at my interview
[for *Fen*] they talked about wanting dancers and singers,
but in the end it was actors doing what we could . . . This
was the time when performance art was very strong and
Caryl was going into a sort of dream/performance art
exploration.

One of the first illustrations of Churchill's growing interest in
movement and dance came with *Midday Sun*, a performance
art piece to which she contributed. She collaborated with
Geraldine Pilgrim from Hesitate and Demonstrate, Pete Brooks
from Impact Theatre, and John Ashford, who had directed
Churchill's *Traps* in 1977. She produced what was described as

'a cracking centrepiece script . . . which neatly captures the subtle beastliness of the English on holiday'.[12] The script consisted of a fragment of dialogue for five characters on a Moroccan beach. Either side of Churchill's script were two surreal scripts, one imagining the Moroccan scene before it occurs (Pilgrim); the other recalling the sequence (Brooks).

Midday Sun was one-third of a project devised by the founder of the Mickery Theatre, Amsterdam, Ritsaert Ten Cate, and called 'Fairground 84'. The other two-thirds of the project consisted of work from Chapter Theatre of Cardiff and the Traverse Theatre, Edinburgh. Ten Cate seated the audience in three thirty-foot-long boxes built to move on a cushion of air around the 'fairground'. The boxes went round the 'stalls' in a different order. It was a way of manipulating the audience, and altering their perceptions of theatre. *Midday Sun*, according to *City Limits*, had 'José Nova swathed in gold bobbing to the strains of Judy Garland; a figure rising mysteriously from a fountain; a radiant set of amber and azure and many tiny shining moments. The problems are that the themes of anticipation and memory are under-exploited so that if you haven't read the blurb, you've no idea what's going on'.[13]

Between *Midday Sun*, and a fully fledged attempt at combining several expressive arts, *A Mouthful of Birds*, came the production by the Royal Shakespeare Company (RSC) of *Softcops*, originally written in 1978 and revised for its 1984 appearance. Churchill wrote the first version immediately after her television play *The Legion Hall Bombing*, and *Softcops* is related to it thematically. Both plays are concerned with the depoliticisation of crime, 'or calling things crimes that other people might call political acts'. The period 1978–9 was the time when Churchill was thinking about 'methods of social control . . . how you can control people without the necessity of violent means once you have a whole lot of systems to fit people into'.[14] It was at this stage that she read Foucault's *Discipline and Punish*. Foucault analyses the change in methods of control and punishment 'from tearing the victim apart with horses to simply watching him'.[15] Enter Jeremy Bentham, the inventor of the panopticon, the tower from which one person may watch and control society. The effect of reading Foucault was to place the play in nineteenth-century France and centre it around Vidocq, the criminal who became chief of police, and Lacenaire, the murderer and petty thief.

Financial constraints at the time of the first version meant that large casts and multiple-set plays were largely things of the past, especially for theatres principally concerned with new writing. Churchill knew this very well, but for once:

> I thought I'd just write a play on it, and I wrote quite fast these massive scenes. I thought I'm not going to worry about who's going to do this and whether we can do this one with six people and a chair! In this one we will have crocodiles of schoolchildren and *mobs*, and *executions* and all the things I know it is completely impractical to have. Then I put it aside and forgot about it until some time later when Howard Davies was approaching me about doing a play for the RSC. I remembered that I had this and showed it to him, and he liked it and read the book and said, yes, finish it. We can have executions, mobs, no problem.[16]

The play had, in fact, appeared on the Royal Court grid to be read between October and December 1982. It was habitual to read anything by Court writers, even if the play was going somewhere else. It is, however, likely that the Court would not have been able to afford to mount *Softcops*. According to Rob Ritchie, then Literary Manager of the Court, 'the discussion was about whether we were missing out on a great play and so should try and pinch it. I didn't think we were . . . We all went to see the show when it was done and I don't recall anyone having a massive fit of jealousy.'

Churchill's Production Note stated that it was developed:

> by the director, designer, composer, choreographer, actors, musicians and myself in a way that I have not attempted to

describe [in the printed text] . . . Nor have I stipulated that the set is a neglected room in a great house, that the actors are in evening dress, or that there is a string quartet on stage throughout. These things come from Howard Davies's production and it does not seem right to appropriate them as part of the play.[17]

In addition, the performance area (the Barbican Pit) was draped in white muslin. There were lighted candelabra against a background of paintings, furniture and suitcases. Twelve male actors played multiple parts. Choreographed groups dealt with mob violence, disciplined formations and stillness. The dominant colours of the production were black and white, off-set by red, as stipulated in the text.

A central figure in *Softcops* is Pierre, who dreams of a perfect system of control, a balance of terror and information, as he supervises the building of a high scaffold. Around him is a crocodile of uniformed young boys who, says their headmaster, have stood motionless already for three hours. Their stillness contrasts with the general bustle of the scene, as workmen put the finishing touches, and people come and go. Pierre's efforts are always under pressure. He dithers about whether to keep red ribbons on the scaffold, he takes them off, but one remains. The procession of the magistrate, the executioner and a prisoner arrives and, because the minister is slightly delayed, has to go round again. When the minister arrives, he deflates Pierre by telling him that most of the crowd cannot read. Pierre cannot read his own writing. He has to coach the prisoner, Duval, in his prepared speech, who then has his head cut off, and the minister laments the good old days: 'What brings a crowd, it's very simple, is agony.' Once the mob has that they are controllable via fear. As the next prisoner, Lafayette, refuses to read his prepared speech, so a riot begins, dispersed by soldiers.

Pierre dreams of a 'Garden of Laws', where 'there would be displayed every kind of crime and punishment. Different coloured hats. Different coloured posters. Guides to give lectures on civic duty and moral feeling . . .' Above, an iron cage suspended for 'the worst crime. Parricide'. Pierre's listeners consist only of the headmaster and the children. Then Vidocq, the master criminal, becomes chief of policy and bases all justice on a card-index system to keep track of all known criminals, together with a newly organised police force led by himself. Pierre is bewildered by Vidocq's tactics and seeks some more theoretically sound system. He wants to put a regicide in his iron cage to make a great spectacle, but is persuaded instead to make a spectacle of Lacenaire who is 'pretty. He writes verses. He'll do.' He is also a complete incompetent and is executed. Pierre turns to the methods of the headmaster, who so controls his charges that physical punishment becomes unnecessary:

> I use the cane very rarely now I have perfected the
> timetable. I enjoy my work. I see the results of it. Their
> bodies can be helped by harnesses. And their minds are
> fastened every moment of the day to a fine rigid frame.

However, Pierre only finds his solution via Jeremy Bentham, who says: 'you don't need to be watched all the time. What matters is that you think you're watched. The guards can come and go. It is, like your display, an optical illusion.'

Yet in the final scene, the system of control, operated by one man, Pierre, begins to fragment. He sits on a beach, while some of his charges splash about in the sea. As he talks to a holidaymaker, one of the men tries to attack him, and is shot dead. Pierre's final speech of the play is one rehearsed to produce in front of the minister. As he becomes very confused, the terminology slips. The incoherence of the language reflects the innate incoherence of any system which tries to operate in this way. If a prisoner, in spite of the system, tries to kill Pierre, and Pierre cannot formulate precisely how his system works, then it is resistible – but not incredible. Churchill added a 'Further Note' to her Author's Note in *Plays: 2*:

Softcops was originally written in 1978, under a Labour Government, when the question of soft controls seemed more relevant than in 1984, the year of its first production, when Thatcher was dismantling the welfare state . . . In 1985, as this edition goes to press, the Government are attempting to depoliticise the miners and the rioters by emphasising a 'criminal element'.

While *Softcops* was staged at the RSC, Churchill's main theatre business was with the Court and her new project with Joint Stock. And in 1986, at the Court's Council for 13 January, the issue was raised which was to lead to her resignation in 1989:

Ms Caryl Churchill raised some of the problems of sponsorship and a full discussion ensued . . . The consensus of the discussion was that sponsorship and outside fundraising was a necessary part of survival, but that a certain integrity had to be exercised. Ms Churchill asked that her objection to sponsorship and royal patronage be recorded.

While it is true that the Court was threatened by the Arts Council's questioning of its role, and the fact that the Court's grant for 1984–5 was an across-the-board increase of 2.9 per cent, barely one-half of the rate of inflation, it is also the case that supporters of the theatre's survival argued the importance of keeping it running. The eighties saw this debate as a central and irresolvable dilemma. It was pragmatism versus principle, and it was to force out one of the Court's most important writers.

One of the consequences of Churchill's preoccupation with dance, choreography and expressive movement at this time is that the published text of *A Mouthful of Birds* is even less revealing about a particular production than a text consisting only of words. She says in her Introduction to *Plays: 3* that: 'One can only get a rough idea of the piece by reading it because a large part of it was dance.' The same is true of *The Skriker*, 'a play I was working on from before *A Mouthful of Birds*'.[18]

A Mouthful of Birds is Churchill's fourth work for Joint Stock, whose project committee interviewed a total of six writer/director teams: 'Caryl Churchill, Les Waters and David Lan were then informed that their project using *The Bacchae* as a base had been chosen as the 86 Project'. From the comparative opulence of the RSC to the comparative poverty of Joint Stock.

The collaboration between David Lan and Churchill was the first time Churchill had truly collaborated with another writer. David Lan, a playwright and anthropologist, was good friends with Churchill, who believes it was Lan who first thought of *The Bacchae*:

> . . . and his interest was from the point of view of possession . . . he'd spent some time in Zimbabwe finding out about spirit mediums and their relationship with the guerrillas during the war. He'd recently had a book published based on his research there. Les [Waters], by coincidence, was reading *The Bacchae* at that point and one of the things that led him towards it was that I had been saying that I was interested in doing something about women and violence, and women being violent, rather than having violence done to them.[19]

Of the team assembled for *A Mouthful of Birds*, Churchill, Waters and designer Annie Smart had of course worked together on *Fen*. As well as David Lan, Ian Spink (co-founder with Siobhan Davies, of Second Stride, a dance company admired by Churchill) joined the group as co-director and choreographer with Waters. The company of seven consisted of four actors (Tricia Kelly, Dona Croll, Christian Burgess and Amelda Brown), two dancers (Philippe Giraudeau and Stephen Goff) and Vivienne Rochester, an actor who had trained as a dancer.

What needs underlining is that this was a hugely experimental venture, groundbreaking and risky. It also made massive demands on the whole ensemble. As Lan commented: 'It was very interesting really because I don't think any of us had the faintest idea what we were doing really when we were doing it.'

Joint Stock ventures demand an absolute commitment to the process, and a willingness to trust everyone concerned. This was a twelve-week, continuous workshop with no writing gap, as was usually the case in Joint Stock. Spink was involved in the workshop from the beginning, developing the skills of the group and creating sequences often from a simple direction from the writers: 'Dance a pig'. The learning curve for the company was complex. As Churchill said:

> For the writers the time still fell into something of the usual structure – roughly the first four weeks were spent by us all looking into possession, violence and other states where people felt beside themselves; then David Lan and I stayed home and wrote, coming in with scenes as they were written; the last few weeks were something like a normal rehearsal. Ian Spink worked with the company continuously, making some material before any text was written, and some to fit specifically into scenes that were written to have dance in them.[20]

The research period involved talking to spirit mediums, a transsexual, an exorcist, prisoners.[21] Churchill herself, in order to pursue ideas of 'tearing up and destroying and eating', brought back from Smithfield market a sheep's head and a dead rabbit.[22]

The structure of *A Mouthful of Birds* consists of, initially, seven scenes which display who and what the characters are before extraordinary events take over. There is then a middle section, imbued with the concept of 'the undefended day', when there is no protection, as there normally is, from the disturbing forces inside and outside the self. There are also the possession stories in this section. They deal with violent women and men who are weakened or made uncertain by possession. The final sequence consists of seven monologues, in which the figures talk about what eventually happens to them. And if the piece's attempt to impose a holding structure on the material is at times a little precarious, the brilliance of individual episodes is compelling.

Within a frame expressed by the figure of Dionysus, the seven figures signal their unhappiness, distress, unease. They are all vulnerable to attack, either from their innermost fears or from an external source, summoned by a sense of weakness. Lena is subject to 'Psychic Attack', as a spirit, seen and heard only by her, urges her on four successive days to murder her child. The banalities of everyday life are counterpointed by the intensity of the assault upon Lena. Intercut with such narratives are moments from *The Bacchae*, and expressions of the effects of possession. Paul, a businessman, falls for a pig. As Paul recites dreary business statistics, the pig dances a solo. Paul's colleagues do not notice the pig. Paul is drawn steadily to it. The pig is slaughtered in the abattoir before he can be rescued. But the pig, wrapped in clingfilm, is unwrapped and 'Paul and the Pig dance, tenderly, dangerously, joyfully'. Derek is translated into a woman from a weightlifting macho figure. Doreen, however, is mired in her alcoholism. Her violence is a function of her despair.

The seven figures traverse the dangerous territory of their undefended day to arrive at the play's conclusion of seven monologues. For Lena: 'Every day is a struggle because I haven't forgotten anything.' Derek, now a woman, is in love with a lion-tamer from Kabul. But Doreen cannot rest, and presents a frightening image of terror as she carries on her work as a secretary.

A Mouthful of Birds opened as a co-production with Birmingham Repertory Theatre at Birmingham on 2 September 1986. After a twelve-week tour, it opened at the Royal Court on 27 November. The Birmingham opening was noisy. As David Lan put it:

> I think the audience thought what they were getting was 'Top Girls 2' and they got this very disjointed, broken-up piece, which was unhappy when it opened . . . it really came together on tour . . . by the time it hit the Court it had found itself.

In fact, the play did only 29 per cent business at the Court, but it did find an appreciative coterie audience for one of the most adventurous pieces of its time.

A month before the play opened at the Court, its Council for 29 October raised the question of another play, *Perdition* by Jim Allen, the controversy over which produced the worst crisis in the Court's history. As a Council member, Churchill was closely involved. *Perdition* dealt with the behaviour of Hungarian Jews in 1944, and stated that the deportation of Jews from Hungary in the last month of World War Two was made possible only by the co-operation of Jewish leaders in pursuit of the creation of a Jewish homeland. The play examined the Zionist doctrine of Nazi collaboration in pursuit of this goal. When *Perdition* arrived at the Court in August 1985, reports were commissioned as to its historical accuracy and, some felt, its anti-semitism.

The Court's Artistic Director, Max Stafford-Clark, failed to notice the impending storm. As well as the play itself, there were those who thought an opportunity had presented itself which might see the end of Stafford-Clark's reign. Council met to debate the matter. Stafford-Clark felt that he received support from Bill Gaskill and Caryl Churchill, but others were not so supportive. Churchill is minuted thus:

> Caryl Churchill said that she had read most of the play and felt there could be no possibility of seeing the play as anti-Semitic. She felt an enormous amount of compassion came through. She would hate to think that the fact that the play was a polemic would go against it. She felt the Council should respect Jim Allen's reputation and right to his position.

Stafford-Clark eventually withdrew the play, and the Council vented its anger at the affair. Churchill's support, however, was unwavering. Six days before *Serious Money* opened, Churchill wrote to the *New Statesman* in response to a letter the periodical had published from Tony Garnett attacking the Court. She replied with some asperity:

Tony Garnett accuses the Royal Court Council of keeping their heads down over *Perdition* . . . maybe it's time I stuck mine up. It's easy to see how from the distance of Hollywood he has misunderstood the situation. He imputes all kinds of scurrilous motives to the Council, overlooking the simple and honest one of supporting the artistic director, Max Stafford-Clark. The Council of the Royal Court, unlike that of many theatres, has no say in what plays are put on – that is left entirely to the artistic director, and it seems to me important that he should be free from interference by a managing body (I'd prefer to see theatres without them).

. . . It is as Tony Garnett says, a time when many of us may find our work under attack from the right; please don't confuse things by thinking the withdrawal of *Perdition* is an example of this. I still believe the Royal Court to be a theatre that supports radical writing. Allen, Loach and the actors have my sympathy – what happened has been horrible for them and no one connected with the Royal Court has any pleasure in it. But Stafford-Clark has my support, both in his decision to do the play and his painful but honourable decision to withdraw it.[25]

Serious Money was rehearsing while the *Perdition* row developed and while *A Mouthful of Birds* was touring. Stafford-Clark had organised a workshop in September 1986, lasting two weeks. The participants, apart from himself and Churchill, included eight actors, the composer Colin Sell, the Court's Literary Manager Philip Palmer and Mark Long of The People Show. The working title of the project was LIFFE, the initials of the London International Financial Futures Exchange. Two of the workshop actors got jobs on the floor of LIFFE. The group met stockbrokers, Metal Exchange traders, traders on the Baltic Exchange and financial advisors. As Stafford-Clark's Diary noted:

> The first session of each day would be a group rehearsal. One exercise was for each of the actors to pursue a story

from the *Financial Times*, which meant that we all became involved in comprehending the financial world and its jargon. But the main purpose was to report back to Caryl. We would set up improvisations replaying the interviews with the people we had met the previous day . . .[24]

At the end of the workshop, the actors performed a twenty-minute piece, based on what they had learned. It was left to Churchill to decide if she wanted to write the play based on the workshop material. She did, and researched further for the rest of the autumn of 1986. At this point, a series of financial scandals became public. The London Stock Exchange had deregulated in October 1986, which opened up a hitherto private club to anyone able to make money. It was known as 'Big Bang'. Following this, scandals like that of Ivan Boesky came out. He was charged in November 1986 with insider dealing, served two years of his sentence and fined $100 million. In the UK, the so-called Guinness Four were accused and convicted of a huge share-trading fraud. A play about this could hardly be more timely, although Stafford-Clark had been interested in the subject for some years.

Out of the mass of material came a piece written in verse, which helped to bring the mass under some kind of control. The rarity of verse in modern British theatre reflects the strange and enclosed world Churchill depicts. Stafford-Clark noted in his Diary for 7 February: 'Caryl's bravery and boldness to the fore: she's written it in rhyming couplets. I mean, in verse of all kinds, which sometimes doesn't give it much room to stop and be serious. It's caricature and it's funny'.

The reaction of the actors to the play was mixed. In his Diary, Stafford-Clark noted the moment 'where actors say how good the play is but just that their own particular parts are underdeveloped. The play . . . doesn't go into the psychology of the characters in any detailed manner.' Nor was Colin Sell's music much to the actors' liking. On the other hand, Ian Dury's songs, which appeared in the final version, worked well. A further alteration came, as Stafford-Clark noted on 7 March. A concern had been expressed about the structure of the first act, because the extract from Thomas Shadwell's 1692 play, *The Stockjobbers*, was embedded in the act:

> After a reflective weekend Caryl came in with a completely restructured first act. She moved the extract from *The Stockjobbers* to the start, where it became a kind of prologue. Most of the music was cut – it seemed to hold up the action – and we were left with Ian Dury's magnificent and obscene anthemic numbers to end each half.

One of the consequences of the deregulation of the Stock Exchange was an end to what was termed 'open-outcry' trading on the floor of the Exchange, which closed within two years. This form of trading was replaced by computers and telephones. The impersonality of the new system stands as a metaphor for the impersonality of the business of making money. As Zac, a banker, observes:

> Pictures of starving babies are misleading and patronising. Because there's plenty of rich people in those countries, it's just the masses that's poor . . .

The facelessness of the operation mirrors the facelessness of the poor. It is therefore far easier to deal in numbers than people. The huge and, in some ways, attractive energy of the people involved in making money is concentrated only on that one thing – profit. There are only two dominant emotions expressed by the inhabitants of this strange world. They are greed and fear. Greed to make as much as possible, at whatever cost, and fear of disclosure of the method used. Consequently, the figures become their own stereotype. As in a Restoration or Jonsonian comedy, character is subordinate to action, and the situation matters more than the personalities involved.

The central story of *Serious Money*, which ends without an ending, is of the death of Jake Todd, and the search for his killer by his sister, Scilla. Yet all Scilla actually wants is not justice for her brother but any money he has accumulated. The only difference between her and the new, young traders, labelled 'oiks' in the play, is her upper-class accent. The arrival of the 'oiks' as a consequence of 'Big Bang' gravely unsettles the existing denizens of the City and ruffles the hierarchy, which replicates that of society at large. There is no difference between either group as far as greed is concerned. The difference is that the newcomers are raucous, obscene and loudly indifferent. The older inhabitants, as devious and amoral as anyone, prefer discretion and the quiet murmur.

Serious Money bursts into life after an initial excerpt from Shadwell's *The Stockjobbers*, where it is asserted that 'the main end verily is to turn the penny in the way of stock jobbing, that's all'. Three different dealing rooms are shown simultaneously. The rooms buzz with frantic activity. Since most of the audience will not understand the process of, say, the gilts dealing room, concentration focuses on the strangeness of the figures as they in turn concentrate on the work. The actual trading is interspersed with ordinary conversation, or bits of conversation. Thus the effect is mosaic-like. The vulnerability of the new system is comically displayed when power is lost and all the systems crash. The sense issuing from the LIFFE Champagne Bar is solely to do with rising to the top of the heap:

> Think of the ones at the top who can afford
> To pay us to make them money, and they're on the board.

LIFFE is pronounced 'life', an irony which will not have escaped Churchill's notice. The structure of power is changing, as Zac the banker tells how in the USA a new brutalism sees patrician members of finance houses ousted by the new breed of trader, uninterested in clubs, golf and buying Picassos for the sake of it:

> If you're making the firm ten million you want a piece of the action.
> You know you've got it made the day you're offered stock options . . .
> Now, here in England, it's just beginning to hit.

Zac likes England:

> London, I go to the theatre, I don't get mugged, I have
> classy friends,
> And I go see them in the country at the weekends.

He hunts with his friends, a motley crew of upper-class country figures, including Greville Todd, a stockbroker, father of Jake and Scilla, and representative of what he thinks England ought still to be. It does not involve 'the most frightful yobs'. A lonely figure is Frosby, an old-fashioned jobber, full of self-pity and nostalgia for the old Exchange and for the old system. He telephones the Department of Trade and Industry (DTI) to leak some information, and, as the DTI begins to look at some of the murkier deals, the City panics. With Jake's death, it is assumed that trouble is on the way. Marylou Baines, an American arbitrageur, on hearing of the death immediately tells her assistant: 'Put anything from Jake Todd in the shredder.'

The most characteristic representative of the new order is Corman, a corporate raider, whose passion is buying companies, stripping them of their assets, making an enormous profit and moving on. He wants Albion Products, run by Duckett, prefers the acquisition to be difficult – 'if it was easy it'd bore me' – and goes about raising the finance to acquire, quietly, Albion shares. He is a fantastical character in a crude operetta. He is also deadly. He hears that Albion's chief has acquired a white knight (a company which is the target of an unwelcome takeover bid may search for a white knight, an alternative bidder acceptable to it), Ms Biddulph. She tells Duckett:

> You're a sweet English maiden, all shining and bright.
> And Corman's the villain intent upon rape
> And I'm the white knight . . .

Corman swings into action:

> From today we're coming to the crunch.
> Nobody's going out anymore to lunch.

(You can cancel dinner too.)
From today, we're going for the gold.
Put your family life and your sex life on hold.
A deal like this, at the start you gently woo it.
There comes a time when you get in there and screw it.
So you get the stock. And I don't care how you do it.

In Corman's world, exotic and vicious creatures swirl around. They include a Peruvian businesswoman Jacinta Condor, who quickly takes her money out of copper mines when the price falls, and leaves the workers to shift for themselves. Jake brings Jacinta in to buy Albion shares for Corman, as he does Nigel Agibola, an importer from Ghana. Apart from these strange figures, there is a group of new traders, which closes Act 1. The five gather on the floor of LIFFE. There are four separate companies, each with telephones. The scene builds in volume as trading develops. Out of the noise emerges the song which concludes the act. The 'Futures Song' is breathless, obscene and designed to bring the house down at the interval.

Corman's image is massaged in a way which bothers even him. Duckett has cornered the market in 'fatherly, blue-eyed, babies, workers' friend'. Dolcie Starr, a PR consultant, urges Corman to present himself as a villain. If Duckett sponsors orchestras, then Corman can sponsor the National Theatre:

Theatre for power, opera for decadence,
String quartets bearing your name for sensitivity
and elegance,
And a fringe show with bad language for a thrill.
That should take care of the spiritual.

Starr also recommends a sex scandal: 'sexy greedy *is* the late eighties'. This thread of the play, the makeover of greed via the arts, exercised Churchill through the decade and beyond. To this extent, *Serious Money* reflects her sense of the logic begun with Marlene in *Top Girls*. In exchange for dropping his pursuit of Albion, so persuaded by a cabinet minister in the interval at the National of a performance of *King Lear*, Corman becomes chair of the National and a lord. The minister is anxious about the impending general election. The play predicts a Conservative victory. Three months after it opened, Margaret Thatcher was returned as prime minister for the third successive time. The play concludes with the song 'Five More Glorious Years'.

Serious Money opened at the Court in March 1987. It transferred to Wyndhams in the West End and ran for a year. It ran for five weeks at the Public in New York with the original cast, and opened with an American cast at the Royale, New York, in January 1988. It won an Obie in the USA for 'Best New American Play'.

At a Council meeting of 13 April 1987, it was reported that two performances of *Serious Money* 'had been sold out to individual companies, the price including a substantial profit margin; everybody attending would be given a letter outlining sponsorship opportunities'. At the same meeting: 'It was reported that Caryl Churchill was opposed to speeches from the stage at the buy-outs encouraging future sponsorship. This provoked discussion . . .' What Churchill had attacked in her play was coming true in her own theatre. Not only Churchill: Hanif Kureishi at the 13 July Council 'voiced his concern at the acceptance of the need for commercial sponsorship and its recruitment of people who represented the kind of society to which the [Court] was opposed'. Ironically, the success of *Serious Money* bailed the Court out of its financial difficulties. The proceeds from the transfer were estimated in September at £70,000.

The City world flocked to see itself on the stage, and the enthusiasm with which they greeted it was evidence of their ignorance of satire and irony. The money did help the Court. The Court chose to exploit the play in using the buy-outs to promote sponsorship to the very audience the play attacks. *Serious Money* in 1987 was very much a play addressing the eighties. A play for that day. Given the current prominence of private equity dealers and the growth of hedge funds, it appears to be a play for today as well. Later in 1988 a conference of 'British Theatre in crisis' heard from Churchill:

> That the debilitating reductions in public funding for the arts marked a recognisable impetus by the government towards the privatisation of theatre . . . [She] called for a concerted rejection of private sponsorship because of the intrinsic inequalities which the system promotes, and because of the level of control which it gives to business organisations whose values are ultimately those of Thatcherism.[25]

In the same year, Churchill collaborated once more with Ian Spink on a twenty-four-minute television piece, *Fugue*, described as a play with dance. It is the story of the death of a father, of the cremation of the figure, and the subsequent funeral tea. It has thirteen sections and, together with Spink, it featured seven dancers, two of whom, Philippe Giraudeau and Stephen Goff, had worked on *A Mouthful of Birds*. The piece went out on Channel 4 on 26 June 1988.

The structure of the piece reflects the circumstances of the funeral of J. S. Bach, pre-eminent in the composition of fugues. Here, the dance is to Bach's 'Contrapunctus Ten' from *The Art of Fugue*.[26] The first section tells the story of the father's death, elements of which are then repeated in twenty-two very short sequences. The mother telephones her daughter: 'He'd just got out of the bath. I thought I heard him call so I came out of the kitchen. And he was already falling down the stairs'. This information of her watching him fall is transmitted to and by the daughter, the son, the girlfriend, the husband. On the one hand, the method cleverly shows the news reverberating through the family; on the other, it reflects, comically and accurately, that that is the only relevant information at such a time.

At the crematorium, Bach's fugue comes in, as they prepare to bury the father. Within this structure, there are two scenes, studio based, where the father, smiling at the mother by his coffin, moves into a fifties dancehall. It is the son dressed in fifties' clothes. The mother is then played by the daughter before the scene dissolves to the crematorium. Father is duly cremated, and appears as an angel, with a crown, wings and a harp, waving from above. The funeral tea mixes parts of the mother's initial phone conversation with the usual chatter on such occasions – the traffic, the motorway, no flowers from Phyllis: 'No she's the one who went to Canada.' The enforced banality of the occasion reinforces the repetitive nature of all such occasions.

There's then a flashback, set on a beach, thirty years ago, with the family happy and enjoying itself. This reverts to the funeral tea, where it comes out that the son did not like the father. Out of nowhere, the father appears only to yell at his children. The father and his habit of making up music in the evening now become important, since he had gone missing for six months and had lost his memory and his music. As the relatives leave the funeral tea, there is a sequence showing father going missing again. In the panic, the son rushes to his room to find it full of model planes. The daughter's room is full of falling music stands. Father's death is re-enacted. He stands at the top of the stairs, 'falls forward but flies up into the air'. The son, husband, daughter and girlfriend play the fugue for four pianos. Then they wash the father's naked body and burn it on a funeral pyre. The piece ends when the same four dance the fugue to incorporate all the previous elements.

All of Churchill's work demonstrates invention and re-invention, ways of saying which take the discussion further on. The givens of *Serious Money* are succeeded by the subtleties and apparent surfaces of *Icecream* and *Hot Fudge*. *Icecream* concerns two American visitors to the UK to find family. Lance and Vera duly find cousins Phil and Jaq. The narrative line sees Phil killing a man, and persuading Lance and Vera to help bury the body in Epping Forest. After ten scenes, the play moves to the USA, where Jaq takes off in Lance's car, gets involved with a hitchhiker and his mother, who are preparing for the imminent end of the world, pushes a groping professor off a hill and ends up in an airport, perhaps to go off with a South American passenger.

None of the above says what *Icecream* is doing. Churchill herself said that she:

> wrote it very much as a story and as a road movie . . . The starting point was an American couple who came to England and find it not as they expected . . . I suppose it is a play about people constantly trying to place themselves and make sense of the world in which they live. How do you understand all the things that have happened which you don't know about, the hidden things?[27]

And Les Waters, who directed the play in New York, said: 'There's nothing on the surface of one scene that prepares you for the next scene. The play reflects what the characters are going through – things happen to them and they don't understand their own behaviour as they're doing it.'[28] The title plays with the fact that an American would pronounce 'ice cream' with the stress on the first syllable (a trochee); the English pronunciation would stress both syllables (a spondee). Same word, different pronunciation, different culture.

Lance and Vera entertain notions of what the UK is like consistent with a romantic view of the ancient, green and pleasant land. But from Lance's hardly remembered song from *Brigadoon* in the opening scene, a vagueness which demonstrates how unreal his vision is, to his awe at the history of the UK, there is the picture presented by Phil and Jaq of an erratic, aimless and restless time and place. In the absence of any clear view, these two simply move with the circumstances. A main idea is developed of how each couple regards the other couple's country, a fascination which was to surface in *Drunk Enough to Say I Love You?* in 2006. Phil is thrilled with the mere mention of American things and places and, just as forcefully, filled with loathing about hamburgers and American cops. Lance loves England: 'The green fields. The accents. The pubs.' Vera is anxious not to provoke anyone, but to love Jaq and Phil for Lance's sake because they are family.

Throughout *Icecream*, violence simmers: from Scene 1, and Lance's great grandmother drowning herself in a well, to the death of Miss Glade, to Phil's German shepherd trained to attack, to the murder of a man who may be Phil's landlord in Part 1, to Vera's dreams, the incipient violence of the hitchhiker, the death of Phil, the aggression of the professor. All through, barely subdued, the threat of, usually, random, violent events is present. The arbitrariness of the events, the lack of connection or of logic, creates a sense of dislocation. Churchill pointed up the subject:

> Writing the play from the basis of a simple story meant that it didn't have a subject that I could identify quite so clearly. I knew that a lot of the scenes were about people trying to find out where they are – Lance trying to place himself in terms of his family history, Lance and Vera trying to work out whether Phil is mad or sane, people generally trying to find a grid with which they can make sense of things. But I didn't realise until after I'd finished writing it how much there is about death and ways of facing death, and about things which are buried rather than being faced.[29]

The end of *Icecream* is inconclusive. Jaq waits for a plane. She may go with the South American who approaches her. It is not stated. The rootless air which pervades the play persists: 'it is about a girl in Thatcher's England living quite an aimless, violent, limited life: a girl who begins to see more possibilities . . .'[30]

The play, directed by Max Stafford-Clark, opened at the Court on 6 April 1989. Worried about its brevity (about seventy-five minutes), he suggested to Churchill that she write something to go with it. In her Introduction to *Shorts* she 'wasn't sure [*Hot Fudge*] did go well with *Icecream* and was afraid it would somehow spoil it. But when we did *Hot Fudge* as a reading anyway we found we liked it.' Stafford-Clark noted in his

Diary of 15 March: 'Decided not to do *Hot Fudge* . . . as it would distract and defocus the statement from *Icecream*.' *Hot Fudge* was given a 'performance reading' Upstairs in May. It had to wait for a full showing until April 1990, when it appeared for fifty-six performances in New York, directed by Les Waters, under the title of *Ice Cream with Hot Fudge*. For Waters, the play is about 'how exhausting and scary it is to try and tell another human being the truth about yourself'.[31]

Hot Fudge is in four short scenes. It takes place over one evening in a pub, a wine bar, a club and a flat. In the pub, Matt carefully explains a scam involving building society cheques to a doubting Charlie, who is an old-fashioned bank robber and car thief: 'I like cash in my hand . . . I don't like plastic.' The scam has been developed by Charlie's daughter, Sonia, regarded by her father as incapable of anything so clever. The group decide to try the trick on a bigger basis. Even Charlie. New technology ousts old.

Meanwhile, Ruby, forty, and one of the group, tells her sister she has a new man, Colin, who is in 'media monitoring'. She has told him she runs her own travel agency. Colin and Ruby in the wine bar systematically tell each other lies about what they do. The audience knows about Ruby, but not Colin who, in Scene 3, takes Ruby to meet some friends: a global manager, a virtual tennis teacher and an estate agent. The conversation is entirely predictable. The final scene erupts into violence as Colin's ex-wife turns up at his flat. She angrily reveals that Colin has had a nervous breakdown. He knocks her over. She does the same to him, and leaves. Warily, Ruby and Colin begin again, this time perhaps telling each other the truth. The fantasies are sidelined. The play ends with the possibility of some new growth. The bulk of the play has shown and derided the image-conscious banalities of those who prefer not to speak the truth.

Icecream and *Hot Fudge* begin to mark a movement in how Churchill writes. Neither of the plays was workshopped. There was no pressure to respond to a brief. A consequence of that, perhaps, is that 'more subconscious things can come in and start connecting up. Your research just comes from your life and what you're thinking about.'[32]

Some months after *Icecream* opened, Churchill resigned from the Council of the Royal Court (3 November). As has been seen, her objections to corporate sponsorship were profound and had been voiced. When it emerged that a potential sponsor was Barclay's Bank, she made her feelings plain at Council on 23 October, and left. A day later, Stafford-Clark reflected in his private Diary on the situation. He was aware that Churchill would oppose any liaison with Barclay's but:

> did not fully contemplate it being a resignation matter. She made her objections clear, but was not present at the executive meeting when the decision was ratified, nor did anybody present realise or fully take on how upset she would be . . . After Caryl's speech yesterday [at Council], I felt my view was opportunistic and shallow, and that I had supported the wrong decision. If a theatre director cannot keep his writers and their loyalty, then I've got no right to stay . . . Because the bottom line is that the Royal Court is led by the principles of its writers . . . Because when Caryl spoke it seemed like the voice of the Royal Court, and the pressure to fundraise has probably led us at least one compromise too far.

The dilemma of theatre generally in the period is accurately expressed in the above. More powerful, because from a writer, is Churchill's letter of resignation to the Court chairman, Matthew Evans. It speaks for her and future generations of theatre workers, and it mirrors the state of affairs as the eighties drew to a close:

> Barclays are of course no longer boycotted by Anti-apartheid but I still can't accept the Royal Court being used to launder the image of a bank. It's clear to me though that the issue is not just Barclays or the way the decision was

made. The Council has been supportive of the search for private funding and sponsorship and though Barclays was sufficiently stark to give me a jolt it is not essentially out of keeping with recent Royal Court policy.

I've been opposed to this policy for a long time and occasionally speak out, and it has been clear that almost no one on the Council agrees with me. Though it will probably need to be decided what companies are or are not acceptable to the Court, I don't feel happy with any company sponsorship. It means the theatre and those involved with the show endorse not only the product but also the government's policy of privatising the arts, along with medicine and water. I would like to see the Court resisting this policy, and making it clear to the Arts Council that we are not going to help them carry it out. For this to happen the artistic director, staff and Council would need to feel committed to this position and inspired by the kind of theatre it could create, and I don't think it's likely. I would urge you all at least to make the distinction between accepting donations (small thank you in programme) and accepting sponsorship (large name linked to specific project on posters and advertisements) and consider rejecting sponsorship; and not to accept money when the idea for a show or kind of show comes from the people giving it.

I can understand and respect the view that what matters is to keep the work going and so the theatre should take whatever money it can get. But I can't share it. I feel that my plays are saying one thing and the theatre something else. It is a serious problem and not just for me, because if the theatres are making a political statement by their acceptance of this government it's very hard for anyone who doesn't agree with that to work in them with any spirit. There's been a lot of talk in the building about 'the times' as if they were a force of nature – we are part of them just as much as the government, the city and business interests, and our opposition can be part of them. It's been put to me that under this government the theatre can't survive without embracing sponsorship and all that goes with it but I question what it is that's surviving. I think we and others will look back at this time with astonishment at what we went along with. So I can't be part of the Court's administration any more.[33]

4

Mad Forest to *Our Late Night*: 1990–1999

The nineties begin with *Mad Forest* and Churchill working with final-year drama students. It ended with a rare foray into directing as she put on *Our Late Night* at the New Ambassadors. The play, by her friend the American writer Wallace Shawn, was a production without décor by the Royal Court, on the set of Mark Ravenhill's *Some Explicit Polaroids*. In between these two productions there were: *Lives of the Great Poisoners,* renewing her work with Ian Spink, and beginning work with the composer Orlando Gough; *The Skriker,* which began its life in the early eighties; a translation of Seneca's *Thyestes*; *Hotel,* an opera for Gough, with Spink directing and choreographing; *This Is a Chair* for the Royal Court; and *Blue Heart* for Out of Joint. It is a formidable list.

Max Stafford-Clark reported to the Royal Court's Council in January 1990 that: 'Caryl Churchill could be delivering her new play in March'. By 19 March, he said in the Council: 'Caryl Churchill had stopped work on [her new play] for the time being.' The play was *The Skriker*. By the time Stafford-Clark made his announcement, Churchill had been approached in January by the director Mark Wing-Davey, Artistic Director of the Central School of Speech and Drama's acting course, to consider working with his final-year students on a project to do with the revolution in Romania. Between 3 March and 7 March, writer and director went to Romania. At the end of March, writer, director, designer, lighting designer, one stage manager and ten students went to Romania to meet people and carry out research in workshops. Back in the UK, Churchill wrote the play in three weeks, and *Mad Forest* had its first performance at Central's Embassy Theatre on 25 June. The company was invited to perform at Bucharest's National Theatre on 17 September, and on 9 October the play went to the Royal Court. Typically, Churchill's interest was less in the affairs of Romanian politics and more in the effects: 'I wouldn't have agreed if the RSC or the National had asked me. But I was interested in working away from the mainstream with students of the same age as the people who made the revolution'.[1]

The play was workshopped, rehearsed and performed amidst the revolution and its aftermath. In this sense, the piece is addressing events which were still unfolding as it was being written. Briefly, the dictatorship of Nicolae Ceausescu of Romania, together with his wife, Elena, which had started in 1965, began to crumble at the end of 1989. It began on 16 December with a demonstration in Timisoara in western Romania to protest about the harassment of László Tökés, a dissident ethnic-Hungarian priest. The demonstration became a mass protest against the Ceausescus, who ordered troops to fire on the crowd. On the 21 December, Ceausescu's speech in Bucharest was shouted down. The following day, the army went over to the people, and street battles ensued. On Christmas Day, the Ceausescus were tried, found guilty and shot.

It was in mid-January that Mark Wing-Davey suggested the project to Churchill. The death of the dictator did not end the affair, for at the same time a new party was created, the National Salvation Front, led by Ion Iliescu. The Front contained many of the dictator's former supporters, and it was unclear whether there had been a genuine revolution, or a putsch. The Central actors were thus surrounded by suspicion and unease while there in late March and early April. They saw anti-Front demonstrators block the centre of Bucharest, and, on 20 May, the Front achieved a large majority in the elections.

Mad Forest thus shows apparent and radical change while at the same time charting the doubts and disbelief of the ordinary people of Romania, as well as demonstrating the effect of decades of repression. It in fact ends deliberately abruptly, for there can be no ending to a fluid and ongoing situation. While there, a friend of Churchill's testified to the unease: 'People now don't want to tell stories about what happened (during the revolution). Before it seemed true, it was wonderful to say it, but now they don't know, they think perhaps it is a lie'.[2]

The play has three sections. The first and third feature weddings. The second section has a number of characters who, independently of each other, give an account of the events of late December 1989. The weddings link two families, one working class, the other middle class. Each scene, with the exception of Section 2, has its title read out: 'Each scene is announced by one of the company reading from a phrasebook as if an English tourist, first in Romanian, then in English, and again in Romanian.'[3] The effect of this device is to frame the action, and emphasise the relationship of an English company to a remote country's problems. There is a process of education going on for both Romanian and foreign audiences. The notion of a tourist coming to grips with a language reflects the pre-revolution fear of speaking loudly and truly about a situation.

Neither the Vladu family nor the Antonescu family is able to speak freely. The Vladus are used to increasing the volume of their radio in order to speak to each other privately. Radu Antonescu, an art student, whispers 'Down with Ceausescu', while standing in a queue for meat. The reaction is to pretend that no one heard anything. Declamatory speech is only apparent in praise of the leader. Flavia Antonescu is a teacher, and she 'speaks loudly and confidently to her pupils'. The Vladu family is under suspicion because the daughter, Lucia, is engaged to be married to an American, Wayne. Everything slightly out of the ordinary is automatically suspect. Bogdan Vladu is told by the Securitate to 'make a report once a week' about his own daughter who obtains an abortion by a written conversation with her doctor while a conversation goes on between them for the benefit of the listening security people.

Everywhere, the atmosphere is tense. People wait. Some tell jokes. Others are silent. Religion is irrelevant, as a scene between a priest and the archangel Michael shows. The priest talks to the angel: 'no one's ever known an angel work for the Securitate.' Michael himself remains apolitical, but flirted a little with the Iron guards who carried his picture about. For him, they were not fascists: 'They were mystical.' In a typically daring scene, Flavia and husband, Mihai, sit with Flavia's grandmother 'who is dead. She is an elegant woman in her 50s.' The grandmother rebukes Flavia for not living the only life she will have. In her life, she has welcomed the Nazis because she thought they would protect her from the Russians, and then the communists because they might protect her from the Germans: 'But at least I knew that was what happened to me. There were things I did. I did them. Or sometimes I did nothing. It was me doing nothing.' The contrast is drawn between activity, however mistaken, and the stagnation created by Ceausescu. A dead woman speaks to her grandchild about living.

Section 2 recreates the events of December, as the revolution unfolds. Churchill is clear in her stage directions: 'None of the characters in this section are the characters in the play that began in Part 1. They are all Romanians speaking to us in English with Romanian accents. Each behaves as if the others are not there and each is the only one telling what happened.' They therefore speak of the events unfolding in soliloquy and in an English which identifies them as not English. Each figure – from a painter to students, to a doctor, a house painter, a flower seller, a Securitate officer, a soldier, a bulldozer driver – offers a memory which, collectively, moves towards the execution of the Ceausescus on 25 December. The figures are still on the stage, lost in the act of recalling events only recently enacted. As figures, they therefore speak of the same events, but as figures they are also in isolation as they recall their apparent liberation.

The final section of *Mad Forest* is called 'Florina's Wedding'. It opens with the startling image of a vampire and a dog. 'The Vampire was not dressed as a vampire.'[4] The Vampire has come 'for the revolution. I could smell it a long way off.' He and the dog talk about an alliance: 'Don't throw stones at me, I hate it when they throw stones, I hate being kicked, please please I'd be a good dog, I'd bite your enemies. Don't hurt me.' The five-hundred-year-old bloodsucker talks to the emaciated six-year-old dog, and makes him into a vampire dog at the end of the scene. The Vampire, moreover, speaks of the utter tedium of his existence:

All that . . . happens is you begin to want blood, you try to put it off, you're bored with killing, but you can't sit quiet, you can't settle to anything, your limbs ache, your head burns, you have to keep moving faster and faster, that eases the pain, seeking. And finding. Ah.

The dog without an owner finds a new master, being unused to anything else. The post-revolution period has arrived.

After the opening, both families meet up in the hospital where Gabriel Vladu is receiving treatment for wounds sustained in the fighting. He is now a hero of the revolution, but the hospital contains other images and sounds and suspicions. A patient asks: 'Did we have a revolution or a putsch? Who was shooting on the 21st? And who was shooting on the 22nd?' He was wounded in the head and asks numerous and valid questions, which stand for the other characters in the play. Nothing is resolved. The revolution has created more doubts and fears, as Lucia returns from America to describe a land of enormous plenty and enormous waste. The questions are not answered.

Post-revolution, old fears and prejudices surface. Florina, Lucia, Radu and Ianos visit Florina and Lucia's grandparents in the country so that they can meet Radu before his marriage to Florina. The grandparents automatically hate Hungarians and gypsies. Florina confesses she felt freer under Ceausescu than she does now: 'It's because I could keep everything out.' Radu hates the leader of the National Salvation Front, Ion Iliescu. The grandparents comfortably assert their prejudices, and Ianos, Radu, Florina and Lucia make a wish list. It begins with holidays, fast cars, fame, riches – when Lucia says: 'not be frightened'. Churchill's stage direction is: 'The pauses get longer.' The sequence runs: 'Make Florina happy . . . Make Toma happy . . . Live forever . . . Die young . . . Go on lying here.' The pauses are: 'Longer silence . . . Very long silence . . . Very long silence'. A simple and masterly evocation of upset and wanting to hide away.

Towards the end of Part 3, the young group bring Gabriel home from hospital. Drunkenly, they re-enact the trial of the Ceausescus with Gabriel acting with vicious enjoyment. The depth of their anger at the couple is marked by their enjoyment of the freedom to act. But in the heat of it all, Gabriel's racism is shocking. He hits out at Ianos with his crutch: 'Get your filthy Hungarian hands off her . . . Just joking.' It is important that the play shows the dark side of liberation, and the prejudice still inherent in some. It is apparent as well in the play's final scene as everyone gets progressively drunker. The atmosphere becomes emotional and aggressive. The National Salvation Front has won the election, and the victory splits the wedding party and terminates in a free-for-all fight. As all calms down, they begin the fashionable dance of the Lambada. The group includes the Archangel and the Vampire, dancing together. All of them talk in Romanian, using words previously spoken in the play. And the Vampire closes the play with his speech in the opening scene of Section 3:

> You begin to want blood. Your limbs ache, your head
> burns, you have to keep moving faster and faster.

A dancing crowd, words largely indistinguishable, concluding ambivalently, neither optimistic nor pessimistic. In her Production Note, Churchill describes the arc of *Mad Forest* as going 'from the difficulty of saying anything to everyone talking'. The play's title refers to the large forest where Bucharest now stands: 'impenetrable for the foreigner who did not know the paths'. The play suggests that the forest is still to be negotiated.[5]

If, as has been seen, *A Mouthful of Birds* is difficult to read because dance is near impossible to represent on the page, then

Lives of the Great Poisoners is even more so. The play had its first performance at the Arnolfini, Bristol, on 13 February 1991. Churchill noted in her Introduction that the printed text 'gives more weight to the sung and spoken characters because description can only give a glimpse of what was going on physically throughout the piece'.[6] It may be thought that even the music, though published, remains inaccessible except to the trained reader.[7] However, the piece is the most ambitious collaboration to date in Churchill's work. It derives from her fascination with forms other than the purely verbal, given expression, as she explains, in her response to dance and singing in the early eighties (see pp.92–3). The difference from *A Mouthful of Birds* was to do with the singing. It was decided that actors, dancers and singers would, as it were, stick to what they mostly did best. Orlando Gough decided that the singing should be *a capella*, that is, singing without instrumental accompaniment. And the effect of this decision was that words were written first and, in the event, so was the music. The movement was made last.

Gough's view of the process was that singing *a capella* meant that it was much easier to hear the words, but it placed a heavy duty on the singers to keep in tune. Given that characters are very often in some kind of tension with each other: 'most of the music is counterpoint of some kind . . . So, from one point of view, the piece is like a play in which some of the dialogue happens to be sung.' Gough also in the *Production Dossier* addresses the implication of dance:

> I was also trying to keep in mind that it is at the same time a dance piece, and to write music that would inspire movement. In particular, the lengthy 'Death of Creusa and Creon' is intended specifically as a dance number. The music tells the story of their deaths; but there is scarcely any text – the singers sing syllables that I chose for their sound rather than for their meaning . . . When the singers sing these meaningless syllables, they are in the strange position of being half

in, half out of character. Fortunately singers do not seem to mind this ambiguity as much as actors.[8]

The piece was designed by Antony McDonald who, as a member of Second Stride, applied to the piece the precepts of the dance company in seeing design 'not as decoration but an essential part of the production'. One of the questions to be resolved concerned both the number of short scenes and variety of locations and also the fact that the show toured. As with Joint Stock, the production needed to deal with the different configurations of the venues. For McDonald, it was crucial that scenes flowed into each other, that no furniture should slow the development and that the small number of props should be reused. His Introduction in the *Production Dossier* describes the basic set as three units which, using hydraulics, could function in a variety of ways and angles. It enabled performances to appear in, above, around and in the gaps between the walls.

The fluidity of design met the fluid requirements of the piece, which evolved in discussion between Churchill, Gough and Spink. They began to meet every few weeks, and played with the idea of poison stories. The stories, after a brief Prologue, are of Dr Crippen, Medea and Madame de Brinvilliers. Dr Crippen killed and dismembered his second wife, Cora. Medea, spurned by Jason in favour of Creusa, daughter of King Creon, poisons Creusa and Creon, who attempts to save her. Madame de Brinvilliers poisoned her father, brother and two sisters in order to inherit their property, with the help of her lover, army captain Godin de Sainte-Croix. She was arrested, beheaded, and her body was burned at the stake. There is one figure who appears throughout. He is Thomas Midgley, an American mechanical engineer turned chemist. He was honoured for the invention of lead in petrol to stop 'knocking' and CFCs in refrigerators, both now implicated in harming the Earth's atmosphere. Midgley wanders in *Lives of the Great Poisoners* as the embodiment of the inventor without responsibility.

The progression of the piece sees figures evolving into a second and third guise as three stories fuse into one. Thus Cora, murdered by Crippen, becomes Medea in Part 2 and Madame de Brinvilliers in Part 3; Ethel, Crippen's lover, becomes the poisoner Creusa and then Madame Sainte-Croix; Crippen becomes Jason and then Sainte-Croix. The worlds of late nineteenth-century, aspiring middle-class society; of ancient Greece; and of seventeenth-century France reflect a common cruelty, indifference to life and a vicious self-regard. Crippen's world is shown via an evening at his home, Hilldrop Crescent. His wife, Cora, is an aspiring music-hall performer, who has her own group of theatre friends. Crippen's dislike of her and them is made clear, as is Cora's second-rate ability. He poisons her, dismembers the body and sails with his lover, Ethel, to Canada. His hatbox (Churchill's invention) contains Cora's head.

The veneer of civilisation covers a vicious and uncaring world of one who kills solely for his own purposes. Cora is empty headed, vain and posturing. Crippen is a destroyer by stealth: 'Drink your cocoa, my love, and we'll go to bed.' Cora dies to a Chorus of Poisons who 'appear above and start singing her to death'. Her music-hall friends grow suspicious and track Crippen and Ethel to the ship, with the hatbox. Crippen drops the hatbox over the side, while the ship's captain and a sailor dance 'a curious dolphin dance, like formation swimming, in which we can only see their legs upside down'. Comically, Cora's head suddenly appears over the edge of the ship. She will always be with him. As the section ends Cora has transformed into Medea for the second section.

The serio-comic, almost larky atmosphere of the Crippen section now gives way to Medea's revenge. The hatbox has become a metal box of poisons. Medea has opened the piece in a Prologue in which she restores Jason's father, Aeson. Revived, he does 'a small youthful dance and bounds up the wall as it lowers into the next scene'. Midgley, fresh from his naïve observation of Crippen's activities, tells Jason about his experiments with lead. Jason is candidly and cheerfully dismissive about his rejection of Medea:

> Look, Midgley, you don't live with her. She was wonderful in her own country, dealing with monsters, I owe her a lot. But when you get back to civilisation. Not everyone's as tolerant as you.

His engagement to Creusa is 'a brilliant career move'. He could almost be a character out of *Serious Money*. What Medea has given up for Jason is dismissed by him as unimportant. He pays the price. He offers to buy her a house. A nervous Midgley tries to arbitrate: 'Try not to hate him. Things may turn out for the best.' The modern figure, always dressed in his forties' suit, watches as the poisoned dress does its work, and ends the scene thinking through his idea for CFCs. Medea transforms to Madame de Brinvilliers.

Brinvilliers kills by poisoning patients in hospital. Her elegy for them reverses the song of Medea in the play's Prologue. Poison is now a commodity to be marketed from the laboratory: 'We'll corner the market', says Sainte-Croix to the notorious Italian poisoner Exili. Historically, Sainte-Croix and Exili met in the Bastille. Midgley is now tutor to Sainte-Croix's children, while Madame de Brinvilliers is poisoning her husband. The atmosphere is sour and debauched. Even Midgley senses something is odd: 'Something strange is going on here. There's something in the air.'

He becomes increasingly infatuated with Madame de Brinvilliers as the group plays a game called Hoca. Midgley plays, wins and loses his winnings. But the real point of the sequence is to make the equation between personal selfishness and the state of the nation. Sainte-Croix tells Midgley that: 'The whole political life of the country depends on poison . . . Everyone in public life drinks antidote every morning.' He is in turn poisoned, and Madame de Brinvilliers is killed.

The element in the production of *Lives of the great Poisoners* which was the last to be realised was the choreography by Ian

Spink. After the development of the score and the text: 'Improvisations with the performers led to movements which were later developed separately into dances which were then fitted into the written scenes.'[9] Added to this was the evolution of the 'mixed-form' scenes: 'Whist', 'Music Hall Song', 'Death of Creusa' and 'Hoca'. They began as separate layers of text, music and choreography, 'and were woven together so as to allow each element its own integrity'. For Orlando Gough, the piece did not resolve the inherent issues of music and dance:

> So what about the alliance of dance and music? Well, we managed to make a piece in which there was no hierarchy of musicians and dancers and in which they were able to rehearse productively for a long period; but the problem of the composer and choreographer as middle-men remained. It turned out to be just another experiment in linking dance and music, but from my point of view a very instructive and worthwhile one.[10]

On 4 December 1991, Max Stafford-Clark read a copy of Churchill's *The Skriker*, a play which puzzled him and which was the cause of some friction between the two. His Diary recorded that the author had been working on it for eight years. Churchill herself told her friend Nicholas Wright that: 'I had an idea which had been around for about ten years until I finally finished it last year [1992]:

> For some reason I couldn't make it work till then. A lot of the energy and feeling of what it was about kept turning up in completely different plays, which had apparently nothing to do with each other. That was odd, and it was the only time it's ever happened to me, it usually all happens very fast.[11]

This means that what became *The Skriker* began to occupy Churchill a little after the time of *Fen*. In other words, the period of the early eighties when Churchill and others were interested in alternative forms of expression, when dance and song began to re-appear in the vocabulary of the theatre. Churchill's account of the play's evolution is in her Introduction to *Plays: 3*. The form arrived at finally was to create three speaking parts, with the rest of the characters played by dancers. The underworld section of the play was written as a libretto for composer Judith Weir. The crucial section of her Introduction is how her experience enabled her to write in this fashion:

> I'd never have written *The Skriker* that way if I hadn't already worked on other shows with dancers and singers. It brought together what had been for me two separate strands of work, plays I worked on alone and dance/music theatre pieces.

It also brought together a group of artists with whom Churchill was very familiar. Director Les Waters had worked with her from 1979; designer Annie Smart from 1983; Ian Spink began with *A Mouthful of Birds* as did dancers Stephen Goff and Philippe Giraudeau. *The Skriker* was a Second Stride show, and the play marked Churchill's debut at the National Theatre.

There is extraordinary trust in handing over a piece of writing to a company with a text for three characters, but the rest of the piece contained in stage directions for Spink to develop. However, Churchill had seen in *Lives of the Great Poisoners* how precisely this procedure could work. In effect, with her director and designer, she had virtually a repertory company to bring *The Skriker* to the stage of the Cottesloe.

The play is for three actors, thirteen dancers, singers and a stilt-walker. Its story centres around the Skriker, described as 'a shapeshifter and death portent, ancient and damaged'. Churchill describes the Skriker as: 'a polluted, not-believed-in nature spirit who comes up to the world to get love, attention and revenge'.[12] The opening of the play concerns Josie, in a mental hospital for apparently killing her child, and Lily, her visitor, who is pregnant. The Skriker attaches itself to the two young women and tries to lure them into the world of spirits and underground, adopting a variety of different disguises. Josie goes to the underground, and returns, after what she thinks of as years, to find only seconds have elapsed. Lily, on the other hand, ends the play by leaving her child in the modern world, believing, like Josie, she will be back in a few seconds, only to find herself forever trapped in the world of her granddaughter.

The power of the play's opening cannot be overstated. A stone-throwing giant riding on a pig-like man gives way to the figure of the Skriker, who, in an extraordinary and long soliloquy of puns, word play, alliteration, free association, bits of sense and nonsense, demanding a virtuoso control of pace and rhythm from the actor, and, cumulatively presenting a frightening spectacle of linguistic disintegration, prowls the underworld and talks of this 'real' world from which it has become estranged. Its own world is now alien, disregarded by humans. The hurt and the damage are visible as the Skriker begins to look to reconnect: 'Revengeance is gold mine, sweet'. The violence of the language presages disaster:

> They used to leave cream in a sorcerer's apprentice. Gave the brownie a pair of trousers to wear have you gone? Now they hate us and hurt hurtle faster and master. They poison me in my rivers of blood poisoning makes my arm swelter. Can't get them out of our head strong.

The spirits fill the play. The hospital sequence with Josie and Lily contains 'the KELPIE, part young man, part horse', whereas the conversation between the two women is perfectly naturalistic. The surface naturalism knocks against the visual effect. Josie, however, knows the Skriker is about, in the hospital, and she duly appears, disappears, arrives again as a derelict woman, as a drunken American woman. Around her are spirits: a Green lady, a boggle, a spriggan, a brownie. The world of the spirits fills up the world of humans. The Skriker wants to belong and be loved. When Lily impetuously hugs and kisses the Skriker, the stage direction is: 'Pound coins come out of her mouth when she speaks. She stops talking and examines the money.' In a nicely comic moment, Lily fails to explain how

television works to an increasingly exasperated Skriker –
'Don't fuck with me' – after which the Skriker, in plain English,
explains who she is. She describes herself as 'an ancient fairy
. . . not a major spirit but a spirit'. There was a time when 'we
mattered'. Lily is stuck with the Skriker because Josie made a
wish that she should be. But Lily, like most people, cannot
explain how television works, just that it does. The analogy
may be with the world of the spirits, who exist in the play, but
it's not said how.

The Skriker continually changes. Josie and Lily sit on a sofa.
The Skriker is part of the sofa, and invisible to them. Suddenly,
she leaps up, wearing a short pink dress and gauzy wings. Her
insistent presence, her demanding, irresistible need dominates
the play. In a park, she is a small child who wants Lily to adopt
her. Lily effectively does this: 'Give me a cuddle. Let me sit on
your lap.' And Josie decides to go with the Skriker to the
underworld, where there is a feast laid out, and an exotic
assortment of spirits, lavishly dressed, contrive to give the
appearance of a palace – except that 'it is all glamour and here
and there it's not working'. The stage direction instances the
food which is partly twigs, leaves, beetles. Where Josie and the
Skriker speak, all the rest sing. They are characters in an opera.
Josie is told by a Lost Girl not to eat or drink anything. She did
'and now I'm here forever'. But Josie does eat and drink, and
seems condemned to stay in the underworld for an eternity. Yet
she does go home – to the park, Lily and the Skriker as a child.

As Lily, with her child, sits with the Skriker, now a thirty-
year-old man, he delivers a kind of elegy about the change in
the world:

> It was always possible to think whatever your personal
> problem, there's always nature. Spring will return even if
> it's without me. Nobody loves me but at least it's a sunny
> day. This has been a comfort to people as long as they've
> existed. But it's not available any more. Sorry . . . I'm going
> to be around when the world as we know it ends.

The loss of the conventional world by human neglect is paralleled by the loss of human imagination in favour of logic. Lily drives herself to go with the Skriker. At the hospital, she agrees to go, believing it will be like Josie's experience and feel as if she's been gone for a few seconds. Now the Skriker becomes the ancient creature as at the beginning of the piece, and exults in her actions: ' "Oh I was tricked tracked wracked", cried our heroine distress, "I hoped to save the worldly, I hoped I'd make the fury better than she should be" . . . So Lily bit off more than she could choose. And she was dustbin.'

The separation of the imaginative, creative life and ordinary existence is portrayed as a catastrophe. The natural world is raped and left to die. The world of the Skriker has run mad in its isolation, and the two young, damaged and friendless women have no comfort or sustenance. Children are killed, lost or devoured. A dead child sings of being put in a pie and eaten. It is a desolate world and it is a warning about what is to come.

The Skriker opened at the National Theatre in January 1994 and at the Public Theater, New York in April 1996.

From the stunted world of *The Skriker* to a translation of Seneca's *Thyestes* or, as Churchill put it, 'a collaboration with a dead writer',[13] which had its first performance in the Theatre Upstairs on 7 June 1994, directed by James Macdonald. It received its first performance at The Green Room, Manchester, as a co-production with Manchester as City of Drama. Tantalus was punished by the gods for serving them his son Pelops for dinner. Pelops was brought back to life and had two sons, Atreus and Thyestes, who were supposed to rule the country in turns and keep the symbol of power, a ram with a golden fleece. Thyestes seduced his brother's wife, and they stole the ram. Atreus, after a civil war, drove Thyestes out. The play begins with Atreus as king, thirsty for revenge on Thyestes, who is in exile with his three sons. At the end, Thyestes' three sons are dead. As Churchill noted in her Introduction: 'The play ends bleakly except for our memory of a chorus who'd hoped for something better.'[14]

The precision of the translation, the stress on the desensitisation of humans to horror, was well served in the first production by the design of a bare, dark room, with monitors. A world of surveillance. The audience entered through a small box room, with a dining table for Thyestes' meal of his children. The company were casually dressed and seldom raised their voices. The seventy-minute piece begins with Tantalus rising through a trap, forced by the Fury to contemplate the killing of Pelops:

> Then let
> rage harden and the long
> wrong go into the
> grandchildren

Churchill's translation uses lines of, often, alternative five and seven syllables: 'fives to move faster, or sevens'. The effect is compression, barely suppressed emotion beneath the lines. When Atreus comes on, he is consumed with rage at not having had his revenge:

> Not brave. Not clever. Not strong.
> What I'm really ashamed of
> not avenged. After all that.
> My brother's tricks.

Thyestes, urged by Tantalus, and despite profound misgivings, returns to see his brother. He knows, however, that:

> You have vast power if you
> can manage without power.

Atreus sees him arriving, and unleashes a torrent of five syllable lines:

> I see him, it's him
> and the children too.
> At last my hate's safe.
> He's coming into

my hand, Thyestes
is coming, the whole
thing.

The translation is pared and economical. It shows a stunningly indifferent world, so used to cruelty and violence that it is hardly noticed. A family is devastated by its actions. The consequences are visited on the next generation. A pervasive sense of horror and nihilism concludes the piece. This is a world not far removed from that of *The Skriker*. Both are parables for today.

Between *Thyestes* and Churchill's fourth collaboration with Second Stride, *Hotel*, there is a gap of nearly three years, when nothing new of Churchill's saw the stage. Not that she wasn't writing. The minutes of the board of Stafford-Clark's new company, Out of Joint (OJO), for 15 February 1995, recorded that:

> The Director confirmed that Caryl Churchill is to write for OJO. Not at liberty to discuss the project further, he stressed she was working with a sense of purpose . . . The Producer reported that Nottingham Playhouse were keen to co-produce. The Director felt Caryl Churchill was OJO's strong card for approaching regional venues.

On 25 May, OJO's producer and co-founder, Sonia Friedman, wrote to Elizabeth Adlington, the senior touring officer of the Arts Council about the project:

> Caryl is set to write an 'epic' and satirical piece for ten actors dealing with 'Freedom'. It aims to look at how the word and notion of freedom has been exploited and misunderstood through the ages.

Stafford-Clark wrote to Ruth Mackenzie at Nottingham on 3 July to tell her that the play 'now has a title, "Britannia And The Bad Baby", and Caryl has very clearly got an epic subject in her sights and is pleased with the work she has already done'. The play was never delivered.

However, 1997 saw the performance of both *Hotel* (15 April), *This Is a Chair* (June) and *Blue Heart* (August). *Hotel* opened at the Schauspeilhaus, Hannover in April, and transferred to The Place, London, in the same month. *Hotel* is 'an opera for Orlando', and brings together for the fourth time Churchill, Gough, Spink and Second Stride. The piece is in two parts. Part 1 is 'eight rooms'. Part 2 is 'two nights'. The first superimposes eight rooms. The second shows the singers singing a diary left in a hotel room. The umbrella title of the process is: 'In a room anything can happen'. For the first time Churchill's text is entirely sung. There are thirteen singers, two dancers, three instrumentalists. The television and a ghost were played by the same performer. The image of a hotel is one of transience, used for all kinds of reasons, and then abandoned. Few stay permanently, if any. Those occupying the hotel rarely engage with other occupiers in other rooms. Perhaps the only thing in common is the television, used frequently to counter-act boredom or waiting. Churchill's idea was to superimpose eight hotel rooms on each other to make a single room, within which disparate experiences might fuse into 'a single stream of human experience'.[15]

The hotel guests range from a silent couple to an American couple, two people having an affair, an elderly French couple, a lesbian couple, two drunks, a woman with a birdbook and a businesswoman. There's nothing extraordinary about the group. Their ordinariness is choreographed and woven together. They are unaware of the existence of the others, but as they communicate with each other as couples, or talk to themselves, the effect is of some kind of connection. As Gough in the Introduction pointed out: 'Their lives intersect in the realm of shared emotion, in the realm of counterpoint and polyphony. The action is everyday, consciously undramatic.' Part 2 contains three narratives. The singers as chorus perform the song of the diary of someone who disappeared, while the dancers, who have spent different nights in the same room, dance a need to vanish. The second piece is elegiac and darker, mysterious in a way that

Part 1 is not, but the printed text cannot, inevitably, portray the connections and movement made by the choreography.

In the course of her Introduction, Churchill described how she arrived at the text. Asking herself what she wanted from words in an opera, she decided: 'a situation, an emotion, an image'. Referring to the underworld sequence in *The Skriker*, she noted that it had 'words without the usual structure of sentences . . . but it was easy to understand what was happening':

> So in *Hotel*, how little need the characters say to let us know enough about them? I decided there would be no complete sentences, just little chunks of what was said or thought, that could be absorbed first time round or in a repeat or even never.[16]

This notion of a minimal dialogue, a prompt implying more becomes the basic procedure of both *A Number* and *Drunk Enough to Say I Love You?* It is an important idea which infuses the two most recent plays.

In June, Churchill's *This Is a Chair* was performed at the Royal Court's Duke of York's Theatre, where the Court had moved during the refurbishment of its Sloane Square base. It is a piece of eight scenes running for half an hour and played twice nightly for four nights, 25–29 June. Critics were specifically not invited, although some did go and reviewed it. Directed by Stephen Daldry and designed by Ian MacNeill, it was decided that the piece, given that it asked fundamental questions about the nature and purpose of theatre, should be presented in an unconventional manner in the heart of London's West End. Thus the audience sat in tiered seats on the stage, and the actors performed on a platform spread across the centre stalls. At the end, the cast sat in the front row of the dress circle, while the audience onstage saw the programmes floating down to them from the grid. The cast assembled for the performance as part of the London International Festival of Theatre included some of the theatre's most prominent names for this one-off event.

Each of the scenes was preceded by music and its title marching on to a screen above the circle. Thus Scene 1, 'The War in Bosnia', gives way to Julian waiting with flowers for his date, Mary, who arrives to say she has double booked and can they do this another time. A scene called 'Pornography and Censorship' is actually about a family at dinner, with the father threatening the child as to what will happen if she does not eat up. The powerful disjunction between title and content refers indirectly to the Belgian surrealist painter René Magritte, whose painting *The Treachery of Images* showed a pipe with the line attached: 'This is not a pipe'. The disjunction is also the case between the play and its reception. Each of the scenes portrays, whatever the title, an excerpt from a larger scenario. Actor Desmond Barrit played with Timothy Spall and Andy Serkis in 'Hong Kong' and said that 'the lines had been taken from a 24-hour period and strung together. Thus Character A said something at 7.00 a.m. Character B then said something at 7.15 a.m. There was no connection between the lines. One line followed another chronologically, but was not a response.'

Linus Roache, who played Julian in the first sketch, said that 'Hong Kong' was the funniest sequence in the show, and that the entire cast used to assemble in the wings to listen to it. It is remarkable for another reason. Churchill's idea, set out in her Introduction to *Hotel*, of not using sentences, but bits of sentences sufficient to establish a character or a point, has its first try out as spoken text (the words were sung in *Hotel*) in 'Hong Kong' where a three-handed scene contains only three question marks and four full stops. The full stops only occur when a sequence of dialogue ends and a new thought begins, just as *Drunk Enough to Say I Love You?* will do a few years later. The last line of the sketch – 'love it when you' – could have come from the latter play. The scene is effectively a prototype. The technique is also partly present in 'Genetic Engineering', another scene in the play.

The titles, with the contents of each scene, ask where the domain of the theatre lies: 'The Labour Party's Slide to the

Right'; 'Animal Conservation and Third World Economies: the Ivory Trade'; 'The Northern Ireland Peace Process'. The final one, 'The Impact of Capitalism in the Former Soviet Union' has no action at all. What is theatre for? What now is its role? More than that, aside from our daily concerns and preoccupations, do we notice anything other than living our lives? One of the titles is 'Genetic Engineering', a topic which will surface in *A Number* in 2002. The piece asks about the playwright's job. Is it possible to write both about the mundane and the global, to find the link between the two? And if it is, how best to represent that line? *This Is a Chair* lays out a manifesto for future works.

If the epic play 'Britannia and the Bad Baby' did not materialise, Stafford-Clark reported in May to the board of Out of Joint that he 'was looking to open the double bill of *Heart's Desire* and *Blue Kettle* in June 1997'. The play was to preview at Bury St Edmunds, and go to the Traverse for the Edinburgh Festival. It would form part of the 'British Council Showcase' and if Council delegates liked the play 'there could be the possibility of an extended international life'.[17]

The plays were not originally intended as a double bill:

> Caryl came to me with *Heart's Desire*, and I thought about putting it on as a short play. Then Caryl mentioned she had another one she'd been working on, and we decided they suited each other well enough to be shown together.[18]

Both the plays, in the sense that they ask questions about the mechanics of theatre, follow hard on *This Is a Chair*. *Heart's Desire* is two lines in when the stage direction is: 'They all stop, BRIAN goes out. Others reset to beginning and do exactly what they did before as BRIAN enters putting on a tweed jacket.' Two more lines and the same stage direction. Each sequence adds more information each time. The only other thing to change is Brian's red sweater to begin with, which becomes the tweed jacket and in turn an old cardigan. This resetting runs through the play with its starting point moving through the text.

The effect is akin to a loop endlessly repeating itself, except that the demands vary and intensify. After the first entrance of Lewis, drunk, the play resets to the beginning but 'at double speed, all movements accurate though fast'. On another occasion, only the beginnings of the lines are to be said; on yet another only last words are said. The demand on the actors is considerable. On each reset, they have to reconstruct the tiniest of their gestures, whether laying cutlery, patting hair, arching an eyebrow. The characters are caught, suspended in an agony of waiting for the return of their daughter from Australia. As each sequence takes place, it becomes clear that the daughter is the nominal subject, as is so often the case with Churchill. The real subject is the family. Brian and Alice bicker sarcastically. Their son, Lewis, is a drunk. Brian fantasises about eating himself. He catalogues the process of eating, beginning with his fingernails, to the accompaniment of Alice's sarcastic questions 'Is this something you've always wanted to do or—?' and ends with his mouth eating his mouth. The image of a sterile and loveless group grows stronger. In this bizarre world of apparent naturalism, set in a kitchen, the surreal makes its visitations. At one point, lots of small children rush in, round the room and out again. At another: 'Two GUNMEN burst in and kill them all, then leave.' A uniformed man demands their papers and, gloriously, after the doorbell rings: 'A ten foot tall bird enters'.

In one of the funniest pieces Churchill has written, the insistently dull routine of the family in the kitchen is constantly subverted by the fantastical, where the daughter appears very briefly – 'Mummy. Daddy. How wonderful to be home' – and the play immediately resets, and the effect is of the strain of waiting. It brings to the surface matters normally hidden. Each of the characters constructs his or her own reality and fantasy as they seek to escape from their situation. The end of the play resets to its beginning, and 'She's taking her time' begins the agony again.

Blue Kettle appears to be the story of a heartless con man, Derek, forty, whose trick is to persuade older women that he is the son they gave up for adoption. Each of the women reacts differently. Mrs Plant asks if Derek hates her; Mrs Oliver brings family photographs; Mrs Vane wants Derek and his girl-friend Enid to come to dinner, but not to let on to her husband; and Miss Clarence, the don, briskly tells her story in as much detail as she can remember. All of them share their memories with Derek. All of them speak compulsively of a part of their lives, of past and current relationships. In Scene 8, however, Derek talks to his real mother, who is in a geriatric ward. She barely listens. Enid, on the other hand, questions Derek's rea-sons for acting as he does: 'Is it a contrick or is it a hangup?' And this addresses the heart of the play. What is Derek doing all this for, if not money? In the play's last scene, Derek tells Mrs Plant about knowing her real son in Indonesia, that he died and that Derek took his documents. The idea of seeking out women whose child was adopted came from this one moment. He appears to lie to her that his mother died when he was a child. The longing he expresses is of a bereaved child, rather than an amoral man preying on others.

Derek's world is as fragile as the world of the women he invades. As he seeks his identity, they live with a past which his presence forces them to relive and re-experience. Mrs Plant has to recall an affair when she was sixteen with a twenty-two year old and a lambretta: 'I've been in fields since but I've never seen buttercups comparable.' Mrs Oliver never told her husband about her child, and he is now dead: 'I mean I look at you and you could be anyone . . . You shouldn't expect to be loved.' Mrs Vane discussed the whole matter with her husband in a very civilised way. They decided against keeping the child: 'We thought it would make us unhappy.' And Miss Clarence was thirty-seven: '. . . nobody looked at me to see me, they regis-tered my presence and we talked about anglosaxon'. The women express their private feelings to a skilful interrogator.

However, feelings as well as ideas begin to come under alarming pressure as the language of the play steadily disinte-grates. As early as Scene 2: 'You don't have to blue anything up.' Later in the scene comes: 'having the kettle of seeing your son or not . . .' From that point, the frequency of the two words increases, so that in the last scene, 'blue' and 'kettle' are reduced to 'b' and 'k'. Like a computer virus, all normative language is replaced. But the sense of what is being said remains. Remarkably, the absence of language is not an absence of coherence. Rather, it reinforces the fractured world of its inhabitants, and paints a picture of longing and distress. Family, as so often in Churchill's work, is frequently dislocated and fragmentary. Memory is a constructed affair, read differently by different characters. *Blue Heart* demonstrates the work of a writer experimenting with the nature of language. It is a constant preoccupation, and it is to do with the adequacy or otherwise of the tools available.

Out of Joint's producer felt that the double bill was 'the most fantastic response from a writer who couldn't write the epic. It was all about a writer's journey, and I felt we were completely blessed to have just those two pieces.' And Stafford-Clark's view of the play was that it itself 'becomes a character, a naughty play that doesn't behave'. He used the image of a frisky pony galloping round a circuit: 'It comes to a fence and refuses, so it goes back and tries another route . . . Sometimes it thinks, "If I run really fast I'll get over this fence", so it goes at double speed and clears it and then hits another fence.'[19]

Blue Heart opened in Bury St Edmunds in August as a co-production with the Royal Court, and at the Traverse, Edinburgh five days later before playing at the Court from September. In February 1998, the director reported to the Out of Joint board that: 'it had been a hard play for the actors to repeat consistently, with the emotional demands being rather less than the technical'. The play then opened for three weeks at the Brooklyn Academy of Music's Majestic Theater in January 1999. The board minutes for 16 November 1998 recorded Churchill's objection 'to the sponsorship by Philip Morris Inc of the BAM Season of which *Blue Heart* was to be a part'. The issue which caused Churchill to resign from the

Council of the Royal Court in 1989 had not gone away. In the same month of November, the rumour arose that the Jerwood Foundation was to supply the £3 million needed to complete the refurbishment of the Royal Court, but wanted its name attached to the theatre. Churchill and others objected:

> To have a sponsor's name on a building is the start of a very slippery slope . . . We're not saying that we shouldn't accept the money, or that the name shouldn't be associated in some way. We're saying it would be more appropriate if it was in the inside rather than the outside, like the Cottesloe Theatre at the National. You could have the Jerwood Studio, for instance.[20]

The Royal Court became the Royal Court Jerwood Theatres.

It was around this time that Churchill translated three plays by Maurice Maeterlinck, the Belgian symbolist playwright. The translations remain unperformed. The plays were *The Intruder* (1890); *Interior* (1891); and *The Death of Tintagiles* (1894). They were used by her former director, Les Waters, in his teaching at the University of California, San Diego:

> I taught a class for the third-year Master of Fine Art Directors and Actors . . . in site-specific theatre, and we used these three texts to initiate the process and as part of the performance. We never produced the entire text – there was never an actual production of the plays – but used them as fragments. The performances were for one night only in 1998 and again in 2002, and the site was . . . a mansion in the hills of Rancho Santa Fe, overlooking the Pacific. The house has a strange, haunted history. I am still looking to direct the plays in their entirety. It would be possible to create a double bill out of *The Intruder* and *Interior*. *The Death of Tintagiles* is one of the most terrifying plays written. Maeterlinck is a sadly neglected writer.[21]

Elsewhere, Churchill lent her name to the official launch of the Shadow Arts Council on 24 March 1999, in the company of

Tom Stoppard, Harold Pinter, Richard Eyre, Judi Dench and many others. It aimed to fulfil what it regarded as neglected aims by the Arts Council. And Churchill's was one of many signatures in a letter to the *Guardian* of 10 April 1999, deploring the British government's imposition of sanctions in the former Yugoslavia. There were to be many other occasions in the following years where the activity of the British government abroad appalled the artistic community as well as many others.

Churchill's final public work of the nineties was her direction of Wallace Shawn's *Our Late Night*, which opened at the New Ambassadors Theatre on 20 November. The play had premiered in New York in 1975, winning an Obie. Churchill's account of the play was a late-night production without décor, that is, at least theoretically, without set, design or sound. In fact, the existing set was strewn about with white cushions. It was lit by Johanna Town of the Court; and there was a sound track by Paul Arditti. A rather upmarket version of a production without décor was described as having 'a glint in its eye of the best of Churchill's work, as Shawn traces the sexual currents flowing round a party in a Manhattan loft apartment . . . Shawn's is a satirical portrait of an audaciously shallow, decadent society, obsessed with self-gratification but lacking the imagination to seek it beyond sex . . . Churchill directs with a keen eye and ear for the absurdity and desolation.'[22]

Far Away to *Drunk Enough to Say I Love You?*:
2000–2006

The new century saw the appearance of *Far Away* at the Court in 2000; two years later came *A Number*, also at the Court; *Plants and Ghosts* by the Siobhan Davies Dance Company, with text by Churchill, opened at the same time in a hangar on a former United States Air Force (USAF) base in Upper Heyford, Oxfordshire; February 2005 saw a version of Strindberg's *A Dream Play* at the National Theatre. Churchill wrote the lyric for Orlando Gough's *We Turned On the Light*, performed at the BBC Proms, July 2006; and *Drunk Enough to Say I Love You?* was premiered at the Court in November 2006.

At the end of December 1999, Churchill sent *Far Away* to Max Stafford-Clark. It occasioned some upset, as he recorded in his private Diary:

> I spoke to Caryl in the course of the morning. She has written a half-hour play which she has sent me. Later, she rings to tell me she wants Stephen Daldry to direct it . . . I ask if she's bored with me. She says the play is not realistic. I'm not sure why this makes it more suitable for Stephen, but I'm pissed off and upset. Of course she's entitled to have whom she likes, but I feel unreasonably angry . . . She always wanted to wander off and have other directors from time to time, but it is not good news. Oh, for fuck's sake. I should console myself by thinking that someone as unremittingly inventive as Caryl needs to be reinvented by her director as well. What a day.

On 11 December, he described the play in his Diary as 'an elliptical, political fable . . . surreal and powerful'. At a Court script meeting in March 2000, *Far Away* was discussed. Stafford-Clark's Diary recorded part of the meeting:

> I say she's developed her own response to a political agenda which she has discovered she cannot effectively address directly any more. The play is compressed and surreal but epic, and also functions like an installation. We disagree about whether it should go on Upstairs or Downstairs. Apparently, Caryl doesn't want the focus of Downstairs. I understand, but she's evading her own significance.

Far Away has a large cast, only four of whom speak. A note prefacing the text refers to 'The Parade' in Scene 2:5, which says 'five is too few and twenty better than ten. A hundred?' The note does not disclose the grim contents of Scene 2:5 to the reader. The events and effects of the play creep up on both audience and reader. In the first production, a painted front cloth opens the play. On it are images of that rural arcadia which so impressed the Americans in *Icecream*. A farmhouse nestles by a lake, with a background of trees and mountains. It was designed by Ian MacNeil. Churchill writes only 'HARPER's house. Night'. Behind the cloth, a song, 'There Is a Happy Land, Far, Far Away'. It's not in the published text, but Churchill increasingly in her work delivers her text to those she trusts to create it in performance, just as her solution to *The Skriker* had been to make three speaking parts, and list a group of other parts to be imagined onstage by director, choreographer and dancer.

In *Far Away*, the cloth rises to reveal the singer in a chair by a table and a lamp. Beyond the playing area it is black. A child arrives, trailing a stuffed lion and opens the play with: 'I can't sleep'. An air of normality is established, with the aunt comforting the child and trying to persuade her to return to bed. It is 2.00 a.m. The child admits she left her room and got into the tree outside because she heard a noise. With surgical precision, Churchill begins to ratchet up the foreboding and tension. The aunt begins a series of explanations as to what the child heard and saw. The child rigorously insists on what she witnessed: 'It was a person screaming.' It is the last word here which is frightening, as in her moving to that from: 'It was more like a person screaming.' Hers is a truth convincingly told. Harper (only the text gives the name) works hard to resume normality, but the girl inexorably goes into detail: crying, blood on her feet, children in the shed. The aunt tries to explain away the detail. The blood is from a dog, 'Black with a bit of white', which got run over. Yet she can't evade the child's insistence, and appears to concede: 'You've found out something secret.' And, unforgivably, she corrupts the child's sense of truth by constructing an entirely plausible set of reasons about the situation. The reason her husband is acting as he is outside is so that he can help the people escape. At this moment, the child begins to be convinced, and the aunt is in the ascendancy. She concedes there was no dog, no party, and the admission persuades the girl that here is the truth. It is an appalling corruption, as the child is now appropriated to the lie. She is 'part of a big movement now to make things better. You can be proud of that.' She agrees to help her aunt clean up in the morning. And finally agrees to get some sleep. Arcadia has become an abattoir. Joan's acceptance of a perverted view of the world carries through the play, as she tries to do the right thing. Intended or not, Harper's view of the world is imprinted on Joan. She is damaged.

Act 2 is divided into six short sections. It begins several years later as Joan and a young man, Todd, sit at a workbench in a hat makers. It is Joan's first professional hat. She has a degree in hat making. Each scene, apart from Scene 6, follows on the next day. Initially, the atmosphere is light, playful. Reference is made to a parade, where the hats are worn. What starts to build does so gradually. In Scene 2, Todd says that he stays up until the early hours 'watching the trials'. Against the careful normality of the conversation, and the interest generated by the steady and elaborate growth of the hats, the idea of trials is mentioned three times in the scene. Todd and Joan are concerned that they are being exploited by the owners of the hat factory. Todd intends to speak to someone about it. By the end of Scene 4, the hats are now 'enormous and preposterous'. And then Scene 5 explodes the normality as 'ragged, beaten, chained prisoners, each wearing a hat, on their way to execution', flood the stage. There is a sense of a never-ending procession of men, women and children spread out across the width of the stage. Their heads are bowed, hands chained together, a placard placed around each neck with a number, colourless and beaten, but with a hat. One parade among many. In the first production, lines of prisoners appeared upstage out of the black, and shuffled forward. The significance of Churchill's initial note becomes clear: 'A hundred?' As Todd says in Scene 6: 'There's other parades.'

The parade of prisoners who make no sound, as if part of a silent movie, is a carefully choreographed happening in the middle of the play. The parade is an occasion to make public those deemed to have offended. The hats make for good public interest, a competition for the best hat. Nothing demonstrates the utter contempt the prisoners are held in that they are fodder for millinery. Daldry's production also choreographed the process by which Todd and Joan, at the end of each workbench section, synchronised the placing of the hats they were working on under the work surfaces, replacing them with ones more advanced. Creativity becomes automatic.

All of this horror has no effect on Joan and Todd. Joan continues in the way she was taught by her aunt, and is delighted that her hat, her first one, has won and, terrifyingly, laments that it seems sad for the hats to be burnt with the bodies. This enables Todd to muse philosophically on the ephemerality of art. Only three of the three hundred he has made won and were placed in the museum. The Act is a numbing, spare account of the extent to which quite ordinary figures like Joan and Todd are able to live their lives in the context of obscene events.

Act 3 is several years later and the world is destroying itself. Todd and Joan have married, and are part of a world war. Todd is on leave at Harper's house. Joan has escaped from her bit of the war and, unlike Act 1, is sleeping. She appears here only for her speech which closes the play. It becomes apparent that the very elements themselves have taken sides in a war of unnamed alliances. The whole of the animal world is engaged in bloody slaughter. Everything is running amok. And this nightmare is discussed in vaguely outraged middle-class voices. There's not an exclamation mark to be seen. The calm tones produce a mix of the comic and the horrific:

> Mallards are not a good waterbird. They commit rape, and they're on the side of the elephants and the Koreans. But crocodiles are always in the wrong.

Or more directly:

> And I know it's not all about excitement. I've done boring jobs. I've worked in abattoirs stunning pigs and musicians and by the end of the day your back aches and all you can see when you shut your eyes is people hanging upside down by their feet.

This is the same Todd who, throughout the scene, frets about Joan.

Joan then enters to be scolded by Harper for acting and thinking selfishly: 'Maybe you don't know right from wrong yourself, what do I know about you after two years, I'd like to be glad to see you but how can I?'

Joan's speech ends the play. The little girl of Act 1 tells of her journey to Todd. The horrors she encounters are spoken matter of factly. That is the tragedy. She is, after all, telling of her journey to see her husband. But the telling involves her, almost incidentally, in killing 'two cats and a child under five', of seeing rats bleeding 'out of their mouths and ears, which is good, and so were the girls by the side of the road'. A different normality has been established, one accepted by those involved. It is absurd and terrifying at the same time. The play powerfully asks where the responsibility lies, who is to blame for what has happened, and it clearly lays that at the audience's feet: 'The water laps round your ankles in any case.' In the first production, the idyllic front cloth hurtled to the ground at the end as if broken.

Far Away opened in the Theatre Upstairs on 24 November 2000. Demand was so great that it played twice nightly. On Sunday, 4 November, it formed part of an evening in aid of the Stop the War Coalition. And on 22 February 2001, at the Albery, to which the production transferred, there was a special performance of the play in aid of Al Kasaba and Inad Theatres in the Occupied Territories. The Court has a long-standing connection with both theatres. New York saw the play at the New York Theater Workshop in November 2002, and at the beginning of 2002 *Far Away*, directed by Peter Brook, opened at his Paris theatre, the Bouffes du Nord.

Given Churchill's preoccupation with international affairs, especially at this stage with the Occupied Territories, she reacted strongly to an article by Michelene Wandor in the *Guardian* for 20 June 2001, about Arab and Israeli theatre. Wandor saw a Hebrew version of *Top Girls* in a theatre in Haifa by final-year students from Haifa University. Churchill responded in the *Guardian* of 23 June to say that she 'was surprised and uncomfortable to read about a student production of a play of mine . . . I recently turned down the offer of a production of a more recent play, *Far Away*, by an Israeli theatre. I don't know if other playwrights share the feeling of not wanting their plays done in Israel at the moment.'

In September 2002, *A Number*, with Michael Gambon and Daniel Craig, opened at the Court to almost unanimous acclaim. It was directed by Daldry and designed by MacNeil, the third time they had worked on a Churchill play. Churchill's ability to catch the *zeitgeist* is uncanny. Equally uncanny is the ability to turn such material into issues of wider concern. Ostensibly, *A Number* is about cloning. That is its nominal subject, important for what it leads to.

The play is in five scenes. There's one set, 'it's where Salter lives'. Salter, early sixties, has three sons, all played by the same actor. They are named B1, B2 and Michael. B2 discovers that he is one of a number of clones created from B1 whom Salter asserts was killed in a traffic accident. Salter says that B2 is the result of Salter's attempt to begin again by recreating B1. However, B1 is actually alive, but abandoned by Salter a good while ago, and badly neglected before being abandoned. B1 now learns that he has a cloned brother. B2 is unnerved by B1 and leaves the country, followed by B1 to seek revenge. In the final scene, Salter meets Michael, another of his cloned sons.

Initially, B2, who is thirty-five, is curious to know how he came into existence. As he tells Salter of the number of clones in existence, Salter appears unaware of it all. Salter calls the clones 'things'. The son objects, but is totally confused as to what he thinks about the discovery. Comically, Salter wonders if they can sue whoever is responsible for illegally making copies. He is also trying to deal with what his son knows and does by diversionary tactics. But B2 tells him that none of the clones is the original, and Salter lies about his first son, who, he says, with his wife, was killed in a car crash. None of it is true. At the end of the scene, it is clear that Salter regards B2 as the real thing and, importantly, the same thing as the allegedly dead first son.

What makes the scene, and the subsequent ones, remarkable is the nature of the dialogue. It is a deployment of the technique first seen in the 'Hong Kong' section of *This Is a Chair*, and reflects the view set out in Churchill's Introduction to *Hotel*: 'how little need the characters say to let us know enough about them?' In *A Number*, characters take refuge in the fragmented dialogue, particularly Salter who frequently tunes his response to his sense of or interpretation of what is being said to him. Salter is constantly preparing to evade whatever issue is raised, trying little forays into argument, changing tack or altering the line. Sometimes figures falter and the confidence drains away. Sometimes eye contact is the last contact wanted. The effect of this is complex. It establishes a clear, verbal choreography between the speakers. It implies a dependency one on the other, or, paradoxically, it can imply a terrible distance between them.

More becomes clear in Scene 2, where the surprise is that his first son, B1, is alive. Salter is instantly convicted of lying to B2 by the audience. He now wants an alliance with his forty-year-old son and denies any kind of responsibility for the original cloning. B1 is full of loathing for a father who 'sent me away and had this other one made from some bit of my body . . .' B1 faces the man who has had created a new version of himself. Salter tries the same tack as he did with B2: 'I think there's money to be made out of this.' But B1 paints a terrible picture of his neglect as a child, with Salter on the defensive. The rage at what happened to him has rendered him incapable of any understanding of his father and his actions. B1 vents his hatred on B2 when they meet, an account of which is given in Scene 3. B2's reaction is to think of leaving the country. Salter's remorse at what he was when B1 was a child drives the second attempt to be a better father: 'I did some bad things. I deserve to suffer. I did some better things. I'd like recognition.' But B2 points out with remorseless logic that he is the person he is, and that underlines all his actions. It is true of anyone, but Salter opts to deploy modern technology in order to act differently. Having damaged one child, he then treats another well. But that does not alter the fact that he damaged one child. The responsibility remains. The science does not resolve the mess.

Just as the meeting between B1 and B2 is described, and takes place offstage, so in Scene 4 B1 describes the killing of B2. And Salter completes the picture of his neglect of B1 as a child. Images emerge of B1 under the bed, or being put into a cupboard by his father. And the child was finally put into care. Salter begs for B1 to tell him anything he recalls of that time, but if B1 remembers he denies access to his father. It has taken four scenes for the real picture to emerge. Salter is left to his own miseries. Yet the real surprise is Scene 5, where Salter finally meets another of his cloned sons, Michael, married with three children, and a maths teacher. Salter is desperate to hear real details about Michael who cheerfully rambles on about anything but. None of his sons gives him anything to hang on to. Michael is unfazed by being a clone: 'I think it's funny, I think it's delightful.' But Salter is now numbingly searching for anything and tells Michael that B2 is dead, and B1 has killed himself. And Michael can exist happily without him. He delivers a summarising speech about genetic make-up, which pleases him:

> We've got ninety-nine per cent the same genes as any other person. We've got ninety-eight per cent the same as a chimpanzee. We've got thirty per cent the same as a lettuce. Does that cheer you up at all? I love about the lettuce. It makes me feel I belong.

Michael exists freely of Salter, who is left to contemplate his misery and his mess.

Though the case against cloning is strongly made in most of the play, the last scene upends the point and shows a happy and contented clone. But, crucially, the play debates larger matters to do with the nature of free will. Is free will genetically determined or constructed by social environment? Is the conflict irresolvable between nature and nurture? It is a debate that occupies Shakespeare's last plays, and it is still germane. The effect on Salter of his actions reflects this larger context. Sam Shepard, who played Salter in the New York production, described his character, who

> is dealing with a terrible, terrible mistake he tries to correct, and in trying to correct it he created an even worse disaster. On the surface he deals with anger, arrogance, denial. But underneath he's haunted by guilt and remorse. Underneath the language is this tremendous emotional base that you have to be vulnerable to. You have to listen very closely. You have to follow the veins and the rivers and the creeks and everything the language is leading you to. Every once in a while, it just erupts.

The play asks what makes us what we are, how that is determined and how our responses to what we are affects what we do, especially relationships. It argues that genetic make-up is not the sole determinant of identity. The one per cent dissimilarity is sufficient to create individuals, such as Michael. What is done with that one per cent is crucial to any understanding of behaviour. *A Number* has no interest in the morality of cloning. As Samuel West who, with his father, Timothy, performed the play in Sheffield in 2006, said: 'It's about fathers and sons'.

As *A Number* played at the Downstairs Theatre at the Court, Upstairs mounted a season of Caryl Churchill events. It consisted of three productions without décor: *This Is a Chair, Not/Oxygen* and *Identical Twins*. And there were also four rehearsed readings of: *Seagulls, Three More Sleepless Nights, Moving Clocks Go Slow* and *Owners*. At the *Evening Standard* Theatre Awards, *A Number* won 'Best Play'. *A Number*'s American premiere, directed by James Macdonald, was at the New York Theater Workshop in December 2004.

In the same month as *A Number* opened (September 2002), the Siobhan Davies Dance Company, commissioned by Dance Umbrella, opened *Plants and Ghosts*, for which Churchill produced a story. As Davies said, Churchill

> came to watch the early rehearsals of *Plants and Ghosts* and one day she brought in this piece of writing which had the first sentence 'she bit her tongue'. From that she built up this story, each time with different additions like 'she bit her tongue quite hard, accidentally'. It was a very witty choreographic device, which I then used to create a dance sequence where one dancer works at speed with sign language, while another uses pure dance language.

The story was told as a voice-over by Linda Bassett to add to the dancing. Davies's show opened on the USAF former airbase in Upper Heyford, Oxfordshire, and toured to Oslo, the London Victoria Miro Gallery, Salts Mill, Saltaire, a former tea warehouse in Bristol, and the old Corn Exchange in Brighton.

Churchill's involvement in political protest had begun by the seventies when she, for example, marched with members of Monstrous Regiment to protest against the war in Vietnam. And in February 2003, she was one of an estimated half million people in the protest march to oppose an attack on Iraq. In March 2002, she was part of the Lysistrata Project, which gave readings of the play in Parliament Square. The same readings were performed at 830 venues in forty-nine countries. On 6 March, she reacted in the *Guardian* to a statement by the then foreign secretary, warning that Washington would abandon the United Nations and NATO unless Europe acquiesced in US proposals over Iraq: 'So Jack Straw's latest justification for the war is that we must all do what America says because otherwise, in future, we'll all have to do what America says.' It is difficult not to think that *Drunk Enough to Say I Love You?* stems from this period. In November 2003, the Stop the War campaign staged 'A Royal Welcome' at the Court for George W. Bush's visit to the UK that month. Martin Crimp and Tony Kushner contributed material, while Churchill showed 'Iraq.Doc', a collection of quotes about the war from an Internet chatroom, many of the calibre of 'I hope we nuke you and the camels you fuck with'. On 17 March 2004, the Court staged 'War Correspondence', with work from Martin Crimp, Rebecca Prichard, Tony Harrison and Churchill. Churchill appended her signature to two letters to the *Guardian* of 25 March and 16 April 2004, as part of the Palestine Solidarity Campaign protesting at American-backed Israeli activity in Gaza and the West Bank. And she was one of very many, as reported in the *Guardian* of 16 February 2007, to call for British troops to be withdrawn from Iraq and for MPs to vote against the replacement of Trident.

After *Plants and Ghosts* came a new version by Churchill of Strindberg's *A Dream Play*, directed by Katie Mitchell for the National Theatre. More accurately, Mitchell in the end used about forty per cent of Churchill's version. The rest came from her actors' dreams, Jung and Freud. Mitchell later said: 'At the point that I asked Caryl to do the version I had no idea that I would only use such a small proportion of the original text'.[4] Mitchell and Churchill met a number of times while the text was developing. The playwright went to several rehearsals, and was kept abreast of changes and cuts. Relatively speaking, Churchill was hardly there during rehearsals, unlike rehearsals of her other work. She was, however, quite happy with the addition of other material and the cuts 'so long as it was made clear that my production was not her version of Strindberg's text'.[5] In her Introduction to the published text, Churchill noted that:

> on the whole this version stays close to the original. What I've mostly done is tighten the dialogue and cut out a few chunks . . . I've cut things that seemed repetitive; sometimes I've cut bits that just seemed to me or Katie not to work very well. And I've cut the meaning of life.

One of the actors in *A Dream Play* was Angus Wright, who recalls that two or three weeks into rehearsal the decision was taken to create a dream on stage rather than a play. The consequence was that

> the text was going to need to be thinned out. At this point a less flexible and understanding playwright would have been well within their rights to cry foul at the direction our work was taking, but Katie Mitchell and Caryl Churchill have an excellent working relationship and this, combined with Caryl's outstanding generosity with her version of the play, allowed us to take her text as a starting point from which to begin to explore.[6]

The play opened on 15 February 2005. There were some predictable cries that it was not Strindberg's play. Nor was it Churchill's, which remains unproduced.

As with many artists, the issue of climate change occupied Churchill. In September 2005, she took part in what the *Guardian* (24 September) described as an 'unorthodox conference', hosted by the Environmental Change Institution at the

University of Oxford, where thirty scientists and thirty artists were brought together 'to discuss how art and science might collaborate in fighting climate change'. And the Royal Court, on 12 May 2006, put on an event featuring two leading climate-change scientists, and introduced by Churchill. It, according to the Court, underlined 'the need for cultural engagement with climate change'.

In July, Churchill renewed her collaboration with Orlando Gough at the 2006 BBC Proms. For part of a day celebrating the voice, Gough's choir, called The Shout, performed *We Turned On the Light*, with a text by Churchill, based on a medieval poem, 'There Was a Man of Double Deed'. The original poem tells how an innocent action leads eventually to disastrous consequences. Churchill's version of this is to do with climate change and the impending disaster. Gough described it as 'a musically sophisticated piece of agit-prop'.[7] The piece was performed twice during the one day (29 July).

The two-hander *Drunk Enough to Say I Love You?* was first seen at the Court on 10 November 2006, in previews. It was originally scheduled to have its first night on 15 November, but the date clashed with the opening of *The Sound of Music* and, consequently, press night was moved to the 22nd. Critical reception of the play dwelt mainly on the idea that Sam equalled Uncle Sam and Jack stood for the Union Jack. Churchill pointed out that:

> Sam is Uncle Sam all right, but Jack was supposed to be
> just a person. I shot myself in the foot by calling him Jack
> . . . I didn't, stupidly, think of Union Jack. I should have
> called him Jonathan or Fred . . . What I wanted to write
> was about the way most people (in Britain, or other
> Western countries, or anywhere, almost) are a bit in love
> with America, whether it's movies, ice cream or ideals, and
> are then implicated in all this stuff it does.[8]

Thus Jack is a figure in a story 'about a man who fell in love with America', as the Court's publicity has it. And 'Jack would do anything for Sam. Sam would do anything.' The play is not centrally about the 'special relationship'. It is clearly not about George W. Bush and Tony Blair, although there are moments that echo aspects of that particular relationship. It is about a love affair between two gay men, with all that follows, including a dominant figure and a generally submissive one, who fall out, row and reconcile. The love affair spans decades. At one point, for example, in Scene 2, the reference is to Pol Pot, leader of the Khmer Rouge, and prime minister of Cambodia between 1976 and 1979. Pol Pot exterminated between one and two million of his people, all in mass graves, and died of natural causes, in hiding, in 1998. Sam wants to help Pol Pot but cannot afford to be seen to be involved. And Jack suggests: 'so why don't we help China help him . . . because no one can blame us for what the Chinese'. Sam's admiring reply is: 'knew I was right to bring you'.

The historical frame of reference in the play is from the Vietnam War, 1959–75, to Allende's Chile, 1970–2; from North and South Korea in 1945 to the Korean War, 1950–3; from the assassination of Patrice Lumumba, first democratically elected prime minister of the Congo, 1960; to Greek military dictatorship, 1967; from the Huks, a communist guerrilla group in the Philippines formed in 1942 to Hamas taking the Gaza strip in June 2007, and to President Hugo Chávez, a strong critic of US foreign policy, and currently President of Venezuela. All these have in common US-inspired activity or hostility or war or funded overthrow. The love affair implicates Jack and what he represents in these activities. This means that the play does not solely indict the US as the arch enemy of other nations. It indicts all who support America either directly or by looking the other way.

Jack is intoxicated by close proximity to power. He is talking directly to a country with the greatest military capability on Earth, and his reaction is: 'so much fun in my life . . . god must have so much fun'. In the first production, the two sit by a sofa. There is a dense black surround. The picture was framed by a proscenium with dressing-room light bulbs which stayed on during scenes. The effect was theatrical and deliberate. Between scenes, the light bulbs dimmed. Each scene ended with a blackout and music. At the beginning of Scene 2, the sofa had risen from the ground. By the last scene, it was only a little way from the level of the circle. The effect of this was to increase both the lordliness of the dialogue, and the sense of remoteness from the rest of the context. Churchill, of course, specifies nothing in her text. Indeed, there are only two stage directions in the whole piece, both in Scene 7: 'SAM alone' and 'Enter JACK'. The overall design, by Eugene Lee, was visually arresting, as it contained the domestic intimacy of the sofa with the epic scale of the dialogue.

It is apparent from the beginning that Sam is the dominant figure of the two. Jack is quick to declare undying love. Sam casually says: 'to be honest I'd forgotten till you'. Jack leaves his wife and children and is inducted into the world of foreign policy, which in Scene 2 is partly about propaganda. The policy uses deepest fears or beliefs to persuade people to behave as the Americans want. So the slogan 'Christ has gone south' in Vietnam stems from the fact that the country was originally occupied by the French; or Chileans are threatened with their children's being taken and 'disappeared'. Countries are invaded, such as Grenada in 1983, Lumumba is killed, 1960, Allende killed in 1973. Nations are used against other foes, as Afghanistan becomes Russia's Vietnam. Jack in the main complements or repeats whatever Sam says.

Only occasionally does he falter. A reference to the Iran–Iraq war, 1980–8, has Jack saying: 'lot of dead in that one'. In Scene 3, amidst recitations of death and destruction, Jack refers to 'civilian injuries', to which Sam replies: 'not that interested . . . not that interested in numbers of civilian . . . need to get on'. Jack eagerly learns as he goes: 'and the children dead from sanctions we don't count that because'. By Scene 4, Jack is homesick, but brought back into line by Sam's explaining the economics of destroying other economies 'because our economy is the priority here'.

Sam behaves in some sections like a sulking child, quick to react if crossed. Whenever Jack brings up the subject of Israel, the response is quick:

> Israel seems to get the largest share of
> you want to go home?
> . . . keep saying you love me and then we have all this

He feeds Jack a line of cocaine, and explains how drug trafficking works to his advantage. And how local resources are appropriated, manufactured and sold back to the local population. It is, of course, necessary to do all this because of American need: eight billion dollars on cosmetics; ten on pet food. Jack's reaction is that it is 'enough to provide health, food and education for the whole of the third'. And Sam explodes with fury over Jack's lack of commitment. There are no shades in Sam's world. He thinks globally only for the promotion of US interests. Jack, occasionally, detaches himself to find another perspective. But only occasionally.

Not only the world is processed according to American beliefs. Space is to be similarly treated via the construction of star wars as a shield against attack. Sam argues the necessity because of the proliferation of weapons of mass destruction, and lists the American nuclear and toxic arsenal around the globe. They discuss the effect of weapons such as dioxin, sarin, and the consequence of exposure to depleted uranium. The build in the play is relentless and unforgiving. The indictment is massively felt. The figure of Sam is sometimes virtually out of control, a blinkered, fanatical figure, with only one objective, as he looks around him down into the blackness of the stage. As they bicker at the end of Scene 6, they are witnesses to 9/11. From reciting past acts of aggression, there arrives the brilliant moment of the collapse of the twin towers and they watch. Sam has only one word, a hugely ironic 'evil', given what he has been talking about all along. At the scene's end, Jack leaves because he says he can't live with Sam any more.

Scene 7 opens with a horrifying soliloquy by Sam played in a subdued tone, only his upper torso lit. It is a catalogue of torture techniques made the more terrible because clearly not the ravings of a lunatic but more like reading from a manual. The scene develops the range of tortures practised by US and other authorities, including the use of extreme rendition. On this basis, what is done at Guantánamo needs necessarily to be exempted 'from rules forbidding cruel, inhuman or'. The lovers are united, and all is well.

The final scene centres on climate change, which Sam dismisses as 'junk science'. He doctors a report pointing out the threats, and insists that technology will come up with an answer. The refusal to sign the Kyoto Protocol of 1997, which set targets to cut greenhouse gas emissions, is rationalised as 'price of electricity in California'. By the end, Jack has given up on Sam, who insists on being loved. The ending literally leaves the play in the air. Jack left once, and returned. He can't love Sam, and can't leave Sam. And Sam demands, like a child, limitless love. The stasis at the end of the play is deeply disturbing. The settee rises.

An extraordinary feature of the play is the development and extension of the style of writing seen in *Hotel*, 'Hong Kong' and *A Number*. *Drunk Enough to Say I Love You?* has no complete sentences, very few full stops, and no capital letters apart from proper names and the first person singular. If Salter and his sons on occasions retreat into incomplete expression as a way of not being definitive, Sam and Jack are playing a different game. Sam does not feel the need to explain in detail what is being done in his name. Jack hesitates to cross his dominant partner. He mainly echoes or rephrases. The two are locked together in an endless batting to and fro, a sort of linguistic dance without end. The one complements the other. Sam assumes that he is perfectly clear. Jack does not, apart from specific moments, object. The lines are incomplete because the assumption is of certainty, rightness of purpose. Sam's arrogance in not explaining but endlessly demanding love is akin to a conqueror dealing with a client state. The part lines brilliantly underscore the essence of the situation. The two, isolated and comfortable, survey the world as a toy to be played with, manipulated as and when, brought into line if it strays, and bent inexorably to the will of Uncle Sam.

Churchill's feeling is that with *A Number*, 'It's more a naturalistic conversation, with what's in the text being everything the characters say in real time, while with *Hotel*, 'Hong Kong' and *Drunk*, it's more like a sampling of phrases from much longer conversations, so that we move quickly on'.[9] If Jack at the end cannot love Sam, he appears to have no choice but to stay. The play asks much from its artistic team. It also demonstrates a huge belief in that team's ability to show this dance of death in its true light.

Part 2

Voices and Documents

This part of the book deals both with Churchill's collaborators, and with material relating to her work. It also includes some previously unpublished material by Churchill herself. 'Voices and Documents' is presented chronologically and begins in 1975.

Any unattributed material is drawn from correspondence with the writer of this book.

Strange Days (1975)

Churchill was appointed Resident Dramatist at the Royal Court for one year from autumn 1974. The director of the Court's Young People's Theatre Scheme, Joan Mills, reported to the Council of the English Stage Company on 8 April 1975:

> *From next week, for a term, Caryl Churchill and I are going into a junior school twice a week, working with a group of nine and ten year olds via improvisation, games and discussion in an attempt to give Caryl the basis of a play for that age group. This is a pilot project which we hope will show us the problems and advantages of this type of scheme.*

The first section here is part of Joan Mills's account of the project (1); the second consists of extracts from Churchill's own notes of the process, which ran from 14 April to 10 July (2); the third section sets out the initial seven scenes of the play, called Strange Days *created and performed at the William Tyndale Junior School, Islington (3); coincidentally or not, the school became the focus of a heated debate the same year (1975) about 'progressive' versus 'traditional' teaching methods.*

1. Joan Mills

I think the idea emerged from discussions about writing for young people, informal talks Caryl and I would have had over a drink or lunch. She had three children at that time, two of whom were in Tyndale School, Islington. So I guess this influenced our choice for the site for exploration. Quite simply it was easier for Caryl to ask the school if they would be interested in having Caryl and I come to the school to do these workshops. The heart of this discussion was that writers who create plays for children may not necessarily understand a child's imagination.

Caryl and I decided to visit the school twice a week for a whole term. It was about twelve weeks and we went in the afternoons, something like 12.45 to 3.15 perhaps. Our aim was to explore the dramatic ideas which engage these children who were about nine, ten years old, I think, and to tap into their story telling and idea of character. I was to lead games, exercises, improvisations and Caryl would take notes on the dialogue, ideas, characters that started to emerge, and discuss the writing with the children and eventually help the children to write the text. And then I would 'direct' the play and help facilitate its staging in a simple manner. So we worked very much together on all of that. The school agreed to this proposal.

What I remember about the first few sessions was sitting in Caryl's house having a cup of tea after the sessions and feeling pretty daunted because at first it seemed the children were not interested in anything but television. We asked about their hobbies and what they did and they said they didn't do anything; they just knew about television programmes. They were rather distractible, fidgety, weren't able to concentrate for more than a few minutes it seemed, and the girls and boys wouldn't go near each other, never mind hold hands and touch as needed in some exercises. There was a lot of shrieking and giggling and 'ugh'. Of course this is all usual with kids of that age, but in order to reach their imaginations we had to break through all of this surface or nothing would have happened. Despite feeling it was all a little bit of a struggle and a fear that we were getting nowhere, we continued patiently and, after a few weeks, we really saw some progress. The children got used to us and to the strange games which became a bit more familiar; the rules and structures became their possessions and territory and suddenly their initial reserve and silliness fell away. And they began to develop skills and talk to quite a different level in their story and character explorations with Caryl.

I remember one session where we began to explore what scared us, and this bore fruit. The room was full of stories, monsters, people you couldn't trust, bullying, overbearing authority figures, the supernatural; these all filled the room. They told us about moments of television programmes or films, which had stuck in their minds and scared them later. And then the discussion turned to kinds of people or characters who are frightening and so on. And after about nine weeks we'd created a series of strong ideas, characters and potential themes and then we spent a few sessions ordering it all and creating a story. And we began to think about how to stage it; what costumes, props, settings and ideas we could manage – and to ask the children's parents for help with some of this, and the school. One scene, I remember, involved animals handing on a message which becomes more and more garbled, and it was misheard and re-interpreted, and interestingly this nice idea emerged and it got misheard and re-interpreted according to the animals' interest. And this idea emerged from a game. I think probably we were playing a game of Chinese Whispers. So quite often some ideas emerged from the exercises and improvisations that we'd explored over the weeks.

And Caryl and I were quite excited by realising that the things the children had come up with, that they were interested in exploring once they began to work with us, were in fact archetypal and quite serious – isolation, friendship, family security, but also the stifling quality of convention, oppression of the new or the different, issues about conformity, loss of identity and the son, of course, challenging and overpowering the father. I think this project with Caryl was quite influential in my development and my work on devising text from then onwards. And interestingly I think I see the seeds of Caryl's interest in working as a writer very closely with actors and directors in a very practical way and in the space, rather than as an isolated writer who only deals with the word on the page and then sends off the script to the agent and is hardly ever involved. Obviously this is not the kind of writer she is. She is a writer, I think, who's learned an enormous amount by being in the rehearsal space, obviously particularly when she worked with Joint Stock. She would then take those devised ideas and then write with her own particular and special vision. But the practice of theatre has influenced her in a way that may not have influenced many other writers in the same way. And in her willingness to explore the physical space and the rhythms and almost choreographic possibilities of space and time, music, dance, visual image and so on, maybe one sees even in this little project a tiny seed of that interest all those years ago.

2. Caryl Churchill
Monday, April 28: Talk about what is frightening
(Tracy, Ben, Linda and Satnam had joined; others left)
Frightening things: sometimes enjoyable, sometimes really horrible.

Enjoyable: Ben – *Dr Who*, Daleks (when little).
William – Horror films.
Vehid – *Moon of the Wolf* with werewolf, not really frightening.
Karen – Shuttered room. Little orange thing tied to a bed that changed into a horrible woman, who had a beautiful sister.

Horrible: Ben – Witch finders, because it really happened; tests for finding if witch. Vietnam.
William – Also witch finders.

Vehid – Film where man threw acid in another's face.

Ben – Man fell out of window on to railings.

Jane – Film with cutting off limbs and building new people.

Insects:

William – Beetles.

Vehid – Spiders.

Ben – Daddy longlegs (not spiders).

Joan – Earwigs.

Vehid – Queen bee.

Caryl – Too many caterpillars.

Blood:

Ben – Seeing so much blood when he cut his arm; nobody in the house.

William – Finger got hit by rusty bar, sight of blood.

Joan – Child cut, blood mixed with milk, coped at time but afterwards fainted.

Paul – Felt sick after being in hospital, not at the time.

Monday, May 5

Quick warm-up with mimic tag, meeting and greeting – fast, slow motion; robots; people with no feelings. (Huge change in ability from when we started.) Trust (liked this very much). Joan talked about ways of making story – where set, kind of character, special effect, e.g., magic, atmosphere (funny, sad, etc.), time (past, present, etc.), how it develops (chronological etc.). Perhaps didn't get through discussing all that. Some talk about style – realistic, like comic strip, slapstick, etc. Don't think got on to thoughts, stream of consciousness, memory, etc.

Children told story ideas.

Someone mentioned tunnel:

Ben   Man alone in dark house. Lots of eyes looking at him but when he goes up nobody there. Man goes mad.

William   Man with woman who cooked him sausages all the time. He liked them but he went mad.

Jane   Aunt goes to America; said street called Hobbsend after the devil. Supposed to be strange goings on and killings. She went into room. Scratches of fingers on the walls. Man lived there visited by devil. Doctors said found skeletons in tunnel. No one lives there except a policeman. And they put a curse on him and he died.

Linda   She hadn't locked door and went shopping; man broke in and put water in their TV and cut rabbit's throat, to punish them.

Vehid   Football hooligans and policeman.

Paul   Man thinks he's the only one who's real; tries to find someone else real. How would you check?

Ben   Normal goes wrong: you wake up and you are abnormal because though not changed everyone else had, e.g., trousers on heads; you think they're wrong, they think you are. Perhaps all your previous life a dream. Or all others dead except you.

Ricky's idea (from Caryl) – Knocking on door, nobody there; repeated, of telephone ringing with silence, in TV film.

Also talked about one person feeling safe within film or play, and how frightening if they turn out not to be. Cf. Caryl – *Les Diaboliques* when woman escapes into bathroom and locks the door, and figure rises out of bath.

Monday, June 16
Knocking game and improvisation; mask sequence. Going into petrified forest with same person. In between they surround him possibly put mask on his face.

We spent some time afterwards working out play in more detail. Sausage man; stranger who comes in with object; days getting strange, e.g., slow motion, physical differences. Boy notices change and others don't. Boy disappears. Man who put object comes and takes boy to help kill ogre. But at the ogre's – mask scene. Ogre tells boy to line up with others but he won't. Mimic. Trick him round into mimicking them. An odd creature helps him escape. Travel scenes. Creature sends message which keeps going wrong. Boy ends up in petrified forest. Creature ambushed – but it had been going to tell boy to go to forest. On Thursday before seeing the group we worked out the end – boy told to go back to castle and when he gets there it's his own kitchen. Destroys object and ogre. Family come alive and now changed, father nice etc., not sausages any more.

Monday, June 30
Steven had difficulty screaming as the baby. Paul Roylance named the creature Tintail (Tyndale!). William good with sausages – I think I'll have sausages *for a change* etc. Worked every morning in the last week, concentrating on weak bits like Ben and the stranger, the guards' ambush, message scenes, where the dialogue hadn't been worked out properly, and group things that needed precision like masks, mimicry, tunnel etc. during travels. Some of this was managed with very little rehearsal. Details put in like red slide for death of ogre, now named The Glump. Joan thought of Christmas tree bauble as object. And the title, 'Strange Days'. More slides and costumes were made by those helping. Rehearsals emphasised loudness (this improved enormously and all were audible in the end); precision (e.g., not showing masks when they came on); lining up straight; speaking in exact unison for mimic scene etc.; not turning back to audience; speed and efficiency clearing set; getting into costumes etc.; being quiet and still when waiting at the side. This all improved very rapidly and was very good in performance. What was impressive was the way in the last few days everyone extended themselves. Near the end we added the

idea of Ben playing boring music at the beginning and lively music at the end, and of Tintail being in a string bag.

On Thursday, July 10, there was a dress rehearsal – the first time they had all the costumes and props. Then a performance for videotape. Then in the afternoon one for the infant school, and one for the junior school; and the evening for parents and other visitors. Amazing day!

14 April–10 July 1975

(about twenty-one sessions before day of performance – fewer for many of children who joined late)

3. Strange Days
by Caryl Churchill
And Joan Mills
And the pupils at William Tyndale Junior School:
William
Ben
Jane
Linda
Karen
Vehid
Tony
Steven
David
Satnam
Paul

Play opens with Ben playing minor scale on piano

I. FAMILY	
MONDAY	*William, Jane, Ben, Linda, Karen*
	(Father comes in and coughs. Children
	stand.)
CHILDREN:	Hello dad.

FATHER: Hello. What's for tea?
MOTHER: Sausages.
FATHER: Good, I like sausages.
MOTHER: Come on you three, go and wash your
            hands.
            (Children wash hands. Pass plates.)
MOTHER: Put that book down.
            (They eat.)
FATHER: I enjoyed that.
ALL: Mmmm.
            (All go off.)

2. STRANGER   *Vehid*
                (Stranger looks through the window,
                climbs in, puts the bauble on the table. As
                he goes off he feels watched. He looks
                round and sees the toy, Tintail. He takes
                the toy and goes out of the window.)

3. TUESDAY   *Same as Monday*
                (Exactly like Monday, still eating.)
BEN: What's that? I've never seen that before.
MOTHER: It's always been there, Ben.
BEN: No, it hasn't. Dad, have you seen it
            before?
FATHER: Yes, we got it for a wedding present, Ben.
KAREN: You got it for mum and daddy, Ben.
BEN: No, I've never seen it.
MOTHER: Be quiet, Ben, and eat your sausages.
            (They eat.)
BEN: Mum, where's Tintail? I left him here.
MOTHER: I haven't seen it, Ben.
LINDA: You're too old to play with toys, Ben.
MOTHER: Your sister's right.
BEN: I'm going to look for him anyway.
            (Ben gets down under the table.)
FATHER: What are you doing down there?

MOTHER:	Get up, Ben, and eat your sausages.
	(Ben gets up and they eat.)
FATHER:	I enjoyed that.
ALL:	Mmmm.
	(All go off.)
4. WEDNESDAY	*Same*
	(Father comes in slowly. All the family except Ben are in slow motion.)
BEN:	Hello, Dad.
FATHER:	Hello. What's for tea?
MOTHER:	What about egg and bacon?
FATHER:	No, I think I'll have sausages for a change.
MOTHER:	Come on you three, go and wash your hands.
	(Children wash hands, mother brings food.)
BEN:	Come on Mum, you're taking all day.
MOTHER:	Don't talk so fast, Ben.
	(They eat.)
BEN:	Do you feel all right?
MOTHER:	We're all right, Ben.
BEN:	You're all so odd.
FATHER:	You're the one who's odd, Ben.
BEN:	But—
FATHER:	I enjoyed that.
ALL :	Mmmm.
	(All go off.)
5. THURSDAY	*Same*
	(Father comes in as usual.)
CHILDREN:	Hello, dad.
FATHER:	Ben, why didn't you say hello?
BEN:	I did.
FATHER:	Oh. What's for tea?
MOTHER:	What would you like?

FATHER:	I think I'll have sausages.
MOTHER:	Come on you two, go and wash your hands.
BEN:	Three.
MOTHER:	Oh yes, sorry Ben.
	(Children wash hands. Ben has difficulty getting a place at table. When the food is passed none is passed to him.)
BEN:	Can I have my sausages please, Karen? I said, can I have my sausages please, Karen?
	(She passes them.)
BEN:	How's your new teacher at school? How's your new teacher at school?
LINDA:	Oh, she's terrible.
BEN:	I don't know why you couldn't answer the first time. How did your exams go? How did your exams go?
KAREN:	Oh, all right.
BEN:	Pass the ketchup please, dad. Pass the ketchup please, dad.
	(He passes it.)
BEN:	Can't you hear what I say? I said, can't you hear what I say?
MOTHER:	Of course we can hear you, Ben. Now be quiet and eat your sausages.
FATHER:	I enjoyed that.
ALL:	Mmmm.
	(All go off.)
6. FRIDAY	*Same*
	(Scene opens as usual.)
FATHER:	What's for tea?
MOTHER:	What would you like?
FATHER:	What is there?

MOTHER:	You can have egg and bacon, omelette, spaghetti, whatever you like.
FATHER:	I think I'll have sausages.
MOTHER:	Come on you two, go and wash your hands.
BEN:	Three.
	(They wash. Ben can't get into his place.)
KAREN:	Look at this.
	(They look at the book, shutting Ben out.)
MOTHER:	Put that book down.
BEN:	Make room for me.
MOTHER:	Does anyone know where Ben is?
BEN:	I'm here.
KAREN:	He's probably down at the garage.
MOTHER:	I hope he comes soon or his sausages'll get cold.
	(They pass the food without giving him any.)
BEN:	Where's my sausages? All right, I'll get them.
	(Ben goes to get his sausages. There aren't any. The rest of the family get slower and freeze.)
BEN:	What's the matter? Etc.
	(The stranger/friend/Vehid comes on whistling.)
7. THE FRIEND	*Vehid, Ben*
FRIEND:	Hello, Ben.
BEN:	How do you know my name?
FRIEND:	Don't you remember me? I'm your friend.
BEN:	No, I don't. But everything's so strange. It's been getting more and more peculiar all week. At least you can see me. They can't. *(He turns to indicate his family but they have gone.)*

FRIEND:	Of course, I can see you clearly.
BEN:	You're all so strange. And now I've disappeared. No one can see me. No one can help me.
FRIEND:	I can see you. And I can help you.
BEN:	Can you?
FRIEND:	Yes, and I've some friends who can help you. We know why things are so strange. It's all because of The Glump.
BEN:	Who?
FRIEND:	Come on, I'll tell you as we go.

<u>Light Shining in Buckinghamshire</u> (1976)

In 1976, the partnership between Churchill and Max Stafford-Clark, one of the two artistic directors of the Joint Stock Theatre Group, began its long trajectory. Their first show together was Light Shining in Buckinghamshire. *Here, the process is described in extracts from Stafford-Clark's Diary (1); Churchill herself reflects on what was to be a seminal piece of theatre (2); and, finally, the journalist Ann McFerran describes a workshop on the scene in Act 1, called 'Claxton brings Hoskins home' (3).*

1. Max Stafford-Clark

25 Oct.	I have another idea in mind which at times seems good and at others a fledgling fantasy. It's about the crusades . . . women, old men and boys left to look after land, half starved life they were leaving behind to become soldiers, skull left in the helmet, women's monologue about why men do it . . . all gloom, wood fires and misery.
29 May	Scene: magistrates examining poor. Church wardens examining poor. Two poor people standing by the poor box.
1 June	Read information about immigrants and

eccentricity. Going naked. Eating veg only. More testimony about lives. Read about vagabonds first. Quaker meeting about beliefs. A day rather like thin gruel. Not enough people in the morning to get anything underway. Personal grievances: talk about them as well as personal inspiration and ecstasy. Did read stuff on vagabonds and tried improvising peasants before magistrates.

2 June   Carole [Hayman] doing her beggar from down the road: do more on that. Utopias – what would we like. Work on scene Caryl has written. More work on characters. A good go at the Putneys.

3 June   Money and clothes are obsessions if you don't have any. Not enough information on Doomsday and Utopias. Caryl suggests doing some improvisations about men and women and their relations. What were things like within a marriage?

6 June   Caryl went to Quakers' meeting. Seats are in a circle. Came in. Settling in silence. Anyone who wishes to speak stands up and does so. Wants to do a Quaker meeting tomorrow. Go back to the eccentrics who would go too far in context of meeting.

Early Aug.   Should Scene 1 be Cobbe or Evelyn? Could do each character by turn. Why shouldn't Claxton know Briggs, and Claxton know Hoskins? Could not Claxton and chairman scene be re-written for JPs 1 and 2?

9 Aug.   Seems a bit arid, dried up and barren at the moment. Must keep it juicy and fertile. Open up the actors and the possibilities of new material. Work on vagrants. Send half of them out on observation and work with the other half on improvising monologues about stages of their lives. How do you make Cobbe more complex? An insightful monologue. Yes . . . talked with

Caryl and decided to make the parts non-specific,
i.e., not have a particular actor identified with a
particular part all the way through. We need to
work specifically on eccentricity, vagrancy and
ecstasy. We need to start with observation.
Finding objects in the street, jewels, firewood, fag
ends. Perform an action and build it into a scene.

18 Aug.   Got stuck again except that we did manage to reset 'Star Recruits' from public to private, but
could not make 'Hoskins and Preacher' work at
all because reactions seemed like acting and the
level of credibility could not be raised. Do it
tomorrow as eccentricity exercise making who
speaks and the level of what they say conditioned
by the end.

7 SEPT. 1976, TRAVERSE THEATRE, EDINBURGH

Max: Is this boring the arse off them? . . . How
much easier it would have been if there had been
a star . . . There is not one laugh in the whole
show except at the idea of Christ coming next
year . . . A Traverse Festival audience is not the
one for this show . . . Are they going to come
back for Act 2? Well, Jim Haynes [co-founder of
the Traverse] clearly isn't . . . 9.21 Max begins to
feel relaxed. Got them going, too. Quiet.

25 Sept.   It's certainly reached the stage where I've got
nothing useful to contribute any more, but then
shows should do. Why is the first half so difficult?
Why isn't it the definitive show I had hoped for?
Why and how and in what way do I know it
hasn't worked out? It's not as good a show as it
would have been had Bill done it with me . . .

26 Sept.   Bill said I should have been there for the first two
weeks of *Light Shining* and he's right. Otherwise,
how would the show improve?

17 Nov.   *Light Shining* has been extended again and will
have run nine weeks in all at the Theatre Upstairs.
I enjoy it . . . it does have a clean, spare beauty
and passion in it. I love watching it. The scrubbed
table . . . the figures . . . the actors lit against the
black . . . the skull, the hourglass . . . The ambassadors . . . emerging from the light . . . soon it will
be gone forever, but it is beautiful.

2. Caryl Churchill

I'd been struck long before by the Ranters and recently thinking about Utopian communities, but none of that was in my
mind when Max asked if I'd like to do a show about the
Crusades. He had stayed at a house in the country where there
was a crusader's tomb and had wondered what would make
someone uproot himself and set off for Jerusalem. He suggested Colin Bennett and I write the play together. The three of us
met often at Max's flat to share what we had read. We were
excited by the ideas but the crusaders themselves remained a
bit remote, and when I read Cohn's *Pursuit of the Millennium*
with its appendix of Ranter writings I was seized with enthusiasm for changing to the seventeenth century. We kept the mil-
lennial dream and Max's question of why you would turn your
life upside down for it, but instead of glimpsing shadowy figures in armour we could hear vivid voices: 'Give give give give
up, give up your houses, horses, goods, gold . . . have all things
in common.'

So there was a new direction for insatiable reading. It leaps
at me from a dense notebook. Hill of course, Morton on the
Ranters, and pages and pages of quotations from the time.
Only a couple of lines about what we did each day at the workshop, but enough to remind me of things I'd forgotten. We
were in a church hall near the Old Vic, it was May, it was
sunny. It was a large, loose workshop with some actors only
dropping in for short visits. We had to learn about something
remote and then find how we related to it, so a lot of reading

history and then finding equivalents – when did it seem to you that anything was possible? The revolutionary hopes of the late sixties and early seventies were near enough that we could still share them, but we could relate too to the disillusion of the restoration and the idea of a revolution that hadn't happened. (Odd that this was only a year after [David Hare's] *Fanshen*; it seemed long after.)

So there was reading and a wall chart; talking about ourselves; and all kinds of things mainly thought up by Max. I'd never seen an exercise or improvisation before and was as thrilled as a child at a pantomime. Each actor had to draw from a lucky dip of bible texts and get up at once and preach, urging some extraordinary course of action justified from the Bible: 'Suffer little children to come unto me' became an impassioned plea to lay children in the street and run them over with a steamroller. They drew cards, one of which meant you were eccentric to the power of that number, and then improvised a public place – a department store, a doctor's waiting room – till it gradually became clear who it was, how they were breaking conventions, how the others reacted. A word in the notebook conjures up half a day's work: 'Songs' – Colin Sell teaching the actors to sing psalms; 'Dives and Lazarus' – we tried acting out parables; 'vagrants' – the actors went out and observed tramps in the street and brought back what they had seen. Already on the third day I find, 'Talked to M[ax] – possibly quaker meeting as setting?' and that idea stayed after the workshop. One day we had a prayer meeting where everyone had to speak; someone wanted to eat an apple but Max made him pass it round and everyone had to say something about it; the last person didn't say anything but bit into it; and that ended up in the play. I condensed the Putney Debates so we could read them, and eventually, far shorter, again they went into the play. In a folder I find a scenario I wrote for a day's work; a character for each actor with a speech from before the war, a summary of what happened to them and what their attitude should be at an improvised prayer meeting, and how they ended up at the restoration. This before-during-after idea was something I took forward into the writing. There were improvisations about real people too, Coppe, Clarkson and the Man Who Ate Grass.

Next, the nine-week writing time. Looking at the forgotten notebooks I can catch for a moment the excitement of being so crammed with ideas and seizing on structure, characters, incidents that might contain them. Colin [Bennett] and I were working fairly separately, though agreed on a before-during-after shape with occasional consultations, and meetings with Max. Two weeks in there is the note, 'C has left'. I establish six characters and a line through for each of them – only one is clearly recognisable, in the final play, as Briggs: 'Poor man, Norman yoke, Leveller, Breakdown, eats grass'. I work out a rather formal structure with many scenes, a meeting in the middle, but what I write not long after is a play consisting almost entirely of one long meeting. Max not surprisingly said it was too static so I scrapped it and started again, intending this time to write a lot of short scenes showing how each character comes to be at the meeting. I played Dylan's 'Lily, Rosemary and the Jack of Hearts' again and again to work up a sense of speed and quick story telling. There next seems to be a version close to the final one, though John Evelyn appeared from time to time, reading about scientific advance from his diary. The play was incomplete when rehearsals started, in that not every one of the six characters had a full enough story, but it was enough to start working on.

Now another church hall near Lisson Grove. Only three of the actors from the workshop went on to the rehearsal, so the first part was like another workshop, making the history real again. The main characters were cast and the idea was that everyone would play minor parts in each other's stories. Then Max and I had the idea, first a joke, then seriously, that perhaps there wasn't any need to write the missing scenes if it wasn't quite clear which character was which and different actors played the same character in different scenes. This solved the problem that the extra material would make the play too bulky and plodding (as well as saving me writing it) and also gave an effect we liked of many people having the same experiences during the revolution. We wondered if the actors would mind giving up parts they had been given but they were quite cheerful, keeping their characters for the meeting and swapping them round for other scenes. I did do some writing during the rehearsal. The new structure meant I could add scenes that weren't part of anyone's story, like the butcher. We went to Max's uncle's farm in Buckinghamshire and read the Putney Debates in the farmyard; the actors were sent to explore the house without anyone in the house knowing they were coming and one of them described being startled by seeing herself in a mirror: that led me to write the scene where one woman gets another to look at herself in the piece of mirror she has looted from the great house. I wrote the description of a battle and Claxton going over the hill after improvisations by Nigel and Will, the first time I'd known the pleasure of giving an actor back a speech in that way, and the only time I remember working quite like that. There was a scene I could never get right despite rewrites and improvisations, a girl tied up to be bled by a doctor, from Hoskins' early life, which ended up, cut very short, in *Vinegar Tom*.

It was August by now, very hot. Did the church hall really have no windows? It had chairs, and Max staged the scenes with these, and that became the set. Sue Plummer designed a beautiful table of scientific instruments and a skull for Evelyn, and then we cut Evelyn. But we kept the table because we liked it so much. Meanwhile Colin Sell was back, and the actors were singing the psalms and the Whitman. Sue brought the dark ragged costumes. Steve Whitson came to talk about the lights. The writing was virtually over and the main work now being done by the rest of the company. There were small alterations through up to the opening. All six characters originally had longer speeches at the end, and I think it was at the dress rehearsal at the Traverse that I cut them all down except for Nigel's Man Who Ate Grass. Max and I share a pleasure in making cuts: 'Look, look, we can go from here to here, it still makes sense.' So there we were in Edinburgh, a solemn, tired, silent company. I remember someone saying he'd been surprised the show was so good having seen us looking so miserable. I don't think we were, even then. This is a slight account of a great deal, and one thing it can't show enough is my intense pleasure in it all.[1]

3. Ann McFerran

One scene involving a preacher and an objector at a prayer meeting caused particular trouble – eventually being abandoned till the next day to allow some work to be done on other scenes. The following morning Max Stafford-Clark returned to the scene, asking that Caryl and I should join in too. Producing a pack of Tarot cards, he gave one card to each participant saying that the number on the card would govern whether we were to support the preacher or oppose him. Eight, nine or ten demanded vociferous support. An entirely different subject was given to the preacher for his harangue – Welsh nationalism instead of the theology of God's elected saints. No one knew who had the joker, the objector's card. The meeting began with Colin McCormack speaking eloquently on the rights of Cymru. The objector Jan Chappell found so many hostile to her cries of outrage that she was forcibly thrown out of the room. We then discovered Stafford-Clark had stacked the deck and dealt out three tens. The scene was conducted again, rewritten, and no longer presented problems of motivation.[2]

<u>Vinegar Tom</u> (1976)

At the same time as working with Joint Stock, Churchill created Vinegar Tom *with Monstrous Regiment, a company established in 1975 by a group of professional performers committed to staging the complexity of women's experience. Three members of the company recall the evolution and playing of* Vinegar Tom. *They are Gillian Hanna (1), Susan*

Todd (2) and Mary McCusker (3); Hanna also discusses the portrayal of Jack and Betty (4) and the arrival of a new company member, Josefina Cupido (5).

1. Gillian Hanna

We had been introduced to Caryl (in Hyde Park, after a march . . .) and she talked about how, in researching her English Civil War play *Light Shining in Buckinghamshire* for Joint Stock, she had come across a mass of material relating to women and witchcraft, and wanted to write a play about it. Her ideas fitted with ours, and we commissioned her to write it. In terms of our relationship with a writer, it was one of the happiest we ever had. There was never any disagreement about the basic argument of the play, although we had long discussions with Caryl about the characters Jack and Marjory, the couple who represented the emerging bourgeoisie. As I recall, their first scene was the only one which was substantially rewritten. Other changes Caryl made were largely practical. A scene in which Jack and another man drag the drowned corpse of the cunning woman through the village and dump it while they go and look for a drink had to be cut because it had to immediately precede the witch-finding scene and Roger didn't have time to change. The part of Betty had to be written in such a way that Josefina Cupido, who had just joined the company as a musician and who had never acted before, could have a part that wouldn't be too terrifyingly long.[3]

The form of *Vinegar Tom* was extremely bizarre. You had a series of quite naturalistic scenes punctuated by very modern songs in modern dress. It all came to some kind of conclusion, and then at the end you had two musical-hall characters coming out of the blue, developing it nowhere. If you took out the music you would have something akin to the traditional play. But we knew that we had to have the music to smash that regular and acceptable theatrical form. We didn't sit down and say deliberately that we need to smash that form, but that is what we did nonetheless; I think we unconsciously felt the need to do that . . .

What we were saying about witchcraft was not necessarily true only of witchcraft, but of women's experience today. We had a very real feeling that we didn't want to allow the audience to get off the hook by regarding it as a period piece, a piece of very interesting history. Now a lot of people felt their intelligence was affronted by that. They said: 'I don't know why these people have to punctuate what they are saying by these modern songs. We're perfectly able to draw conclusions about the world today from historical parallels.' Actually, I don't believe that and, in any case, we can't run that risk. For every single intelligent man who can draw parallels, there are dozens who don't. It's not that they can't. It's that they won't. I believe that the simple telling of the historical story, say, is not enough. It's always a question of choices, and some things are always left out. You have to choose between what you keep in and what you leave out. It's at that point of choice where women on the whole find that they get left out.[4]

2. Susan Todd

Quite consciously, in a very perverse manner, we decided to break the form completely apart by putting songs between the scenes. And though the rest of the play was set in the 1640s, performers appeared in their own contemporary clothes for the songs which were really very aggressive and extremely difficult to communicate. We didn't want to allow the audience to ever get completely immersed in the stories of the women in the play. We wanted to make them continually aware of our presence, of our relationship to the material, which was combative, anguished. The songs had to contain what we sensed as a connection between the past of the play and our present experience.[5]

3. Mary McCusker

It felt very exciting to work with Caryl and there was a strong sense of 'the moment'. What does that mean? Part of a great raft of people trying to connect, to put our skills with our passion and our politics. United by a desire to make stunning theatre. When I read the first draft of *Vinegar Tom* I was thrilled at the thought of getting on a stage and doing it, amazed at how Caryl had distilled all that research into a good story and created great characters. It was theatrical, a piece that belonged on stage.

Caryl not only listened to actors and their ideas but also seemed able to catch the movement of our subconscious sludge and carry it back to her writing space.

My memories of the rehearsal process are hazy – but one thing stands out; the script was there to hang on to when the going got tough. I don't remember ever saying: 'I'm having a problem with this line.' This was not a text that needed editing. And the songs! Some men hated them because they felt 'got at'. I always felt great as I dashed back stage to throw off Joan's rags, put on my shiny grey shirt and jeans, plus a hat to hide the oily hair before stepping on stage with the others to sing one of the songs. Joan was a victim of the 'witch finder' and a lifetime of poverty had left her physically weak. At times I found that uncomfortable; I realised I wanted to play a strong character who 'won'. The songs allowed me to bring Joan's anger and pain and throw it out into the audience. I wasn't asking for their pity. It was my voice, my body.

When I was hanging from the gallows in the penultimate scene, it was a tremendous effort not to panic. Sometimes that noose tightened in an alarming way. On some occasions the harness did indeed nearly finish me off and my ability to play the last scene was impaired. Caryl cared about the discomfort we went through and I think mentioned it when the play was published.

I remember how open and generous she was when we tinkered with the last scene to give it more of the 'old music-hall edge'. I look back over the years and continue to be thankful I was part of that time, that I was able to work with someone like Caryl.

4. Gillian Hanna

My memory is that Jack and Betty needed to represent very clearly the emerging rural middle class – that their anxiety about their place in the local hierarchy and their aspirations to rise higher in the social scale fuelled those anxieties – that's why the question of buying more land was introduced. And hence their viciousness towards anyone they viewed as threatening their social position. These were the areas that were pointed up in the changes. I don't remember that they were new ideas. I think they were already present in the script, but there was a feeling that they just needed to be given greater weight.

5. Gillian Hanna

Josefina Cupido joined the company around the time we began talking to Caryl. She is a brilliant musician which is why we wanted her in the company. We always had music in every show at that point. But we also had a policy that, if possible, everyone should do everything . . . it could have been very isolating for her to be the only person in the company who didn't act. But Josefina had never acted before at all. So we asked Caryl if she could write a character who would be woven into the story (i.e., not just a token part for J) but who, at the same time, wouldn't have a huge amount to say – that would have been very daunting for a novice actor surrounded by actors who were very experienced.

The Legion Hall Bombing (1978)

Churchill's only documentary play was The Legion Hall Bombing *for BBC 1, transmitted 22 August 1978, but only after Churchill and her director Roland Joffé removed their names from the credits. Churchill explains the circumstances (1). Following that, the original Prologue (2) and Epilogue (3) are appended.*

1. Caryl Churchill

The only documentary play I've done was a television play about Northern Ireland, about a trial in the Diplock courts, which were introduced in 1973 because the government felt it was too hard to get convictions otherwise. There's no jury and only one judge. I had the transcript of a trial of a boy who was given sixteen years. A bomb had been planted in a British Legion Hall where some people were playing cards, and a boy walked in, put the thing down, and said 'Clear the hall' and they all went out. Half an hour later, a small bomb went off and nobody was hurt. The trial was extraordinary because there was no evidence to say the boy who was accused did it, except the police saying he'd confessed, which he denied. There was no signed statement by him. And there was an old man who'd been in the hall who said: 'I don't know what boy it was but it was definitely not *that* boy.' There was no positive identification at all, and it was hard to believe you would get a conviction in a normal court. So I did a play for television with Roland Joffé; it meant reducing the nine and a half hours of trial transcript. We put on a voice-over at the beginning and end of the program that explained the Diplock courts, and the BBC took it off because they said it was political comment, and put one of their own in different words, which they said was objective. We took our names off the credits as a protest.[6]

2. Prologue

This is a British court in Northern Ireland. It is different from any court in England. In 1972 a committee was set up under Lord Diplock, an English judge, to find ways of dealing with terrorists other than by internment without trial, which was causing widespread disapproval. According to the Diplock Committee, it was difficult to get convictions in the courts, because of the intimidation of potential witnesses and the difficulty of finding impartial jurors for sectarian crimes. They therefore recommended a different kind of trial for political offences, which was adopted under the Northern Ireland

Emergency Provisions Act 1973. There is no jury. The judge sits alone. And the rules of evidence have been altered so that a confession is allowed as evidence even if it was obtained by threats or force.[7]

3. Epilogue

The Diplock courts were set up to make it easier to get convictions and they have been successful. Recent research at Queen's University, Belfast shows that the rate of acquittals in these courts has dropped steadily each year. If courts can accept unsigned statements put forward by the police with no corroborative evidence and reject the evidence of a defence witness without explanation it is reasonable to ask whether it is worthwhile for the defence to put a case at all. The courts have a tradition of independence, but at the same time they carry out the will of Parliament. In peaceful times the role of the courts is generally accepted. In times of stress their role may change.[8]

Floorshow (1978)

Monstrous Regiment's next work which involved Churchill was a cabaret, Floorshow, *which first appeared at the Theatre Royal, Stratford East, on 18 January 1978. There were four writers: apart from Churchill, they were Michelene Wandor, Bryony Lavery and David Bradford. Gillian Hanna explains the genesis of the piece (1) and (2) and Clive Russell delivers a monologue about fish fingers, transcribed from a live performance (3).* *

1. Gillian Hanna

Now that cabaret has become a cliché of the alternative theatre it doesn't seem like such an extraordinary thing to have done, but at the time we knew we were taking a leap in the dark . . .

---

* As well as the monologue, Churchill contributed at least three songs: 'Hello, Darling'; 'Women's Work'; and the last song, 'Night, Night'.

We didn't even know if women could stand up in front of an audience, without a character, and be funny. So we wrestled endlessly over the problem of each woman finding her 'voice', and the difference between a performer's relationship to a 'persona' as opposed to a character.

A desire to discover if and how women could be funny; to explore as many genres of theatre as we could; to find out if there was such a thing as 'women's theatre' and was that any different from 'theatre', which was always implicitly male. We were searching and our theatrical curiosity pushed us into areas which were new to most of us.[9]

2. Gillian Hanna

I don't know why we chose four writers, as opposed to three or five or any other number. Probably because we wanted a variety of styles and ideas, and we also probably knew that, as we were working in what was at the time very uncharted territory, we needed to be in a position to reject stuff and have enough left over to make a show . . . And any more than four would have been unmanageable.

As I recall, Caryl was a natural candidate as we had had such a good time on *Vinegar Tom* and wanted to work with her again. I think at the time she was also quite intrigued by the idea of cabaret. David was also a *sine qua non*, as he was part of the company, had written before, and I have the feeling that the whole thing was his idea in the first place. I think we contacted Bryony because we had seen her work with *Les Oeufs Malades* and we knew she had a great sense of humour. Michelene, I think, because again we had seen some of her work and liked it.

They didn't write together; they wrote pieces and brought them in and we worked on them. Some were perfect from the start, some needed work of various sorts and some were just inappropriate and were rejected. I can't remember how much of Caryl's fitted into which category, but my sense is that most of what she came in with was perfect and used without much alteration.

3. Clive Russell

Do you remember all those nursery rhymes that you heard when you were a kid? It's funny how they come back to you when you've got kids of your own. Well, I mean, you've got to do something to amuse them, haven't you? So, there you are, hanging over the cot, singing 'Goosey, Goosey, Gander', and 'Wee Willie Winkie', 'Ride a Cock Horse to Banbury Cross'. Amazing the rubbish you keep in the back of your head. How many of you men ever had to look after your children? . . . I don't mean for just ten minutes while the wife's just taking a shower. I mean for hours and hours. By yourself. I mean, it's a funny thing, that you're in the flat, all on your own, and there's the cat, and there's the kids, but there's no human beings, know what I mean? Anyway, there I am in the flat, looking after the kids, looking in the fridge for some lager. No lager. Butter, margarine, fish fingers, bags of fish fingers. Now there's a funny thing. I mean, have fish got fingers? I mean, I've heard about battered wives, and battered babies, who'd ever want to batter a fish finger, eh? I mean, where's the fun in that? I mean, a fish doesn't drive you crazy, does it? Fish fingers. That's what I gave my three wee boys. My wife's first day at work . . .

Letter to the *Guardian* (1979)

Churchill has an honourable record of publicity stating her position vis-à-vis the issues of the day. The position is, of course, contained mostly in her plays. On occasions, however, she responds directly. On 16 July 1979, Polly Toynbee, writing in the Guardian, *decided to patronise a number of women's theatre groups, including Monstrous Regiment. On 27 July, representatives of the five groups written about, replied. Churchill sent the letter below:*

I can't take seriously Polly Toynbee's pretensions to be a critic of women's theatre when she comes out with the old journalistic cliché of worrying who does or doesn't wear a bra. But I must defend the Monstrous Regiment against the defamatory implications slung at 'most of these groups' of lack of drama training, turning up late for rehearsal, looning around on stage. Their professional qualifications are impressive if 'professional' is flavour of the week, and when I have written for them I have found them hardworking, self-critical and impressive, both as actors and musicians. And I certainly don't mean to imply that what she says is true of the groups I don't know so well.

Political theatre raises all kinds of issues about work method and form, for the older left groups, as well as for the women's groups. They have been developing a theatre quite different from 'flag-waving sloganising'. But 'flag waving' is, of course, the uninformed reflex response to the idea of political theatre as 'bra burning' is to the idea of the women's movement.

Not a good article, but I won't let it make me 'uncomfortable about the possibility of women's artistic inferiority' as journalists, nor worry about Polly Toynbee's underwear. I just hope people won't be put off seeing other women's groups by her drastic preference for the enjoyable *Bloomers* [a cabaret].

Cloud Nine (1979)

In 1983, Churchill wrote a long account of the play to the director Richard Seyd during his rehearsals of the play for the Eureka Theater Company, San Francisco (1);[10] Miriam Margolyes, who played Maud and Victoria, describes the original workshops (2); the play's director, Max Stafford-Clark, noted in his Diary the first few weeks of the show's life (3); and Peter Hartwell, the show's designer, writes about designing a Joint Stock show (4).

1. Caryl Churchill

What is important . . . is that the feelings and characters of the
first act should be played for real, so that we do care about them
as people. Otherwise the second act loses out too – you have for
instance to care about Betty in Act One to care about her properly in Act Two, and so on. And of course if the first act does
just go as farce it's for one thing not a very good farce and for
another sets up expectations of a kind of entertainment that
aren't met in the second act. It's important from the beginning
the audience realises what kind of thing they have to pay attention to, and that is essentially the same throughout the play –
the relationships between the characters, their relationship to
their society, the pain and humour that come out of that . . .

The first act obviously isn't naturalistic but should be played
for real; the second act clearly gets played for real but mustn't
get naturalistic. Cathy helps that, of course . . . There's the first
scene that mainly gets the characters introduced. There's the
long scene a couple of months later going from the first Edward
and Gerry through to 'I think I'm a lesbian', the scene where
basically the women (or the female side of things, whatever,
including Edward) are having a bad time, and Betty, Vic and
Edward are all still very neurotic and uptight from their legacy
from Act One. Then there's the goddess scene, midsummer or
so by now, when the women assert themselves, magic happens,
ghosts start to be laid, ending with little Edward and Gerry.
Then there's the final scene, late summer, when everyone has to
some extent been changed . . . The original 'Cloud Nine' song
coming before the last scene, after the goddess scene, helped
mark the change; though there was the danger of a false climax
. . . it did mark a turning point and make the final scene clearly something different . . .

It might be useful to take the characters one by one.

ACT I

Clive has to run the first act with his energy. It's the male, patriarchal, heterosexual, empire building act with a galloping plot,

and a lot of it is to do with him trying to keep together his world, which is starting to crumble at the beginning with murmurings among the natives and Harry's arrival, and is in pieces by the end. Originally I wrote it with a small man in mind, an indoor man, an administrator, a little Napoleon without much natural authority, just the authority of his position. Harry by contrast was glamorous . . . What is important is to see his increasing desperation. At the beginning he is confidently managing the rivalry between Betty and Joshua, by the end he is hastily scrabbling together a marriage that he knows is a sham. He is probably very drunk in the last scene. He is pretending to believe in what is happening; nobody else is, except Maud, who probably does. He has confidently introduced us to his world at the beginning – by the end nobody in it is what he wants them to be. As the play goes on he more and more obviously seizes on excuses for Edward – the first time with the doll is relatively straight-forward, the second time in the beating scene he has for a moment to search more urgently for a reason that makes Edward's behaviour manly, the final time with the necklace it is part of the desperate sham of that whole last scene.

Betty: The pitfalls are . . . obvious . . . If the actor just plays that person in that situation and doesn't worry about playing a woman, it will probably be fine. There are moments when she is more affected than others, like the love scene with Harry (though even that can be played straighter than you might think, the words do a lot without the actors needing to comment much) and there are moments when she can be really strong and forceful, with all the force of the male actor, like when she tells Joshua to go back to the house or hurls herself at Mrs Saunders. That really should be a proper physical attack, a real rugby tackle that brings Mrs Saunders to the ground . . . Mrs Saunders needless to say barely defends herself, the attack is all Betty's. There is nothing particularly weak, poetic, hysterical about Betty, only about Clive's image of her. She throws and catches balls excellently.

Edward changes a lot through the act. He shouldn't be too odd a child . . . He'd be fine if Clive didn't want him to be something different . . . The excuses for the doll start impulsively, and become far more conscious. By the time of the necklace excuse in the last scene, it is quite calculated and plays on what he know Clive will be looking for. He really loves Harry and is really betrayed. By the end of the act he is well set up to be the uptight, repressed, anxious Edward of the beginning of Act Two.

Joshua: Extremely important obviously that he's white and not in black face. He's a white like Betty's a man. Also important that he is genuinely and totally devoted to Clive all the way through . . . He [sings] . . . 'In the Deep Midwinter', a performance for the master by someone totally alienated from his own culture singing about snow that he'd never seen . . . He is completely devoted to Clive in and through the killing of his parents (though obviously still partly of his own world in putting earth on his head). It is only when Clive turns on him – get out of my sight – that he flips.

Maud: Not much of a problem. A strong woman in a dependent position.

Ellen: A clergyman's daughter? Anyway someone who has to have a job and is doing this not because she likes children but because going to Africa seemed a bit of an adventure. At first she just has a crush on Betty I think, and doesn't really know what she feels. There is . . . the difference in attitude to female and male homosexuality for Victorians – male was reviled etc. *à la* Oscar Wilde and Clive-Harry; female was invisible – like Queen Victoria not knowing it existed so they couldn't pass a law against it because it would mean explaining it to her, and the generally accepted lovingness both in words and physicalness between women without anyone thinking it sexual, so that in general it was invisible. It's invisible to Betty obviously – she doesn't realise ever, even when Ellen is declaring her love so directly at the end . . . It seems important that her own feelings are at first invisible even to Ellen – the scene of touching hair etc. should be a discovery for her, rather than a lewd seizing of an opportunity. She realises her passion more as the scene goes on, and has progressed to being really in love by the time of the: 'I'd rather die than leave you' etc. She is shattered by the totalness of rejection and misunderstanding, and 'What if I said yes' is genuine wondering, not an acceptance; it is Clive who rushes it into being that. It's a sad character, and only comic after that and because of it; absolutely not a sly lewd pantomime maid.

Mrs Saunders: She's a strong woman who has been running a farm alone since her husband died. She's fairly humanitarian, doesn't let the servants be beaten, etc. Without putting her ahead of her time she's more aware of what's happening and more progressive than the others. (Or maybe it's better to see both her and Harry, the outsiders to the family who can't possibly fit it or the society, as similar in this.) She genuinely comes to Clive for safety not sex. She sleeps with him when he comes to her bed the first night, out of relief at safety, physical comfort and indeed sex, but that doesn't mean she wants that to be the terms of the relationship. She absolutely is not flirting with him during the 'why ride off now' scene, but is really trying to explain her position. In the end it is sheer physical sensation that takes over briefly . . . She does enjoy it briefly, is indignant when it stops. She's a rather brisk horsey woman. . . . The main point about her is that she's an independent woman, and that Clive interprets her being on her own as making her a seductress. Key lines for her are: 'There's no place for me here.' And 'I shall keep leaving everywhere I suppose.'

Harry: He's a homosexual, genuinely in love with Edward. His betrayal of Edward is serious and appalling to them both. He does idolise Betty, as a good woman, a mother, etc., and rather likes the idea of being her unrequited lover, a far more acceptable role than admitting what he is. When she wants more than that, he at once retreats and tries hard to keep her where she is. Joshua is casual and direct sex by contrast with the romancing Betty. The love scene with Edward can be quite a straight love scene. The crocodile story . . . should have sexual implications but quite veiled for both of them and should really be about the pleasure of being alone together at last. In so far as there's physical contact and rolling around together (if that's even necessary which I doubt) it should be something they can both take as innocent and within their uncle relationship and which only helps lead on to something else rather than pre-empting it. This is quite important. Harry is quite shattered and defeated by the end of the play and not putting a particularly good face on it. He makes a feeble attempt to go back to his old chatting up line with Betty, which she slaps down – I shall get drunk. He is still in love with Edward, though pretending now entirely to be the adult and uncle.

ACT 2

The main thing about the characters is that they all change, slightly. Betty, Edward and Vic bring the tensions and repressions of the first act with them. Simplistically, they are changed by Lin and Gerry (who are both homosexual and working class, which may be relevant). The changes aren't to some idyllic and happy end obviously, but everyone has got a bit less rigid and more open.

Betty: The stages she goes through should be quite distinct. In the first scene she has just taken, is just taking, the decision to leave Clive. (Maybe she doesn't even know it as definite until she's said it, like 'There, I've said it, it's true', in the first act.) She has to run the first scene off her hysteria and leave Cathy hysterical. She is avoiding contact with her children. In the next scene she's left him, is living alone in a flat, depends a lot on Vic and Martin. She's in a near breakdown state of panic and agoraphobia, acute anxiety. She is beginning to relate to people a bit though, especially Lin. Then there's the scene she's not in, the magic or whatever scene. When we next see her she's changed a lot. She still chats on a lot and has moments of not being able to face what's happening but she is basically okay and setting off on her new life . . . She is the same person as Act One Betty and it can help if both actors are aware of that (similarly with Edward) not just as a fact because it's obvious but as something to think about, or the Act Two characters to be aware of where they've come from. A useful key to Betty is: 'I want to be dangerous.' It's something that makes the double with Gerry nice – there's a shadow there somewhere of Betty being dangerous, and it has reverberations for their scene together.

Edward: Not usually a problem, so long as he's sufficiently uptight and even a touch camp at the beginning to give himself somewhere to change him. Actors are usually (rightly) so wary of making him any kind of stage faggot that they end up playing him the same all through. There does have to be reason enough for Gerry to say: 'Just be yourself'. It does have to be clear that it is Edward who is making the relationship neurotic, that he is trying to change Gerry into something he isn't and can't be. The change for Edward is from having rejected being a man if it means being like Clive and taken instead the idea of being a woman but with his only model for that Betty from Act One, to realising through Vic and Lin that being a woman isn't some special stereotyped way of behaving so that he can just be himself, do the things he likes, look after Cathy or whatever without feeling there's a whole old-fashioned feminine behaviour that goes with that. So that by the time he meets Gerry again he's still doing housework etc. etc. and still identifying strongly with women, but in a quite different way which makes him more relaxed, more able to relate properly to Gerry as whatever Gerry is rather than as raw material for a husband fantasy.

Gerry: Originally Gerry's monologue was at the beginning . . . and it was a nice jolt to start the act as clearly somewhere very different. But it gave the audiences a fright and turned them against Gerry, who seemed just the sort of horrible maniac they hoped they'd never meet on a train, which was not the intention. By moving it to after the scene with Edward (this was in England after about a week of touring) it made people more on Gerry's side and able to go off and enjoy the adventure with him. Gerry can be older than Edward as he was originally, or younger . . . that is quite nice as it makes Edward's fantasy of being the wife even more obviously inappropriate. What's important I think is that he's nice, not particularly fucked up. He does love Edward and does not enjoy promiscuity. He genuinely likes being alone, that's not just defensive, but the change he goes through (not a major one, Edward changes more) is realising how much he loves and depends on Edward and would like to get back to him . . . Somehow . . . the love between Gerry and Edward makes up for the hurt of the destruction of Harry and Edward's love. It seems to me really good that the person Betty tries to chat up is Gerry and that he's nice to her, etc., and that that should be the last scene as she reaches out for the first time.

Vic: Fairly clear I think. Goes from the little doll of Act One to someone who still finds it hard to be seen rather than heard, can't talk to Martin, etc. Her feminism and politics are all in books and the head and it takes her relationship with Lin to loosen them up and make them real. So what happens to her is that change, to something less uptight, more feeling.

Martin: He, like Vic, has all his sexual politics in the head, doesn't mean harm, means quite well with nasty flashes, but is so used to being in charge that he finds it hard to stop and talks Vic into the ground with what is meant to be the politics of her freedom. One of the things Act Two is about is how hard it is to give up power (for men, for Britain in Ireland) as well as how hard it is to take freedom. Martin has all the theory of having given it up while keeping it in practice. The change for him is that he does begin to talk less and do more, goes from not speaking to Lin to looking after her child, from theorising about a different form of life to trying to live one. The row with Lin was so as not to make him too perfect or make it seem too easy; and a row is still better than refusing to speak at all. Then the actor originally playing him wanted something to get sympathy back in case he'd lost it by shouting so we put in the bit about holding Tommy on the sofa . . . For me the moment I used to feel sorriest for him . . . was when the other three went off – tell me when you're sober. He and Vic are still fond of each other at the end. Who if anyone is going to go on having what relationship with whom is left completely unsettled.

Lin seems easy enough . . . It's important she should be warm. She (like Gerry) changes less than the others, but she does get a bit of theory from Vic perhaps, and gets less hostile to men, through Edward and then Martin, who she may have a row with but basically has some kind of working relationship with by the end. She's important to Betty too.

Cathy seems to be better the more closely the actor observes four to five year old girls and the less he relies on some fantasy of what they might be. She's not a horrible child . . . The theory of her being played by a man . . . is partly just a reversal of the more conventional woman-plays-boy from Act One; partly I suppose it throws up more clearly the extent to which behaving like a proper little girl is learnt rather than innate; partly that the emotional size and force of a small child in a group is better represented on stage by a large and forceful man than it would be by a child . . . Cathy's change – from being whining and over dependent on Lin to relating to all of them, I suppose. And the negative change by the second scene where she's more conscious of trying to be a proper little girl. I don't think she changes in the sense Betty, Vic, Edward, Martin or even Gerry and Lin do, though.

The Soldier: The last bit of empire, 'fucking' as sex and aggression, a man's life, his anger and pain at what he's been through, and real yearning for something else at the end.

The goddess scene needs to build quite lightly and quickly up through that chanting, the audience needs to be possibly deceived by what Lin sees because for all it knows something will appear, the play might be making a move into the supernatural then rather than a few moments later. Then it turns out to be a joke, to be back to reality and fooling around in the part, then it turns out real magic has somehow started. The soldier needn't just appear at the back in a puff of smoke, he can quite concretely walk on and be like a real person if you prefer. I rather like solid ghosts myself.

2. Miriam Margolyes

They needed a lesbian for a play about sexual politics. I auditioned for Max and Caryl on the phone – shouting across the wires from Italy where I was on holiday. I knew Max and Julie Covington and Carole Hayman – none of the others. On the first day of rehearsal Max explained the work process. I was on a high for weeks; it was the rehearsal process for me which means Joint Stock and I remember the 'truth sessions' – sitting in a circle each day, one of us in the middle, telling everything about our lives, our sexuality and our insecurities – trusting a group of near strangers with buried secrets and private fears . . . The structured improvisation, feeding each others' imaginations, laughter and terror mingling, as we wrestled with Max's witty and malicious comments. It was a spurious democracy – he had the real power but he did try to make us take the responsibility. He forced me to grow up as an actress (which must mean as a person too) and to examine in detail, line by line, my objectives through a scene, an act – the whole play. Lacking a drama school discipline I had never properly worked on preparing a part, and the gaps in my technique were cruelly but necessarily exposed by Max. I remember the 'self-criticism' session, which I had to cancel a lucrative voice-over to attend (Max was very scornful of such earnings) and my inability to find fault with myself but being full of criticism of the others. Max said I was the best *directed* person. I think he might not have meant it as a compliment to me but who cares. The joy of such good work – my moment as the Grandmother trying to murder a doll, Julie's speech as the Mother in Part 2 and Tony Sher as a revolting but accurately observed infant – stuff of which real theatre is made.[11]

3. Max Stafford-Clark

10 Feb.   First run-through.
13 Feb.   Dress rehearsal.

First Performance 14 February 1979

14 Feb.   Dartington . . . world premiere.
15 Feb.   A hard week. The best performance was on Saturday, when the first half was really controlled and tightly played. The jump into the second half is a hard one, but I don't think it's going to get any easier.
22 Feb.   Sparky row between Miriam [Margolyes] and Carole [Hayman] about whether Carole should mop the floor in the dressing room. A big puddle has been left by Carole's umbrella, and Miriam's bag has been made wet. Miriam accuses Carole of being very selfish. Carole says she's going to the meeting and will do it after. A compromise is needed.

Miriam: 'It's not a subject you can tame.' Tony Sher: 'It's much easier dealing with a reactionary society than it is a liberated one. A lack of an overview because we've never had time.' Jim Hooper: 'I've never felt so close to a play I've done, and I do feel defensive about it.' Tony Rohr: 'I'm not getting enough laughs. It's a struggle to go on every night.' Julie Covington: 'Having said I'm thrilled, I'm nowhere near enjoying it.' William Hoyland: 'I came off depressed partly because of the characters I play.' Jim: 'They tire themselves out laughing in the first half.'

The response to the play was warm. The first half veered from high comedy to farce, and there wasn't the difficulty I had anticipated in getting the audience to refocus on the second half.

After two weeks of performances Caryl and I went back and made further cuts which reduced the running time by twelve minutes. It made both halves much tighter, and particularly drew the second half together. Before we arrived at the Royal Court, the reputation of the play had preceded us. The producer Ian Albery came to see the show on tour and offered us a West End transfer after the Royal Court run subject to certain conditions and cuts. The West End always places a certain pressure on a show, and we were in no mood to listen to somebody else's opinion.

6 March   Julie says it would kill the show to go to the West End because it infects and diminishes everything, or it will in the end. Others press for a limited season: three months only. Julie keen to go to Belfast because that's where she's always wanted to go. That leads to a debate about who we want to play to.

We were snobbish about the audience who might come to see us in the West End.

William: 'Tourists from Japan, and bankers from Haywards Heath deserve good theatre as much as anybody else'. Julie: 'I don't wish us to work for a West End manager. I can't articulate why, but I know they are subversive in some kind of way.' Miriam talks compassionately of Julie's special position and how we can see by her unusual emotion it's very upsetting.

If we were to transfer then her name would certainly feature large, and particular pressure would be put on her to undertake publicity. But there's no doubt that the others led by William and Carole would love the focus it would give their careers.

There is no entry in my Diary to mark the success of the first night, or the warm response accorded to *Cloud Nine* in its brief run at the Royal Court. The reviews were broadly favourable, although by no means ecstatic. Michael Billington in the *Guardian*, 3 April, called it 'Cloud three and a half', though, to be fair, he rated Caryl Churchill pretty highly. Among the women writers. He wrote:

> It is a curiously hollow evening. It's so busy covering the waterfront and trying to provide an anthology of sexual attitudes that it ends up illuminating almost nothing.

Billington's disapproval and our own exhaustion were perhaps two of the reasons it took so long to realise that we were involved in a popular hit that would become a modern classic.

24 April   Royal Court run at an end. Feeling tired, skin stretched over face. Awful get out. We wanted to save the set in case we revive the play, but it wouldn't fit through doors. Everybody older, tireder, whiter, paler.

Success doesn't always lead to contentment, but the play was revived with a slightly different cast in September 1980 and was the first new play to be a hit in my regime at the Royal Court. But it was in New York that the full appeal of Caryl's wonderful play was to be exploited. A production off Broadway ran for over a year. None of the team who helped create the play was involved.

4. Peter Hartwell

The design demands of a Joint Stock show were fairly simple for me: affordability, transportability and suitability. The budgets were small but not bad by comparison to other companies. Their fees were much better, so a gig with Joint Stock was good . . . whatever one designed, it had to pack into a red van that would never pass a road test, and another larger vehicle. For *Cloud Nine*, I remember leaving a club in Covent Garden with Danny Boyle (who was the assistant stage manager) driving. We took back roads and forever to get to Exeter for the opening. Everything was to fit into these vehicles and be able to be set up by the stage management, sometimes the designer and cast, and anyone else who could be organised into a crew at our destination.

Cloud Nine at Dartington has one clear memory for me, and though it has little to do with the show it does illustrate what an amazing time it was for mid-scale touring companies and places like Dartington. I remember coming down for breakfast at the B&B we were staying in. I joined Caryl and Les [Waters] at their table. Shortly afterwards, Alfred Molina came down. He had finished performing Dario Fo's *Can't Pay, Won't Pay* the evening before at Dartington . . . it was like the baton being passed from one show to the next . . .

I remember the first read through of *Cloud Nine* after that six-week workshop and the writing period. Act 1 stood pretty much as submitted. The group of actors and Max did not buy into the second act at all. My memory is that, characters aside, the whole structure of Act 2 was chucked out. Something about a garden on the top of a cliff overlooking the sea. I do remember thinking: 'Thank goodness that cliff is gone.' If it had been me who had had half of my play rejected, I would have freaked. But Caryl listened, took notes and seemed to be completely calm. She went away and reworked Act 2, and came back with what turned out to be a winner. I loved her calm, intelligent talent.

Women Live (1982)

'Women Live' was a national campaign run by the group Women in Entertainment during May 1982. Its aim was to highlight women's work in all the arts. Churchill's contribution to the 'Women Live' event was a week-long workshop in the Court's Theatre Upstairs. This is her report.

Caryl Churchill

I thought that for 'Women Live' I would do some kind of workshop for women writers. Annie Castledine agreed to be the director of the project and we decided to include only women. We invited five writers of whom three were able to come (Sarah Daniels, Ayshe Raif and Rose Cullen), and publicised the event at the Actors Centre, the Women in Entertainment office and 'The Factory', accepting the first fifteen performers. They included some quite young and inexperienced actresses and some with a wide range of experience on the fringe, at the Court, RSC, National, etc. There was also one young director (Jo Henderson). The workshop was to last for a week, 11–4, and took place in the Theatre Upstairs.

It was not intended that any piece of work should be produced by the end of the week. The work was to be interesting and enjoyable for its own sake, and it was hoped that the writers would benefit from working with performers and directors. Rather than taking the texts of plays as a starting point we took a subject, the menstrual cycle, with the book of *The Wise Wound*[12] as one of our sources since it has interesting and startling views on the subject.

The first day started with people talking about their experience of puberty and in the afternoon there were some improvisations based on what had come up. During the week this combination of talk and performance continued, though we took care not to spend too much time in discussion and as far as possible discovered feelings and situations through various kinds of exercises and improvisations. One tendency of the work was towards finding external expression for very inward feelings which we had not defined before; another was outward towards a more political look at women's situation.

Unfortunately I had to miss Tuesday because of a meeting and Annie had to miss Wednesday and Thursday because of her commitments at the RSC, but we were together on Friday. On Friday Sarah Daniels brought in a short play which she had written because she felt she had gained so much from the group and wanted to give something back, and the play was read and discussed. I devised a list of events making up a ritual for a girl at puberty, drawing on work that had been done during the week, including poems by Rose Cullen, which was something we had decided earlier in the week that we would like to end with, and this was performed at the end of the day.

Because the subject of the workshop led people to think about their bodies and their feelings and to share things that would usually be private, a very close feeling developed among the members of the group, and there was a general feeling of having gained a great deal from the week. The work had attempted to find dramatic situations and concrete images for things not usually considered in the theatre, and the results though sometimes tentative were often moving and often very funny. Several of the people who took part have hoped that the work can be taken further.

Top Girls (1982)

Gillian Hanna of Monstrous Regiment recalls early discussions of what emerged as the play (1); Max Stafford-Clark, the play's director, wrote in his Diary of receiving and rehearsing it (2); Churchill talks about her play (3); three actors involved in either or both of the 1982 and 1991 stage and television productions – Deborah Findley, Lesley Manville and Lesley Sharp – together with Churchill and Stafford-Clark discuss aspects of their roles, and the play (4); Katherine Tozer describes playing Griselda in the 2001 production at the Battersea Arts Centre

(5); and Churchill dismisses the views of Julie Burchill in the
Guardian, *23 February 2002 (6).*

1. Gillian Hanna

Caryl Churchill was commissioned to write another play. She
was interested in seeing if there was any way of bringing
together women from different historical periods and letting
them talk to each other. In the minutes of our first discussion
with her, 'Dull Gret, Pope Joan, Pocahontas, a Japanese courtesan, Isabella Bird, etc.' are mentioned. None of us had any
idea how their meeting might be accomplished, but we hoped
we might discover that in workshops. *Ms Dante's Inferno* was
floated as a possible title. When we came to do the workshops
with Caryl we also introduced Florence Nightingale, Ruth Ellis
(the last woman to be hanged in England) and Jane Anger (a
possibly apocryphal contemporary of Shakespeare's who
dressed as a man and went round fighting duels).

2. Max Stafford-Clark

Caryl's play. Dinner for the dead at the start does not reverber-
ate through the play. Where do Joyce, Angie come from?
Structure difficult – where to make the act changes. Fuck. How
do we know it's a year earlier? A pity Angie's line: 'She's not
going to make it' isn't at the end.

I saw *Top Girls* at a very early stage when the first scene was
all different monologues, and hadn't been intercut, but I think
when Caryl had taken those decisions it didn't change very
much. It changed a bit in rehearsal because of the overlapping
dialogue. She would say to the actor: 'Oh, I thought that by the
time you'd got there, you would have finished. So, ok, let's start
that overlapping earlier.' And so those things changed.

21 March   With Caryl. She gives the ages of some of the
               play's characters: Marlene thirty-three, Joyce
               thirty-six, Isabella forty, Louise forty-six.

19 July   First day of rehearsals. Marlene clearly the hostess

in first scene. Put yourself in the middle.
Nijo/Isabella relationship central. Dinner party
careers out of control. Pleased with play and cast.
Extraordinary actions reported in first scene.
Dinner party: how does Marlene feel about it?
Each guest – who's your best friend? Each guest –
who are you most interested to meet? Which
guests will be tricky? Find contemporary equivalent to the class and level of each character.
What's the bill? Is it on the firm? Griselda – a
fable so that peasants will believe in the possibility
they could become kings. Pope Joan – difference
between Caryl's story and the facts. Winning
Marlene's attention with their stories.

28 July   All Marlene's references to men in the play. Play is
            about oppression of women by society and, by
            extension, men.

3 Aug.   Marlene doesn't appear to know Joan's story. Run
            through of Scene 1, seeing how much you can
            drink. Dig deep into yourselves to find the pain.

23 Aug.   First Preview. Best play I've ever directed. How
            quickly the audience accepts a surreal convention.

1 Sept.   First night. Peer group approval. Critical disap-
            proval.

3. Caryl Churchill

Thatcher had just become prime minister; there was talk about
whether it was an advance to have a woman prime minister if
it was someone with policies like hers. She may be a woman
but she isn't a sister, she may be a sister but she isn't a comrade.
And, in fact, things have got much worse for women under
Thatcher . . .

A lot of people have latched on to Marlene leaving her child,
which interestingly was something that came very late.
Originally the idea was just that Marlene was 'writing off' her
niece, Angie, because she'd never make it. I didn't yet have the

plot idea that Angie was actually Marlene's own child. Of course women are pressured to make choices between working and having children in a way that men aren't, so it *is* relevant, but it isn't the main point of it.

There's another thing that I've recently discovered with productions of *Top Girls*. In Greece, for example, where fewer women go out to work, the attitude from some men seeing it was, apparently, that the women in the play who'd gone out to work weren't very nice, weren't happy, and they abandoned their children. They felt the play was obviously saying women *shouldn't* go out to work – they took it to mean what they were wanting to say about women themselves, which is depressing . . . Another example of its being open to misunderstanding was a production in Cologne, Germany, where the women characters were played as miserable and quarrelsome and competitive at dinner, and the women in the office were neurotic and incapable. The waitress slunk about in a cat suit like a bunnygirl and Win changed her clothes on stage in the office. It just turned into a complete travesty of what it was supposed to be. So that's the sort of moment when you think you'd rather write novels, because the productions can't be changed.[13]

4. Deborah Findlay, Lesley Manville, Lesley Sharp, Caryl Churchill, Max Stafford-Clark

CHURCHILL: *Top Girls* was a play whose ideas came together over a period of time and in quite separate parts. Some years before I wrote it I'd had an idea for a play where a whole lot of people from the past, a whole lot of dead women, came and had cups of coffee with someone who was alive now. That was just floating around as something quite sort of separate, by itself. Then I started thinking about a play possibly to do with women at work, and so I went and talked to quite a lot of people doing different jobs. One of the places I visited was an employment agency, which later became a focus of the play. Then there was an idea of a play in which all the characters were women; the idea was to offer a huge range of different parts and give women the opportunity to play lots of roles on stage which they don't always get to play. At some point these various elements came together and I began to get the idea for a play about women at work, including women from the past, and a wide range of roles – and all of that fitted into the same play . . .

FINDLAY: [In the last scene] I think Joyce loves Marlene very much, and Marlene loves Joyce very much. It was extraordinary because in the first production Gwen Taylor played Marlene, and we did an improvisation in the rehearsal room (it makes me cry, almost, to think of it). We did an improvisation about what brought the sisters to this last scene, what is between them. So my character, Joyce, said: 'I will take the baby.' That was the starting point, and the improvisation developed between the two of us; we just sort of acted out that little scene [of the sisters deciding who would raise the baby Angie], thinking through what that was like for them. That improvisation stayed with me [through all the productions]. It made me think that there is an enormous connection between the two of them (it was a great big thing for Joyce to take on Marlene's baby daughter) . . .

MANVILLE: When I was rehearsing Patient Griselda I found it quite difficult, because I resisted her, and in the end you have to give in to her . . . I didn't want to come on and be Patient Griselda. I think it's significant that she [Griselda] arrives late in that scene, because what debate could you have with her? She can only tell her story; she's not movable at all. With the other women this great debate goes on, but Griselda comes on and just tells this extraordinary story, and shakes everybody up, and really sets off the mood of defiance that sparked the rest of the scene . . .

Marlene is a very difficult part to play. There's always something about a character that's like a hurdle, and with Marlene for me it was her political passion. It was her belief in

Thatcherism and the individual, and autonomy and selfishness and . . . that greedy color that she has to have . . .

In the early eighties, when we did the initial research on images of women, we were looking at women's glossy magazines, and it was very American, all about just becoming 'new women', and everything was about being hard and dressing male and not having babies, just go, go, go . . . be a women in a man's world, hard, hard, hard . . . And the look was hard: loads of blusher, lips, etc. And looking at the same magazines nearly ten years later, it was just startling because these same magazines were now telling us we had to be everything: we could be career women, and be in powerful positions, but we had to be mothers as well, and have successful partners, and we had to be these fantastic jugglers. We could be soft and feminine, and that was all right [but we also had to be] 'successful' in the world. Now that sounds very simple in itself, but it made us see how women had changed even in that short period of time – which was a tremendous century of change for women . . .

STAFFORD-CLARK: One of the difficulties which was resolved in rehearsal was that it is midway through the second act before the exposition is over. You have a first scene at the dinner table, and this surreal meeting of characters, and then in the second scene you begin to get [a sense of] it and Angie. It's not until the second act, or after the interval – wherever you put the interval – that you see Marlene working in the agency and you begin to get a context and the story threads begin to draw together. So in comparison with, say Shakespeare, where the exposition is handled much earlier, this is a dare: you're titillating the audience by withholding information, and there is a point halfway through the second act when the stories begin to come together, where [in performance] there was always a kind of renewed energy on the part of the actors and the audience, when it became clear where the play was driving. The final scene which begins to resolve the play takes place a year before the play commences; this is both a daring and an elliptical time scale that takes some time to tune into. And the scene is written with such force that the argument between Marlene and Joyce actually sums up what the play has been talking about – that and the final image of Angie saying 'frightening' . . .

CHURCHILL: The dinner party scene was a way of putting Marlene in a context of celebrating extraordinary achievements, so that we would look at her as sort of a feminist heroine who had done things against extraordinary odds, so that we could then have a different attitude to her as the play went on and we could begin to question what her values actually were.

I suppose I put them around a dinner table because it's a place where you can talk and celebrate, and I wanted it to be a festive scene where they were celebrating what they'd done as well as talking about the hard times they'd been through. I thought the conversation would be at the level of amusing anecdotes, of sharing stories and entertaining each other with them.

The choice of the women was fairly arbitrary – it was people who happen to have caught my fancy at that time, and I would have been hard put to it to say why I chose any of them in particular. But when I began to look at what they might talk about, at what they had in common, I began to realise that they had all made big changes in their lives, that quite often they'd travelled, and quite often they'd had difficulties about combining having children with other things they'd done, so slowly I could begin to see what those women had in common. But basically it was just that they were all people with extraordinary stories who were interesting to hear about . . .

STAFFORD-CLARK: [You can do] a simple exercise: seat three people in a line, and [instruct] the two people on the left and right both to converse with the central actor on completely different subjects, one about shopping and one about Wimbledon, for instance. [You'll find that] the central actor can easily cope with two conversations. In fact, in real life we often cope with two or three conversations – often at a dinner party you'll be talking to one person but actually listening to the conversation on the other side. Caryl observed this, and then by incorporating what she had observed into the text she took a step forward for theatre. In fact, writing in dialect form is another way of trying to reproduce, and direct actors to reproduce, real-life [conversational patterns]; by doing that Caryl is trying to direct the actors and then the audience into what she perceives happens in real life . . .

CHURCHILL: I first used overlapping dialogue in another play I'd written a while before, called *Three More Sleepless Nights*. What happens in that play is that there are two couples who are quarreling at night and the first couple have the kind of quarrel where you both talk all the time over each other, and the second couple have the sort of quarrel where you can't really speak to each other, the kind of quarrel that leaves huge silences. In doing that, I set the dialogue out as two columns of talk, and put the odd slash to show exactly where people cut in.

Then when I came to do *Top Girls* I was roughing out the scene in terms of these great chunks of the stories, the things different people had done, and I wanted the characters to be able to tell their stories to each other. But I thought that this approach might be incredibly laborious and boring and contrived, and I decided that one way to make it work was to make the stories overlap, and to have the characters talk in the way that they would more naturally at a dinner party, where everyone would be joining in together . . .

MANVILLE: The overlapping dialogue was horrendously difficult to learn, because you not only have to learn your lines but also the exact moment when you interrupt, and I mean exactly, it's not arbitrary. It's tempting to say it serves the scene by making it very naturalistic, since we do overlap in conversations in life. I suspect it's a more sophisticated decision than that. I worked with Caryl Churchill on *Serious Money,* which is spoken in verse for the most part. Why did she decide to do that? I think it's because she felt that way of speaking reflected the world of the play. And I think that rehearsing with overlapping dialogue means that instead of having somebody speaking and then passing the baton to the next character who speaks, you can have a lot more throw-away dialogue, and of course it isn't all important. With the overlapping, you can rehearse in such a way that [the question becomes]: 'who do we want the audience to look at?' It's not just a question of who speaks loudest; it's a question of passing the baton successfully so that the audience have some of the work done for them. On television it was slightly harder of course, because the camera decided who the audience is looking at, and that inevitably takes something away from the feel of the scene. I think the scene is best enjoyed as a whole picture, when the audience decides where to look . . .

SHARP: Dull Gret doesn't say very much, so that was the first clue to her character: why didn't she speak? The Brueghel painting which Dull Gret comes from is of a woman fighting demons that have come to earth from Hell – a woman whose children have been killed and who is avenging their deaths. I thought very hard about how one would feel if one's children had been killed, about that trauma, and so my interpretation of Dull Gret's silence was not that she didn't have anything to say, but that she had too much to say. Caryl gives her a speech at the end of the act which explains her silence. There's also quite a lot that she does during the course of the first act that isn't speaking, but about acting, about stealing food, for example, which is about her impoverished background, not having enough to eat. So there was another kind of dialogue in her listening, and her ways of communicating with the other characters . . .

There's a cunning and a slyness in Angie that has been nurtured by her isolation. I thought very much that she spent quite a lot of time on her own, and that she thinks things through: even if she thinks slowly, she still thinks very well. The fact that she's managed to get to London on her own, and to telephone Marlene – that she's remembered information that Marlene has given her years ago – actually suggests that she's not stupid but quite bright, and that she might show that in different circumstances . . .

STAFFORD-CLARK: The moment when Angie says 'frightening' is incredibly frightening on stage. The play is also frightening, to use Angie's word, and frighteningly prophetic, written on the threshold of Thatcher's eighties, as it posits the perspective that those who are less talented, those who are weaker, will go to the wall. Of course, that is what happened [in Britain]. Looking back now, when you see the increased number of people begging in the streets, and you realise that [that sight] would have been shocking in the context of the early eighties, or fifteen or twenty years ago, you see that the play is prophetic . . .

CHURCHILL: It's hard to think Angie doesn't overhear that conversation [between Marlene and Joyce] if you're at all naturalistically minded, but I don't think I meant her to overhear, at least, not when I wrote it. In that scene in the hut [which happens chronologically, later] when Angie says she thinks Marlene is really her mother, I didn't mean her to know it; I meant it to be wishful thinking. But of course, if she'd heard it she would have known it; I think when you see the play you can't help wondering whether she heard.[14]

5. Katherine Tozer

I entered through the audience at the Battersea Arts Centre production. I hovered at the edge of the stage and was ushered up by Marlene to a circular table on a very slow revolve. I'm playing Griselda at the moment in *The Canterbury Tales* and it perhaps clarifies my answer to your question about Griselda's late entry. It is completely appropriate that she arrives late and last. As an historical character I think she has always inspired unease in her fellow females. She represents a woman who has such faith in her husband as Lord and literally as Old Testament God that will brook no argument. She is polite and kind but a woman of steely convictions that really sets the cat amongst the pigeons. We need to know what sort of women Griselda is up against. Their inability to agree with her behaviour in a 1980s' context chaired by Marlene sparks the downward spiral into drunkenness and chaos that ends Act 1. Griselda is not a Top Girl in Marlene's sense in as much as she stands for obedience to the male order that Marlene has triumphed over. Her story rewards her for her wifely obedience when she is reunited with her children. She does not bemoan her lot, goes only as far as: 'I do think . . . I do wonder . . . It would have been nicer if Walter hadn't had to' . . . She does not criticise the man.

6. Caryl Churchill

Top Girls doesn't say, as Julie Burchill thinks (16 February), that women shouldn't succeed at work because that's 'acting like a man'. It starts off feminist (hurray for women's success) and ends up socialist (boo to capitalist success). I'm appalled by the views she tries to attribute to me.

Fen (1983)

Actors Jennie Stoller (1) and Amelda Brown (2), two of the six original actors in Fen, describe both the two-week research period in the Fens, and the subsequent rehearsals; a third, Tricia Kelly, adds important details (3). The designer Annie Smart talks of influences and the origins of the set (4).

1. Jennie Stoller

We spent two weeks living in a cottage in Upwell in the heart of the Fens. There were eight of us, sometimes nine, and not enough beds. Amelda Brown had to sleep on the landing, Bernard Strother on the sitting-room floor. We were there to find out about the people of the Fens but we also found out a great deal about each other. Few of us had worked together before. Unlike other workshops we did not go our separate ways at the end of the day so there was an added intensity to the work. We cooked together, read together, combed the village for people, stories, ideas, images – and fought like mad to get into the bathroom.

We had a list of people we wanted to talk to – land workers, church leaders, teachers, children – though we were initially quite apprehensive about whether they would want to talk to us. It proved relatively easy. Upwell is a small village. The people are not used to actors wandering the streets asking a lot of questions. ('Hullo. We're with a theatre group . . .'; 'You never are. Well, well!') Many were intrigued, others simply glad of the company and the chance to have a chat. It is a bleak, isolated place. One Saturday, four of us paid a lunchtime visit to the local pub. As I was buying a round, a man looked at me along the bar: 'You're a *Guardian* woman, aren't you?' I laughed. I had no idea what he was talking about. He followed me back to our table, took one look at the others and announced: 'You're all *Guardian* women.' He seemed both surprised and delighted. When we finally realised what he meant, he confessed he was the only person in the whole of Upwell who didn't read the *Mail* or the *Telegraph*. He was a *Guardian* reader and proud of it. His pleasure at finding four like minds in his local was only qualified by a lingering anxiety about who we were. 'Where you from? Outer Space?' He sat down, cupped his hands round his pint. 'Wherever I go in the village you're talking to people on the bridges or in the shops. There must be sixteen of you. What are you *doing*?' We told him and, whatever he had imagined, the news that we were researching a play didn't come as a disappointment. He began to tell us his life story: 'Lord Melchett and me are the only Marxists in the Fens . . .'

The life he described was wholly unexpected. The black sheep of a Tory family, he had fought and won two industrial tribunals, been ostracised by the village on several occasions, and now worked a small orchard. His story was cut short when the pub closed but later that night he turned up at the cottage clutching a battered suitcase full of newspaper cuttings about the tribunals. Out of this encounter came material which Caryl used for the character of Nell.

Everyone we met had a story to tell or suggestions about who we ought to visit. ('Oh, you want to talk to Tony, my sugar. Runs the goldfish stall at the fair.') And there was always a surprise round the corner. One old woman in a red cardigan waved at Caryl through the window so some of us went in. She talked about her husband's death, her loneliness and a ninety-year–old woman whose father had been a chemist. He used to make opium pills for the poor people to 'cheer them up a bit'. Another woman talked about her convalescence after a major operation. She was lying in bed waiting for her husband to prepare a meal. He eventually appeared with a tin of pineapple and a can opener and asked her to open it for him as he didn't know how.

In the second week, four of us spent a day fruit-picking for a local farmer. We started at eight o'clock in the fog and the wet and finished at five, warmed by the effort and some late sunshine. The farmer insisted on paying us. The standard piece rate was 40p a bushel and we earned £8. It was hard, back-breaking work but invaluable when it came to re-creating the work scenes in rehearsal. To perfect these, Les set up an improvisation during the third week of the workshop back in London. Equipped with buckets of water, we had to move up and down the floor dabbing each wooden block. As soon as we had finished, we were told to go back and start again. We quickly discovered which muscles you need to be a potato picker and what it is to hate your boss. I've never looked at a bag of crisps in quite the same way ever since.

Other improvisations and exercises were devised to analyse the raw material we had gathered in the Fens. In reporting back our findings while we were in Upwell we had acted out the people we met, narrated their stories, described their posture, their clothes. Les and Caryl wrote everything down in little black books. Now we began to explore the underlying social relationships. One exercise involved a farmer and a farmworker.

The worker wanted a wage increase but the farmer insisted on paying the worker in kind. The more gifts he received, the more guilty the worker became about asking for more money. This improvisation led to Frank's exchange with Mr Tewson in the play. Another exercise involved completing a set of physical tasks in a limited space of time. In turn, each of us had to iron a shirt, peel potatoes, sweep the floor, fold a sheet, feed a baby, settle a miserable child and give a man his tea. All in ten minutes. The women we had met in the Fens seemed to do everything – work in the field, organise the home, bring up the children – and as we summarised our impressions at the end of the workshop it was their experience that had left its mark on us all. Caryl's first idea for the title of the play was *Strong Girls Always Hoeing*, not a popular choice among the group but it fixed the monotony and the drudgery we had witnessed.

Several weeks into the tour of the production, one of the people we had met in the nearby town of Chatteris came to see the show. Sadly, we never played in the Upwell area – there was nowhere to perform – but Mrs Parrish made the journey to the nearest venue to see what we had come up with. Her husband came with her, and when we asked him afterwards what he thought, he turned to Cec Hobbs and said: 'You had your hoe the wrong way round'. The mistake was soon corrected, and the process that began so many weeks before in a cramped cottage came full circle. If there is one supreme virtue in the Joint Stock method I would say it is the opportunity to get at the detail – and the chance to get it right.[15]

2. Amelda Brown

I slept on the landing of this cottage because I run and knew I would want to be up early to go off before the day's work, which involved going up to people and asking them if they would like to talk about their lives. I took the opportunity of appearing totally 'crazy' and approaching people while I was out for my run. They would say they had nothing to say, so and so was more interesting, but you'd end up meeting them later, and they'd talk for hours without drawing breath. People told you things you had the feeling they'd never told anyone before, poetry kept in a secret place, artwork.

Cooking in the cottage was shared, and after dinner we got round in a circle and portrayed the person/s we had met. We also read chapters from *Fenwomen*. My memory of Caryl at that time was she was fun, kind, always willing to listen. I had read *Top Girls*, been up for it, not got it, gone to see it and loved it. I was feeling intimidated by her fierce intellect and here she was just lovely.

We spent two weeks in Upwell and returned to London for a final week's workshop in a very large church hall. Here we played games, some theatre, some children's, sang songs, did improvisations. One I particularly remember was to experience the drudgery of field work. There was a very long hall with parquet flooring. Caryl, Les and Annie [Smart, designer] sat at one end while the rest of us started at the other. We were to go along a line marking each block of parquet with our finger, when we got to the end we'd turn round and start again. I'm sure instructions were shouted out and the rebellious nature of being bent over doing this soon set up the antagonism towards the 'bosses'. I do remember the gleeful giggles of those sitting up the other end as they watched and commented on progress. This fed into the potato-picking scenes.

Ten weeks later we returned to a script and rehearsals. We were five women and one man; I think originally they had wanted four/two. We took turns to read different parts but Bernard read all the men's. At the end we all started laughing because he'd been in every scene. Caryl missed this when writing, as had Les and Annie when they discussed it with her. Only on hearing was it obvious. It made me realise even when you're trying to redress balances (of any kind) you have to acknowledge and challenge your own 'historical settings'. Caryl made small changes and some characters became women. There were times when I felt Caryl allowed cuts without it being tried, but of course I should have trusted her more. Long into the rehearsals she asked me something about Angela's last speech. I explained what I was doing and she said: 'Oh, I see, ok'. This made me ask what she had meant by the line, she explained and of course it was quite different to my interpretation. There followed: 'Oh, I'm sorry, I'll do it your way'; 'No, no, it's alright, do it yours', between us. That's what's amazing about her. She had listened to me do the speech for I don't know how long, but instead of becoming more entrenched she let it go as soon as we discussed it. But this was not relinquishing, rather a trust and respect for the actor and their instinct. I thank her for that.

3. Tricia Kelly

You didn't write anything down. You reported in role. It was very intensive, that first period. In the evening, we'd all be reading and writing. Caryl and Les were totally involved in all this. Caryl worked very closely with Les. I think she loves the serendipity the process throws up. That is the strength of it. Because this was about people gathering as well as information gathering, you'd come back and you'd have talked to somebody, and maybe for Caryl there is the phrase or idea. It doesn't necessarily work for every writer, but it would take her imagination and she'd run with it. For instance, the central story of Val and Frank was just a total footnote on the whole workshop. We'd gone out to meet somebody who lived in the middle of the Fens, and she talked about never seeing anyone as far as the eye could see. She had a baby, and she was lonely. She showed us scrapbooks. In one was a bit of newspaper, which was a report about somebody who'd been murdered by the man she left her husband for. And we didn't even really make a big thing of it. It was just something we noticed, but that was in fact the thing that Caryl used.

4. Annie Smart

Fen was the first time Joint Stock took a designer on its research workshop – in fact I was there only half the time because of other work commitments. I'd been working for three years prior to this as a full team member of a Theatre-in-Education and Community group called Perspectives, where design was integral to the playmaking process and so I insisted on participating. This made the designing of the show very easy and 'right'.

Caryl was very interested in being more design/image conscious. And she, Les and I were influenced by a lot of image-based rather than literary-based theatre around at the time. Groups like Hesitate and Demonstrate, Welfare State, IOU etc. affected us . . . In the main part of the village in a stone cottage on a main street we all noticed that behind a pair of lace curtains someone was using their front parlour as a hay store. This integration of the work life with the domestic was, I think, core to the whole thing, script and design. The field inside a room idea was the obvious way to go. And, in fact I had to design the set before the script was finished. I had about sixty per cent of the scenes. Caryl's final draft arrived as the finishing touches were put on the model, but there was no problem because I knew the material intimately.

A Mouthful of Birds (1986)

Some thoughts by David Lan, the piece's co-writer, begin this section (1); Annie Smart, the designer, tells how the design came about (2); the play's co-director and choreographer, Ian Spink, describes his work (3); as does the dancer, Philippe Giraudeau (4); finally, an acting member of the company, Tricia Kelly (5), describes the play's evolution and reception.

1. David Lan

I remember when she did the workshops for what became *Cloud Nine*, I used to see a great deal of her and I heard a lot about the work and how the workshops were evolving and the contribution of different actors. Anyway, so we had been talking about doing something together. I think it was really that it would be a group of four of us: Caryl and me as the writers,

Spink as the choreographer and Les as the director, that made it possible. And I think I suggested *The Bacchae*.

So trying to answer your question, you were saying how did the collaboration happen? It came out of two things: one, it came out of a long friendship and most of our friendship was about the theatre and about art, about life, about politics; and it came out of a long desire to find a way that we could produce something together . . . I suppose one of the things that Spink was trying to do was to find a place for words in dance and maybe Caryl was looking at it the other way round. We did it continuously. We didn't stop to write. We wrote as we were rehearsing. And there was an interview with the woman who had gone through a major schizophrenic experience and she said: 'It feels like my mouth is full of birds.' When we interviewed people during the research process we talked to a lot of people who had relatives who had been through experiences of possession and a number of people . . . I don't know how many, maybe three, maybe more, people talked about 'my auntie . . . this has never happened to me but my auntie, she's a bit crazy', and another title that we almost used was 'My Crazy Auntie'. But we came down to a shortlist of two: 'Mouthful of Birds' and 'My Crazy Auntie'. I would guess that in true Joint Stock style, we got it right. I think we did, yes . . .

It was very interesting really because I don't think any of us had the faintest idea what we were doing really when we were doing it. And I've thought about it quite a lot because the play took a while to take off, but subsequently, and very quickly, picked up speed particularly at universities. It had professional productions in Europe, and it was picked up by the American university circuit and done all over the place.

But there was something in the struggle to find a way for four of us to work together and then there was the lighting designer and there was the stage designer and, of course, there was this very active company who really took that invitation to be deeply involved with the construction and creation of the work – but somehow this thing emerged which is fragmentary.

I think they [the audience] thought what they were getting was 'Top Girls 2' and they got this very disjointed, broken-up piece, which was unhappy when it opened in Birmingham. None of us knew what we were trying to achieve, but it really came together on tour. But it didn't really begin to be a show until a couple of weeks into the tour. And by the time it hit the Court it had found itself. And though it wasn't one of the major Royal Court hits, it found an audience, but an audience which to a large extent went 'What the hell is that? I may like it, I may not like it, but it's a very unusual, wacky, crazy' sort of 'Good God, what a mind-fuck', as we used to say.

2. Annie Smart
At the base village in the Fens, an image that struck us all was an old, derelict house that had only lost its front wall and revealed all the rooms to the elements, all the doors, wallpaper, etc. That actually became the design for *A Mouthful of Birds* . . . but *Fen* and *Mouthful* were designed for touring, so had to be adaptable. *Mouthful* had three configurations to fit different sized venues . . .

3. Ian Spink
I dealt mostly with movement in the piece, but with two writers and a devising, improvisation period the process was quite complex at times. The period from first preview to final performance saw many changes in the production . . . Les, Caryl, David Lan and I had many meetings. The main part of the devising process involved improvisation, research, interviews and quite a lot of physical work to get into the 'spirit' of the subject matter . . . some pieces of movement material were created, or started to form themselves from day one. They were scenes that needed to be part of the 'script' or scenes that were purely physical. But there was also a period of writing when David and Caryl went away and wrote scenes derived from material that the actors had produced over the weeks.

4. Philippe Giraudeau

We were all part of the process from the beginning which was very important for the development of the project. A session if I remember started with some discussion on a topic or idea chosen by Les, Ian Spink, Caryl or David Lan. An improvisation would be set, more discussions would follow, finally we would improvise, discuss the improvisation, do more of it, exercises, but nothing was set for weeks. Sometimes Caryl or David would have written a scene which we would explore. That scene might end up in the show, sometimes not. We were set tasks. We would go out and interview people; I met a wonderful lady in her sixties, who used to be a married man. We spent a weekend camping out in the woods. No tents, hardly any food. We would come back and report, act out those encounters, outings. A normal research process.

I always felt during these years that everything we were doing was new, but really actors and dancers had been mixing in shows for years. Still it felt new, frightening and exciting. It brought me a lot and I enjoyed the different approaches to the work, although sometimes the way actors enjoyed these endless discussions before an improvisation would drive me mad. As a dancer I was not used to discussing things a lot. We would DO: explore, re-explore, feel, find . . . and, yes, talk a bit at the end. It was a very different process for me, a real development as a performer. I felt richer.

I seem to remember that it was a disaster when we opened in Birmingham; there were lots of conflicts in the company, anger, exhaustion, frustrations. Les had broken his foot; we had to cancel the first preview because I had to spend the night in hospital after a small accident, nothing bad, and not the reason why it was so hard to open there. The audience would leave the auditorium by the dozen; Chris Burgess had to stop the show once, as it got so noisy from people leaving their seats. [On stage at the beginning of Act 2] we resumed the show with the audience who wanted to stay or didn't dare to move . . .

5. Tricia Kelly

We read *The Bacchae* and began to explore it and go out look-ing for information and experience. I remember my experience was a day in Epping Forest, where we explored the inner forest for a day and made dens and camps. We were exploring being frightened, being isolated, being away from it all. I went to Greenham to explore being there. Being part of a women's camp. I remember going to meet a woman who was a contact of Caryl's, who was possessed. And she talked to me about being possessed by spirits. How that had changed her life and what that meant for her. I didn't know quite what to do with it. It was very intense, very vivid.

Now this is a twelve-week workshop without a script. For the past three or four weeks we're all going out and doing this stuff and then reporting back in role. And we're doing dance work every morning with Ian, building up a dance repertoire. An hour and a half dance workout. And also building up a repertoire of materials. He's getting us to improvise with phys-ical things, but for those of us who haven't done that it's quite hard because we don't quite know the language. And then gradually pages of text start arriving which we then read. But I think what did start to happen was that people to a varying degree started thinking: 'I don't know what's happening. I don't know what this is about. What are we doing?' I think that varied in intensity depending on where you were coming from. Now I had already done *Fen*. I trusted Caryl and Les a lot. So my thing was, I don't know but I'm quite willing to just believe. I don't know where it's going but I enjoy this sort of exploration. I come from a research background anyway. I didn't feel the need to know exactly where it was going. But it did start to fracture.

The set was a character in itself because the set was a section of the house. It had straw and bits of broken roof and dust and dead birds in one corner and there were about six rooms and I think we each had our own room. And Dionysus in his skirt went from room to room, and sometimes slid down to the next floor. So it was like a house of the different degrees of madness or ecstasy. You know, not everyone understood this, of course, but it was an attempt to explore women's attempt to be free.

The first night at Birmingham was a real baptism of fire. It was very, very traumatic, even though I think we knew as it went on that it wasn't going to be everyone's cup of tea. So, anyway, we opened and all hell broke loose. People really did bang their seats and shout, you know. It was very raw. And the box office and the front of house were having to cope with a lot of very irate people for the first few days. And then it calmed down because people stopped coming. There was always a big dichotomy between people who thought it was a load of self-indulgent wank and people who thought it was fantastic. And I wasn't going to argue with either of them really because it was what people made of it. And I think it was work done in very good faith, but was trying to do lots of experiments all at the same time.

You live in a paranoia . . . because it's very unsettling and you work with people you don't know. You're standing in very close, intimate relationships with them and you're not sure of your own contribution in those situations. And you're very much left to your own . . . I think anyone who's ever worked on a Joint Stock show gets a moment of darkness of the soul where you think: 'Oh, no, what am I doing? I don't know why I'm . . . and is it my fault, or does everyone else know what they're doing and I don't?'

Serious Money (1987)

Max Stafford-Clark, the play's director, wrote about the process in his Diary (1); as did Churchill herself (2); Lesley Manville (Scilla) talks of her reactions to an early version of the play (3); and Peter Hartwell, who designed the production, describes the evolution of the play's setting (4).

1. Max Stafford-Clark

23 Sept.   A good day in the workshop yesterday, but it's not gonna crack easily. How can we think that in two weeks we can become whiz financial analysts, and expose the antics of experts who've spent their lives with it? . . . Visited Futures Market and Stock Exchange. Saw a lot of hanging about. Came back and set up impros of people's behaviour. Terrified by the subject, but we laughed a lot.

Part of the exhilaration was caused by discovering just how much money people in the city were earning. We did an exercise where each member of the workshop had to spend £200,000 in a year. We divided neatly into selfish Hedonists (me, Julian Wadham, Meera Syal), who would go for Porsches, manor houses, swimming pools and flying lessons, and a Politically Correct group (Linda Bassett, Lesley Manville) who declared they would 'give gifts to the ANC. Buy a street in London and rent houses to friends. Help niece who wants to go to RADA.'

People in the city were dismissive about our ability to unravel the complexities of the financial world in two weeks. And of course Caryl read more widely once the workshop had finished. But we had all found the buccaneering spirit of the financial world intoxicating, and a certain admiration mingled with Caryl's inherent disapproval of so much money swilling about.

And in some ways we were progressing quicker than we realised. The actors follow through the intricacies of a particular story. Allan Corduner had been following a story about the price of chocolate in the Ivory Coast. A large portion of the world's chocolate is grown in Africa but is processed in Belgium or France. The French Transport Ministry had determined to phase out transport subsidies to francophone ex-colonies. Allan asked a stockbroker we were interviewing if this didn't mean that inevitably the price of chocolate would rise. The broker looked shocked. It was the early days of mobile phones, and he extracted a telephone the size of a house brick from his immaculate briefcase to phone his office with Allan's tip about chocolate futures.

7 Feb.   *Serious Money* – start rehearsal on Monday. First draft seems a bit breathless. Caryl's bravery and boldness to the fore: she's written it in rhyming couplets. I mean, in verse of all kinds, which sometimes doesn't give it much room to stop and be serious. It's caricature and it's funny. Doesn't show the real feelings of characters like Durkfeld and Morrison, but that's not the point. Jacinta's feelings about her own country could possibly have more weight. The merit of the lunchtime run that we did at the end of the workshop was the sniff of authenticity [that] the Metal Market or the LIFFE improvisations gave us. We should not blow all that away. So the final image I have currently of the play would be nuggets of serious money linked by frenetic and rhymed activity.

9 Feb.   *Serious Money* seems alive . . . I think I've ironed too much verse out of it. The actors do get to play an awful lot of characters; and it will test their powers of characterisation.

11 Feb.   Agonising hours where actors say how good the play is but just that their own particular parts are underdeveloped. The play is an epic account of the financial worlds, and it doesn't go into the psychology of the characters in any detailed manner. Normally, of course, these conversations take place between actors and their agents.

17 Feb.   Kind of get stuck on the 'Take-over Song', which still sounds a bit operetta-ish and should be much more funky. Second half still a bit too much unknown territory.

21 Feb.	Did LIFFE scene with Activists. They're a bit raw but on the whole it went well. I'm not sure how long a trading scene should be. At the moment the audience doesn't know what the fuck is happening. Important not to let it all become high comedy.
4 March	Near crisis with the music today. Actors losing confidence in Colin's music and starting to panic.
5 March	Should try and run first half by the end of the week.
7 March	First run-through of first act. Very far from definitive; in fact a mess. Some of the acting was poor. The music and the songs by Colin Sell still meet with universal disapproval from the company, and will probably have to be dropped. In addition, the structure of the first half is most peculiar. After a reflective weekend Caryl came in with a completely restructured first act. She moved the extract from *The Stockjobbers* to the start, where it became a kind of prologue. Most of the music was cut – it seemed to hold up the action – and we were left with Ian Dury's magnificent and obscene anthemic numbers to end each half.
21 March	Obviously a highly successful First Preview. In fact the first First Preview I can ever remember which was full and which was a real occasion. The first half was superbly played – real ensemble playing – and what a wonderful writer she is.

2. Caryl Churchill

The suggestion came from Max to do a play about the City. He'd been thinking about it for years. The timing was very lucky.

The workshop was two weeks long. We went down to the City and met people. It was a number of actors, me and Max, Philip Palmer who was the Literary Manager of the Court, Mark Long from the People Show, and Colin Sell who is the musical director of the play. We would go to the viewing galleries and watch how the different markets worked and get talking to people and, when we could, get taken down to the floor, and follow up any other contacts we had. After that two weeks I did more research all through the autumn and didn't start writing it until after Christmas . . .

I went back to some of the people we'd seen before and spent some time sitting in dealing rooms hearing what people say. And reading books and the *Financial Times*. There were days when it seemed I did nothing except sit surrounded by newspapers, cutting bits out and sticking them in scrapbooks.

For the first song he [Ian Dury] came to see the LIFFE scene and I gave him a list of phrases that are used by dealers. For the second one I said that we wanted it to be a celebration of the Conservative Party victory – and again included a few possible phrases, like 'five more glorious years' which was already in the play.[16]

3. Lesley Manville

We were all going out and meeting people from the City, and we'd come back to the workshop, and show what we'd got. Then there was a break and Caryl went away to write. She came back and the play wasn't complete in any way, and I think we were on a group outing somewhere in the City, and I said to Max that I thought my part of Scilla was very uneven – this is at the point when the play wasn't at all what it became – and that I was a bit disappointed. I thought the part wasn't representative enough of what I had put into it, and, as it stood, I didn't think I could do it. And Max said: 'Well, let's go back to the Court and talk to Caryl about it. And you tell her what you think.' And I remember getting on the tube, and thinking: 'I'm a working-class girl from Brighton, no 'O' levels, no formal education, and he's telling me to go and tell Caryl what I think!' And I did, and it became a fantastic part. It helped me achieve so much, not just in terms of career, but in terms of finding my voice. I was empowered. A lot of the time as an actor you spend your career being made to feel you're a bit shallow, but Caryl took it all on board.

4. Peter Hartwell

In late December of 1986, when the director asked Hartwell if he would like to design *Serious Money*, the designer replied: 'Great. Send me the script.' 'Caryl's not going to start writing it until 5 January,' Stafford-Clark responded. 'Oh', said Hartwell. 'When do rehearsals start?' '9 February.' 'Max, that's not enough time!'

Stafford-Clark reminded the designer that he had seen a 20-minute workshop presentation six months earlier. Max said: 'What we're doing is what you saw in the workshop,' recalls Hartwell. 'He said that one of the themes of the play would be about the new order moving in, and the old-boy network moving out – one thing growing, the other crumbling.'

'It was the crumbling that stuck in my mind,' Hartwell said. The designer ventured into the City – London's financial district – to check out the major trading sites. He soon found himself at the London International Financial Futures Exchange, right next door to the Bank of England. 'It's really the old Corn Exchange', Hartwell notes. 'It's a middle Victorian building where this ultra-modern Futures Exchange has been literally dumped. They haven't disturbed any of the original building. There are old murals of worthies in alcoves, between old columns all the way around the interior. But they literally formica-ed and portacabin-ed and ran in computer lines.'

'So', Hartwell continued, 'you have this bizarre plastic and carpet tiles and this hideous kind of modern impermanent architecture inside this incredibly orate, expensive, slightly crumbling old Victorian building. It is, in visual terms, a perfect juxtaposition of what Max said was going to be one of the major themes of the play.'

The designer also took bits and pieces from other City structures, notably the high-tech looks of the new Lloyds of London and the Metals Exchange. 'I tried to make a jumble of images', he says. 'Almost like throwing things together and letting the pieces fall where they may.' The first act of the script arrived on the first day of rehearsal. Hartwell delivered the rough model and sketches at the end of the second week of rehearsals and then plunged into his drafting. 'It's the only time it's ever happened to me', Hartwell laughs, 'but the carpenters were actually coming around to my house and taking away the drawings as I finished them. It was rather nerve-wracking.'

Hartwell and the shop managed to get the setting completed for dress rehearsals by which time Stafford-Clark had made some changes – including adding eight supernumeraries to the eight-member cast. The realisation that there were not enough exits, says Hartwell, was painful. 'We were watching this dress rehearsal and all of these people are lining up, trying to get offstage.' Max said: 'You've got to cut more doors in the set.' 'I, of course, threw a wobbly. I freaked.' 'Look,' said Stafford-Clark, calmly, 'you can just cut holes in it.' 'Anyway, that's what we ended up doing', Hartwell shrugs. 'As it happened we were lucky because the set had been built in such a short space of time, it wasn't proper flattage – the carpenters had walloped up three-quarter-inch plywood back walls. So you could just take the jigsaw out and cut a hole. Then somebody just had to touch it up with paint, and it was all right.' Such a short process is not to Hartwell's liking. But, he admits: 'It does stop the dithering.'[17]

Icecream/Hot Fudge (1989)

Max Stafford-Clark directed both pieces, and his Diary illustrated some of his concerns (1); Philip Jackson (2) and Saskia Reeves (3) were part of the cast:

1. Max Stafford-Clark

6 March   *Hot Fudge* sounds great but needs more work. Cast very good. Too many people at the read-through. We should start charging. Began to read

Icecream again in the afternoon. Hard to locate exactly what links both plays. They're terrific, but because they're small it would be easy for them to be dismissed as slight.

9 March   Ran a scene which slipped by in a flash. Problem is that if the play is about weighty matters, the structure of so many short scenes means it may seem slight. Should there be one or two longer scenes to arrest the momentum?

13 March   Sleepless night about *Hot Fudge*. Is it OK, or is it brill? If we just keep going would its best be 7/10 as good as *Icecream*? Is *Icecream* pellucid, brilliant and economical, or just plain underwritten? Could we do *Hot Fudge* as foreplay in advance of the main event or as a kind of platform show? If we do them as a double bill, will it simply take the focus away from the main event? Caryl is now so clearly at the top of her profession that she can write the rulebook. If she wants to do a fifty-minute play, that's fine.

15 March   Decided not to do *Hot Fudge* . . . as it would distract and defocus the statement from *Icecream*. [*Hot Fudge* was given a 'performance reading' Upstairs in May 1989.]

18 March   Once again feel we're scratching the surface and not grappling with *Icecream* in any depth. Hard to enter the world of the kids particularly.

29 March   I could not do the 'Party' scene until Caryl made us make it a much tighter, denser group, and then the sense of confidences being made were much more easily achieved. It's beginning to yield, but with such a small play we seem surprisingly far behind. What have we been doing all these weeks? I have little idea of how it will all go together. When we began, the main problem seemed to be whether we could tune into those short scenes

with sufficient grip to make them make their point before they had gone. The problem remains.

2. Philip Jackson

At one point Carole Hayman and I set out into London in character as the Americans, and spent some time on an open-topped tourist bus. While it was sometimes hard for us to keep a straight face, this actually taught us a great deal about the experience of being American in England and how strange some of our national characteristics would appear to outsiders, and vice versa. We decided that Lance and Vera's home town was Peoria, Illinois, a mid-west town apparently synonymous with, well, nothing of any significance. This decision involved me calling the Peoria tourist office on the phone and taping the conversations, so as to give us a template as to the accent and a certain mid-west *weltanschauung*. This all helped to deliver what I believe was an accurate portrayal of these characters' backgrounds. It also released a great deal of humour, before the horrors of the play descended.

Many people criticised the play as being too lightweight and without a noticeable moral structure. Caryl deliberately wrote this play in a film noir style, the quick, short scenes building up to a feeling of impending doom and confusion, producing a uniquely cinematic theatrical experience. Apart from David Thewlis teaching me to juggle, I can't remember too much else.

3. Saskia Reeves

The information is all there but not spelled out and her over-lapping makes the words a joy to learn and perform. We used to get a huge response from the audience when my character came back to the Americans and admitted 'murder'. Caryl's timing of the dialogue is clever and instinctive, and the over-lapping means she chooses where a word is placed and she chooses when the audience is to hear it. This scene, for instance, worked in performance in a way that I didn't see coming in rehearsals. The play was funny and dark and we had a wonderful time bringing it to life.

Mad Forest (1990)

Churchill's 'Play from Romania' was written about by the author[18] (1); its director, Mark Wing-Davey, describes the process (2); and the then student, and now professional actor, Sarah Ball looks at the play from her point of view (3).

1. Caryl Churchill

I wrote the play *Mad Forest* after visiting Bucharest in the spring with students from the Central School and director Mark Wing-Davey. Now the Quick Change Theatre Company have been invited to take it to the National Theatre in Bucharest.

Sunday	The company are here already and have assembled a new set – old metal, real shrine. Real soldiers' uniforms borrowed from the army. The space is three sides like the Embassy Studio (where we've been playing), 400 seats like the Royal Court (where we go next).
	A friend tells about a woman she saw beaten by the miners in June. 'They asked her for her identity card and then they hit her in the face. I think what happened was so unbelievable that already we are forgetting, but I saw it. It made everything stop, it made fear come again. In a way we are more comfortable now to be again like we were before . . .'
Monday	We're nervous. What will Romanians feel about the play? Full houses, aisles full of people. Laughter of recognition; silence very thick; some people cry. A little group of middle-aged men leaves without clapping. Someone says there were many nomenclatura in the central section of the

audience because it was the first night. Most people seem moved and shocked. 'This is better than
any western aid we have had.' 'This is like a second revolution for us.'

Nothing in the theatre ever means as much to an
audience in England. Does this mean nothing
means as much to us? Or don't we write about the
things that do? Do we know what they are? Or is
it because so much is written that there's no thrill
in it? Or because theatre in Romania has mattered
for years because even censored it was one of the
few forms of opposition?

Tuesday   Sunny day, lots of people, newspapers and pan-
cakes selling in the street. The revolution seems
long ago physically; in April it still felt immediate.
No soldiers about, some police. The candles are
out in the shrines.

Long late-night talk about free market in which I
mention the homeless in New York and London.
'But only because they want. Yes, I read about a
doctor who slept outside for two months in
California.'

Wednesday . . . Discussion with audience. Some feel shame
that anyone should think a Romanian would
scrape up a broken egg from the floor and save it
on a plate. A woman says she did it herself twice.
Someone says the play should have been more
positive and the rest of the audience groans.

Thursday   We do the play for Romanian TV. Two young
technicians giggling gleefully. 'Nothing has
changed.' I say surely some things, the streets feel
different, we're able to do the play, more newspapers. 'Not enough – too much blood for too little
change.'

Friday   . . . No soldiers and tanks now. The play will be
shown on 15 October. Some people don't think

it's possible. It's the first time for 30 years a character in a play has been allowed to say things critical of the president in a theatre – will it be
allowed on TV?

Saturday   . . . Discussion after the last show. Someone says
they are ashamed that Romanians haven't written
a play about the situation yet. I remind them of a
line in the play which a painter said to us: 'I didn't
want to paint for a long time then', and they clap
and agree. Afterwards a young woman says: 'But
really it is because they want to see which way the
wind will blow.' A woman of 80: 'After 25 years
of suffering, your nerves are stiff and your heart is
a stone.' She thanks us for the play and our love .
. .

Sunday   We stay up all night and arrive at the airport
ready to sleep on the plane, but the flight doesn't
leave till the evening. Over the tannoy, a woman's
voice explains the delay. 'It is a great shame for us
and I expect you would like to beat us and kill us.
Do it. But please understand, we try to do our
job.' Everyone claps and we fly home.

2. Mark Wing-Davey

I was an actor with Joint Stock, and got to know Caryl in
1978. She was doing the workshop for what became *Cloud
Nine*, and we became friends. I then worked at Central, and
directed *Cloud Nine* and *Serious Money*. Those early conversations with Caryl undoubtedly informed my directorial values
to this day.

In 1988 I became Artistic Director of Central's acting course,
and introduced to the curriculum some of the Joint Stock workshop exercises I had picked up from Caryl and from Bill Gaskill.
In particular from Bill, there was 'character study'. Students
would be given a different category each week. They would

then go out, interview someone they found, notate it, return to the group a day or so later, and be interviewed as that person, using facts they had gathered, their own observation and their imagination to improvise as the individual they had met.

The Ceausescus were executed on 25 December 1989. I was planning the upcoming season at Central, and realised that many who had risked their lives in the overthrow of the Romanian regime had been the same age as my students. I rang Caryl and asked her if she would go to Romania with my group. She said no, but a couple of hours later she rang back to say yes, as long as the money to do it was not from private sponsors. In fact, it came from the British Council and Camden Council.

So, in March, Caryl and I went to Romania for a long weekend. We prepared a set of questions about the revolution, and began to learn Romanian. We met teachers, students, drama professors, actors. There was a surprisingly pervasive atmosphere of suspicion and distrust in many of the people we met. Two weeks or so later, we returned to Romania with the group.

What we did for eight days was based on classic Joint Stock practice. Each student had to provide a thirty-second to two-minute vignette of an observed incident on the street. We asked for stories about the revolution and before it, and for them to be dramatised by the Romanians. Caryl and I also developed a catalogue of people to find and talk to. This was the primary source of much that went into the play, especially Act 2. The students went out, ours with interpreters, and interviewed a variety of people. Caryl took notes at the end of each workshop, which lasted all day, and every day.

Caryl then had to go to New York for the opening of *Ice Cream with Hot Fudge*. From Romania to New York. The contrast was powerful, and it was there that she heard the story of Lucia who, in the play, marries an American, misses the revolution and returns to Romania to describe the 'walls of fruit' and the 'huge dustbins' of waste.

Antony [McDonald]'s design incorporated many of the specific features he had experienced in Romania. The floor was a worn, blackish, canvas floor cloth. Two L-shaped walls were built out of breezeblocks, one with a shelf in it (replaced by a simple blue peasant window and frame for the second half), and a door. The other L-shape was plain, with a candlelit shrine for the second half. The breezeblock walls deliberately looked hurriedly built. Downstage, a rectangle of breezeblocks, two high, a table and chairs. On the back wall, but only glimpsed, was a Byzantine image, blue and gold of St George and the dragon, patron saint of the fascist Iron Guard. The lighting consisted of bare bulbs to replicate power cuts in Bucharest.

The play was a big hit for two weeks at Central, so Caryl and I, actors and stage management formed ourselves into a collective called Quick Change so named after the very quick change between Acts 1 and 2, where all eleven actors do a complete costume change and get into place.

We rented the place from Central and played a further six weeks. We shared front of house duties. Caryl occasionally sold tickets at the box office, and politely refused free tickets, including to a spluttering 'but I am a friend of Caryl Churchill', to whom she gently replied: 'I am Caryl Churchill'. Then Andrei Serban , as the new director of the Romanian National Theatre, invited the company to play in Romania . . .

3. Sarah Ball
We all stayed with a variety of people in their homes . . . perhaps because it was the best way to experience Romanian lifestyle at a fundamental level. Most of us stayed with students, but I stayed with a female teacher in her fifties. In retrospect, this was deliberate because the main character I ended up playing was Flavia – a female teacher in her fifties . . .

We went to Bucharest and performed at the National Theatre. By then the temperature in Romania had changed, and there was a realisation that the 'revolution' was in fact a 'coup' and that people had died for nothing. The streets were filled with shrines and there was a heavy resignation to the fact that nothing had changed. It was uncomfortable initially performing the play there because the Securitate were still very much an invisible force . . . but when the play finished it was received with rapturous applause, people mounting the stage to deliver hugs and kisses. People seemed genuinely happy that we had captured an important event in their lives, and broadcast their struggle for others to understand what had happened during their 'revolution'.

Lives of the Great Poisoners (1991)

The composer Orlando Gough describes his work for the piece (1), as does the director/choreographer Ian Spink (2) and the designer Antony McDonald (3).

1. Orlando Gough

We had probably about ten meetings with Caryl and Spink. They were mostly about how to make a piece with dancers, musicians and actors together. I decided to make the music *a cappella,* as I thought that the interface between music and speech would work best without any instruments.

We researched different poisoning stories, from the obvious – Crippen – to the most recondite – Madame de Brinvilliers – helped by the fact that Caryl and I were members of the London Library and had access to some very off-piste books. We got very excited by Midgley, the great innocent poisoner, and decided that his presence should be a thread connecting the other stories.

We cast the piece. Because Midgley was such an important character, we cast someone who could both act and sing (though not, as far as I know, dance). The decision not to ask the performers to do things they didn't normally do, e.g., not to ask a dancer to speak or an actor to sing, was entirely a reaction to our previous work in which everyone did everything. We wanted to try something new. We were intrigued by the idea of a 'conversation' between, e.g., a dancer and a singer. On the other hand I needed enough singers to make an interesting vocal texture. The challenge of writing what almost amounted to *a cappella* opera was enormous! Generally, dance and music are not brilliant narrative-carrying media, so we very much relied on Caryl to make the narrative happen. There was a danger in such a narrative-heavy piece that the dancers would be gooseberries. But there's no doubt that dance and music provide a means of expression that is not available in a spoken drama. The piece was very, very rich in texture, though musically it was quite spare because of the lack of orchestra. Interesting.

There's a comfortable well-tried relationship between dance and music (usually music-led), which many contemporary choreographers are trying to subvert, by making dance and music more independent (Merce Cunningham being the obvious example). Here the relationship was both set up by Caryl's narrative and subverted by the spoken word. The dancers did sometimes carry the narrative, while sometimes the dancers simply danced to the music. It's interesting that in the history of Western dance there have been very few pieces with sung music. I'm not entirely sure why – it may be that the lyrics carry too much explicit information, whereas dance is happiest in a more abstract environment . . .

2. Ian Spink

This piece took many months to develop. We had many meetings about a theme and it seemed that environment was the one that stuck. I think at the time there was a ship carrying toxic waste which was being denied entrance to an Italian port, stuck in a bay for months on end. The idea of a community, waiting for this ship of poison to move on fascinated us all. Caryl developed her 'community of poisoners' stretching out over the centuries and Orlando wrote the music based on the words of her 'script'. James Macdonald was brought in later as a director who had worked with Caryl's scripts before.

I cannot remember how we reached the final structure . . . perhaps it was because we found a couple of stories that were too good to lose. The mechanics of how the characters in these stories could transform or mutate into others came about based on how the performers could best express each character. Soprano, bass, lyrical dancer, actor etc. . . .

Working with Caryl was always a different kind of experience for me. She was very much into including movement, even abstract dance as part of her narrative, but there was always a sense that there was a 'play' with 'actors' and that they needed a theatre director to guide them. My usual way of working stems from me not having a traditional theatre background and I tend to break any rules that may seem to exist. This can cause problems and also throw up some interesting new possibilities.

3. Antony McDonald

Although I was present at many initial meetings with Ian, Orlando and Caryl, it was not really possible to begin the design process until the whole libretto was finished and the music was written. I felt it was really important that the piece should feel like one narrative – one strange love affair, not three or four separate stories – and that the design should create very much its own world quite outside the Edwardian England of Crippen, the mythological Greece of Medea or the seventeenth-century France of Madame de Brinvilliers.

A further design challenge, too, was the fact that each section was made up of short scenes in a wide variety of locations that flowed one into another. The production was touring to several venues, so it was also important that the set had its own aesthetic dynamic that would look good and be commanding in different spaces . . .

What emerged as the design was something quite abstract and sculptural that could change by means of hydraulics to create a series of spaces and planes. A permanent set made up of three units – three walls, one of which could also lower to become a floor at different angles. So we created interiors and exteriors, both open and private. Performers could appear above walls or around them and in the gaps or corridors between walls. They could be isolated in their own separate worlds and at the same time be overlooked by other performers. The set itself became, in turn, a drawing room, a courtroom, a ship or two ships, a bed, a gaming table. There was never furniture to remove, so a scene with dialogue or singing could evolve immediately into dance and back again.

Projections were also thrown on to the light-coloured walls and floor of the set, not so much to define location but to give atmosphere . . .

The costumes were not related specifically to any period, although they made reference to several, but were designed again to create a world of their own. Corsets were used for both men and women, worn both on top and underneath other garments. In a way in this production the corset served as the most obvious visual symbol of how we poison ourselves for personal vanity. Layers of clothing were removed as we moved through the different sections of the story. Thus the uptight pretensions of the lower middle-class Crippen world gave way to the exposed exhausted decadence of Saint Croix and Madame de Brinvilliers. As clothing was removed so make-up was added, as part of the self-poisoning process. Midgley stood apart from this scheme of things, dressed always in his forties' suit.[19]

The Skriker (1994)

Ian Spink was responsible for movement in the piece (1); Max Stafford-Clark reacted in his Diary on 4 December 1991 to a copy of the script (2); and the play's director, Les Waters, talks about rehearsing it (3).

1. Ian Spink

She certainly told me about it a number of times, as she worked on it and I was one of the few people who were shown the script when it was finished. It felt very appropriate for me to be involved in the first production . . .

It was very exciting to read when Caryl first showed it to me. When I later directed a student production I realised just how difficult it was to choreograph and direct at the same time. In the Royal National Theatre production Les Waters (director) and I rarely saw each other, because there was so much separate movement and acted scenes that had to be developed on their own in isolation . . . it was similar to working with an opera.

2. Max Stafford-Clark

What she depicts is chaos, which is so hard to present on stage, but the wordplay is so loony and the associations so clever it strikes me you would wish to focus and listen to it. Basically, it's wonderful. How can frogs or money come out of someone's mouth? Some of it is just not worked through like 'a monstrous creature invisible to the others'. How can we possibly know that? A horror story. It could be a film. She's been working on it for eight years. I really can't get into it . . . but I can see that there's a powerful theatrical vision there. *Caryl*: 'There are people to whom it [*The Skriker*] means an awful lot.' 'Who?' 'Almost everybody except you. A feeling you weren't behind the play . . . a choreographer you did not see the point of . . . A play that's disproportionally important to me . . . Other people excited and moved . . . Each time I've talked to you about it I've come away rather low and drained. Perhaps I do need you to say "Wonderful, wonderful".' I am a bit of a pudding at the moment. Caryl upset that I don't appreciate it.

3. Les Waters

I don't know how long Caryl worked on the piece but she certainly would refer over the years to her 'fairy play'.

I would work with Kathryn [Hunter], Sandy [McDade] and Jackie [Defferary], and Ian would work with the dancers and the movers and the ensemble of fairies, both of us on the same section. And then at the end of the day we would put it together, often without any real knowledge of what the other one had done.

The Skriker is one of the great roles written for women. And Kathryn Hunter played it with her characteristic brilliance. I think we would have been fucked if she'd not been available, or turned down the role. The contradiction between the character and the playing of the role is very interesting. The Skriker is a minor earth spirit in decline, but there is a great need for vast amounts of transformative energy in the playing of decline. Similarly, in the opening speech, the language is decaying but needs attack and precision to reveal that kind of decline. Caryl, Kathryn and I spent many hours in a room at the National working on that opening speech, with Caryl explaining many of the puns and word associations.

Thyestes (1994)

Kevin McMonagle played Atreus in the first production.

I was at the Royal Court only a couple of weeks ago and ran into Jeremy Herbert who designed the show; he was saying it was his favourite to work on. He created sets offstage. The banqueting room in which Thyestes gorges his meal was created behind one of the seating banks, and Atreus's lair, where his brooding menace festers, was underneath another seating bank. Images from these sites of awfulness were relayed to the audience via CCTV, so onstage stood only a couple of television screens and a macabre standard lamp.

My understanding of Latin was as an altar server and, often, I was the only respondent, so it was just possible for me to see the translation work. Caryl's challenge to keep to the original and remain within her set syllable counts was really extraordinary. Of course, I can't question her accuracy but did revel in the beauty of the results, and the rhythm of it, especially listening to others, was spine chilling. She was in all rehearsals, and the script was always being tweaked. These kinds of plays dealing with pure passions are almost impossible not to be passionate about.

The peak of pain, if such a thing exists, was when the truth of his supper is revealed to Thyestes, and accentuated onstage by Atreus pushing with his foot, causing it to slide across the stage, a plastic storage box containing the uneaten remains of the boys. Thyestes's questioning face, his limp arms, his future consumed, and soon presumably to be shat out.

'Not brave. Not clever. Not strong. / What I'm really ashamed of / not avenged.' Atreus's opening line I repeated and repeated and repeated as I never felt able to deliver it. Maybe now I can twelve years later – though maybe better not.

Hotel (1997)

Orlando Gough composed the music (1); Ian Spink was the director and choreographer (2).

1. Orlando Gough

Hotel was written for thirteen singers, two (silent) dancers and a tiny band of piano duet and double bass. The singing was very much the heart of the music; the band had a very modest supportive role. When discussing the piece originally I told Caryl that the only bits I liked in operas were the bits where all the soloists sang together; and that's what led her to the idea of the eight rooms. I loved the idea of being able to make a quartet from two very different pairs of lovers who had nothing in common except that they happened to be having sex at the same time in the same hotel. The texture and structure of the music came entirely from the notion of very separate people singing together, sometimes in agreement, sometimes at odds with one another.

The casting was very interesting – we didn't cast opera singers, but singers from many different backgrounds, many of whom had never acted before. Ian was very skilful in working with them in such a way that they didn't have to act, simply to *do*. For me this was a very important project, as some of these singers became the nucleus of my choir, The Shout. The lyrics are very fragmentary – they consist of parts of sentences of which the listener can usually guess the rest. This was a very clever decision of Caryl's, based on the experience of working on *Poisoners*. She had worked out that the structure of my music, based on the accumulation and transformation of short phrases, would be suited by fragmentary lyrics. The music refers to many popular styles without actually pastiching any of them.

2. Ian Spink

The first version of *Hotel* was initiated by Caryl, the idea of simultaneous inhabitants in a single hotel. She had conversations with Orlando about how this might work with singers (they had previously built up a working relationship with *Lives of the Great Poisoners*). The idea of a 'danced' counterpart to hotel then led to me making up the narrative. This time two people occupying the same space, a woman who kills and a man who kills himself. The music for this dance was provided by singers and musicians who could drift in and out, through the walls, like ghosts.

This Is a Chair (1997)

Actors Desmond Barrit (1) and Marion Bailey (2) talk about their experience of the production.

1. Desmond Barrit

Actors always want to know WHY. I remember asking Caryl why the set of plays was called *This Is a Chair*, and why the play I was in was called 'Hong Kong'? Her reply was that there was no reason for either of the titles. The two titles hadn't been used before, so why not? This reply was such a surprise. Thank God she was at the rehearsals, otherwise we would have spent days trying to justify everything. Her reply was also releasing. The image is that authors are always terribly clever (I'm not suggesting she isn't), but it is refreshing to think that she didn't agonise for hours thinking of something clever and tricksy.

Our next problem was trying to make sense of the dialogue. What were they talking about? What was the 'story'? Why did I say what I said, in response to the other character? Again, I was surprised by Caryl's response. There was no connection between the lines. The line was not a response to the previous line.

Caryl had taken lines from a twenty-four-hour period and strung them together. Character A said something at 7 a.m. Character B then said something at 7.15 a.m. Character A then said something at 8 a.m. Character B then said something at 8.45 a.m, and so on. The only connection was the chronological order in which the lines were said. Consequently, we didn't say our lines as a response to the previous one, but as if they were totally independent. There was some sort of sense but this was only determined by the time difference between lines . . . There were no rules with this production which made the whole experience freeing. Nothing was as it seemed for actor and audience alike. It was a hugely rewarding experience. Why? I don't know.

2. Marion Bailey

This Is a Chair was a relatively brief event, performed after a short rehearsal period. I guess it was only ever intended as a one-off. I imagine the expense and overall logistics of engaging a cast of that size and quality (given that everyone only spent a few minutes on stage) for a full rehearsal period, plus a run of a month or so at the Court, would have proved too much to put together.

It was however something of a 'major' event in that it was attended by many of the great and good from the British theatre scene. I guess partly because it could have been the last thing Stephen Daldry directed for the Royal Court, but also I think people were eager to hear what Caryl Churchill had to say next. There was a pretty impressive cast list, and everyone was delighted to be on board.

We performed the play on a small stage which was built in the stalls area of the auditorium, and the audience sat and watched from onstage. I think they mostly had a great time, but I recall some people being quite puzzled at the end of the evening, which I always enjoy, as a performer! However, my daughter, who was around ten at the time, found no problem with it. Perhaps because she had no preconceived notions about the sort of questions she thought she should be asking. Her dad, the playwright Terry Johnson, said that as a writer he understood just what Caryl was talking about.

I'm not altogether sure that I did, but I supposed he meant that somewhere along the line she was asking a question of the audience. What was the territory she should be exploring as a playwright of the nineties? And what is the nature of the theatre? Terrific stuff to perform though. I could feel the audience were completely absorbed by it, whether or not they had any clue about the whats and whys. Fantastically good theatre.

Blue Heart (1997)

Max Stafford-Clark wrote in his Diary about rehearsing the play (1); and two of the actors recount their experience of rehearsal and performance. They are Bernard Gallagher (2) and Eve Pearce (3).

1. Max Stafford-Clark
Caryl and I were finding out how to do the play. I mean the particular problem she set was that every moment you said a particular line in the various different versions of the script you had to, say, have your hand picking up the cup of tea, and so, if you only did the half-line, was your hand stretching for it, or did you actually pick it up on the second half-line? All the technical problems that she set, and the rules that governed that, were things we discovered in rehearsal. She didn't know any more than I did quite how to do it, and so it was how to do that was fun.

2. Bernard Gallagher

I should first say how much I enjoyed playing it. Audiences loved the first play and respected the second (I thought both were brilliant) and doing it was always a daunting but rewarding task. Rehearsing it was something else. When Max first rang me about it I said I wasn't sure about taking it on and that I couldn't understand it; his rejoinder was that neither could he but we'd find out eventually. He was right, and being a very astute individual let us struggle to discover its purposes along with him. My job in the second play was fairly easy and didn't worry me, but the first play was clearly a big problem. Actually, what clinched my resolve to do it was the man's speech about eating himself, which I think is an economical and staggeringly funny short nightmare in which utter logic is used to convey the impossible. I decided the risk of taking the job on was justified by that one speech, and never regretted it.

Max is a meticulous and painstaking worker who will never give up on something until he thinks he's got it right. Fortunately he has a lot of patience and humour, and he certainly needed it as we struggled to get – not so much the words as the actions – right. Each short scene is given repeatedly but with a different and more fantastical close as the play hurtles along. My problem was that each time it broke off we had to replace all the props in a particular order so as to start again, but this was never done in the same pattern because it tailed off in a different way each time. We got it right in the end of course but a lot of weight was lost as we fought our way through.

Having once got a grip on it, of course, its very particular and peculiar process was such that it remained well embedded, and we rarely went wrong. When we did we just pressed on. The play's rhythm is paramount, and you cannot let it be destroyed by any flabby behaviour. Nevertheless, it was the most challenging job I'd ever had until then. Each evening before we went up Mary Macleod, Val Lilley (and later June Watson) and myself used to stand behind the set in a tight embrace, slapping each other on the back. You knew that once you were on stage you simply had to propel the piece with finely controlled energy and that if you started to think about it you'd scupper yourselves.

3. Eve Pearce

At first Max's idea seemed to be that Mrs Vane was the *romantic* mother – *Brief Encounter* was mentioned. I thought this a very good idea and went along with it, and Caryl seemed happy. I had not worked with Max before, and found his method of working – called *actioning*, where the actor has to think of a verb which suggests what effect he is trying to have with every line – very difficult. I know that some actors find it helpful – I didn't – and as time went on rehearsals became increasingly fraught. However, Caryl attended almost every day, and was invariably helpful to me – at the same time managing to support Max as well. Meanwhile the idea of Mrs Vane as a romantic gradually became anathema to Max, and I was told not to think along those lines any more – difficult! Caryl's quiet, reassuring presence was an enormous help – my confidence had taken a big blow, and her first-night card – using the device in the play, i.e., the substitution of words by Blue and Kettle [and] letting me know that she knew I had had a Blue Kettle time but that she was happy with my performance – meant a great deal to me.

Our Late Night (1999)

Churchill directed Wallace Shawn's play as a late-night production without décor at the New Ambassadors Theatre. It was part of the final activity of the Royal Court in the West End before returning to the newly refurbished theatre in Sloane Square. The play had a brief run from 20 October to 6 November. Its evolution and reception are detailed by Jonathan Cullen (1) and Ingrid Lacey (2).

1. Jonathan Cullen

As far as staging goes, the 'production without décor' billing was a euphemism for 'we have to get this on late-night, on the set of *Some Explicit Polaroids*, so let's not raise expectations of a proper *show*, then surprise them by it actually being rather brilliantly lit (by Jo Town, who is an exceptional unshowy talent) and having a *sort* of set – some big cushions – and even costumes . . .' Caryl seemed, generally, unconfident of herself in the new role of director – I can't recall her explaining quite why she had decided to direct Wally's play herself, though she may have done. And as a director she was disconcertingly back-footed: mostly directors tend to exhort, encourage, challenge, cosset, sometimes bully and so on – but Caryl sat shyly as we worked our way through a fairly opaque text, seeming as puzzled by it and how to solve it in performance as we were. Though I came to feel that she was less puzzled than intrigued: as it happens I live with a writer, and I recognise the writer's responses to writing – Caryl would sit, rather quiet, ruminative, appreciative of our struggles but mostly unwilling to intervene in our wrestling with the text. It was refreshing for me anyway – she clearly thought that any choice about acting and particularly the technical management of our performance (by the actors) was nobody's business but ours – hers was to give an overview, to be a sounding board, a sharer in the joint collaborative effort towards elucidation.

Stephen Dillane, however, might have a different retrospect: I recall sitting as he ploughed bemusedly through his long speech three or four times, with Caryl looking on, anxious for his well-being as it seemed, asking whether he'd like to try it one more time. I remember, vaguely, reporting to friends at the time that 'she just sits, mostly and listens . . .', but I remember her as a good listener, and a generous, shy, intelligent, admirable person. One thing she did do, which we all enjoyed naturally, was to organise a cast outing in I think the first week of rehearsal to the Oxo Tower restaurant, or rather bar, for a drink. I think the idea was to establish a shared reference for us all for the party venue; though in fact it was much more useful simply as a way of getting to know each other.

The first night came too soon, and felt under-prepared; but when we found the audience were clearly enjoying the piece, we all cheered up a great deal, and began to believe in it.

I don't remember any of us (including, apparently, Caryl) having any coherent notion of what the play was *about*, or even that such an idea made any sense – but I think yielding to the fragmentary nature of the piece, for me, eased up my worries about it all – which is a long-winded way of saying that I left interpretation up to the audience and just decided to fight Jim's corner, so to speak, and Caryl seemed pleased with that.

Last thought – you ask about the reception of the play, which I'd describe generally as baffled but amused. 'Weird' was a frequently used adjective; likewise 'I didn't think it would be so funny!' was a common response. Those who enjoyed it a lot did so on a non-rational level – and I suppose that's usually true of Caryl's plays lately too . . . they're fiercely intelligent and unsentimental like her but what I remember of them are not specific arguments but a tone, a mood, a startling twist.

2. Ingrid Lacey

I got sent the script for *Our Late Night* and I didn't understand it. It wasn't a case of liking or disliking. I didn't get it. Which is odd as I've just had a quick re-read and now I don't understand why I didn't understand. That may be down to Caryl.

I said to my agent that I didn't think I'd go to the meeting, as I'd be wasting people's time. My agent told me to go. I went.

I liked Caryl. She was very calm. Lisa Makin, casting director, was also there. I can't remember who asked 'What do you think of the piece?' but I do remember the terrible temptation to bullshit. Instead I blurted out bluntly: 'I don't understand it.' Caryl was sublimely serene and said: 'Neither do we; we're going to find out.' And that is my most vivid memory of working with Caryl. Everyone says things like 'We're going to find out. It's a journey. We're going to jump into the unknown,' but hardly anyone actually does it. In truth most people have a mortal fear of any such thing and do whatever they can to avoid the exposure.

Then she gave me the job. And we did find out.

Directors often let you know just how anxious you are making them when you don't get it RIGHT. Caryl was notably lacking in fear. We also made swift progress. The piece came together quickly and vividly. It was like wiping steam from a mirror 'til you can see in it clearly. I remember working on *Our Late Night* with great affection. It was such a relief not to have to pretend to know something. It was such a kick to find something out. I think Caryl should do more.

Far Away (2000)

The designer Ian MacNeil gives an account of the play and its design from his perspective (1); and Katherine Tozer, who played the Older Joan, creates a powerful picture of performing the piece (2).

1. Ian MacNeil

My job is to try and find a way to give a physical expression, to provide a place in which things can happen within our understanding most effectively. It's that simple. What I feel particularly, and I said it immediately about *Far Away*, was 'My God, it's got atmosphere', and that makes my job simple because it's really hard when you're having to create an atmosphere that simply doesn't exist.

A little armchair and a table with a lamp on it, and that's it. Everything caught in space and light. Black on black. But I tried to make . . . all the furnishings and every decision about the few things that were on the table like a painting, like being controlled and telling and provocative and old-fashioned. Ambiguous in its purity, in the way that a house that's slightly isolated might have things in it that were late fifties. A sewing kit or whatever it was. So it had a kind of timeless thing about it. I mean the conversation started about my wanting it to be this allegory of fairytales. Stephen said: 'I think it is actually a table and a chair and a pair of dentures and . . .' And then I enjoyed that and I figured out how to make the transitions immaculate, in a dreamlike way despite the fact that we are in the same space. I mean you could be as close to that table as I am to that pile of DVDs but the flow of it would carry on being dreamlike, so the transition from that first scene, where the little girl finally says 'goodnight', is that she puts her hand on the lamp on the table. Katherine Tozer, some twenty seconds later, comes and turns it on, dressed in the same nightdress and watched the table and chair float off and then watched workbenches and fluorescent tubes above the workbenches come on, and that nightdress was a bit of rag. She took it off, threw her clothes underneath with the next scene . . .

Bless Stephen for worrying the hat-building sequence into believability so that rather than wonder 'What the hell's going on?' you actually get intrigued in the *Blue Peter* story of 'Here's my hat' during the course of the week, and the sort of narrative excitement of his hat looks rather good. 'Oh, my God, her hat's completely extraordinary and she's going to look great.'

But then the prisoners were paraded in groups of four because obviously if you were judging hats you want to look at a set of four, overlap, another set of four, overlap . . . and then peeled off. They were all chained together though, of course, large clanking chains. And huge hectoring women barked instructions. And crowds cheering and there was an awful noise like of a parade ground, like a rally. I think there was a young, slightly good-looking, slightly geeky man in a clean uniform with a peaked cap and a clipboard. Slightly at odds with the badgering and hectoring of the noise beyond. Just that series of ways in which prisoners are humiliated. The cacophony of the bureaucracy of the clipboard, the youth and the kind of banality of the guard. And the lack of intimidation needed because people were so browbeaten.

I think she is a master of not saying anything. It's pretty extraordinary because, for one thing, it is thought nowadays that new plays need to be workshopped inherently, which I know she takes exception to because her plays are fully delivered. You know, the implication that the writer needs help necessarily is not applied in her case. Literally on these three shows [*This Is a Chair; Far Away; A Number*] I think one could count on one hand the number of words that were changed. But the point is she'd worked it out. It's like a poem that has been read out loud many times. It is what it is.

And also what I find very beautiful about it is that, when pushed to say what it was about, Caryl said: 'it's about a young woman who's trying to do the right thing.'

2. Katherine Tozer
The title *Far Away* seems to me to be significant in as much as the nightmare scenario that Caryl describes is really not that far away at all. We would like to hope and think that it is, but the knock-on effect of blinding oneself to the atrocities that are going on in the garden shed is all too prevalent in society today.

Linda [Bassett as Harper] opened the show crooning very quietly to herself the nursery ditty: 'There is a happy land, far, far away.' It was a disconcerting voice; you were left unsure of where it was coming from.

The poster depicts a Savannah scene in what appears to be pulsating heat before a thunderstorm with a menacing shed, terrifying in its isolation and what could be potentially going on in there. It is not very far away from the viewer either.

Annabelle [Seymour-Julien as Young Joan] was in a longish nightie as the young Joan and she dangled a stuffed lion toy that was her own I believe. At the close of the first scene she stood at the back of the stage apparently unwilling to leave, holding the toy. When the lights went down I came from the wings, stood behind her, took the lion and she exited leaving me there in the same position she had been. The stage furniture was on runners, and, as the next scene of the factory established with two workbenches sliding in upstage, the table and chairs upstage slid off and I placed the lion on the table as it left and I walked down into the factory to meet Kevin [McKidd as Todd]. I was wearing a cream calico apron that echoed Annabelle's nightdress and I had had my long hair dyed the same golden colour as hers so it really was very clear that I was her grown up.

As to the evolution of the play, *Far Away* was a fully formed piece of art before we got our hands on it, but Stephen gave it a visual life that is not necessarily evident in the text. For example I completed over 150 authentic actions as the hat maker in Scene 2. It was extremely tightly choreographed and this took shape through trial and error throughout the four-and-a-half-week rehearsal process. Kevin and I had hat-making lessons with a milliner, and we faithfully recreated these skills in the play. It needed to be plausible that I could have created the exquisite Philip Treacy hat. It became evident that I needed a tool kit that was full of the bits I would need. Kevin, I believe, had a more manly box of tools. And I had a roll of them including a silver thimble of my Grandmother's that I lost on the penultimate night in the West End. I had the thimble as I kept pricking myself on stage, and it is a bit disconcerting to be bleeding and acting. I remember that my stitching on stage would reflect the scene. In the furious argument of 2.3 the stitches were wildly erratic. I had to dye and dry peacock-blue feathers, and we were not sure how to do this in a way that would be visually interesting and I suppose that in itself is a clue to Stephen's style. I suggested a salad spinner which I pumped on furiously in the fight. The feathers whizzed around in a very satisfactory way.

You ask me what it was like being in a fifty-minute play. Well, only half of that was dialogue. It was extremely detailed physical work that showed the audience we were getting on with the work competitively and with complete disregard for the victims who would parade them, which incidentally were thirty-strong in our production and, in a bizarre twist, I helped to choose them with the assistant director, Nina Raine. I was absorbed in the finishing touches to the hat when I looked straight out into the audience to muse that it seemed so sad to burn them with the bodies. That floored the audience – I know it did. The combination of action and dialogue. Stephen and Caryl complement each other perfectly in my mind. She is devastatingly quiet and he flamboyant, which I think is why they make such good theatre together.

As to the evolution of the text, again it was pretty much there, but Caryl was in every rehearsal and when I struggled to activate the text of the final speech (I had a tendency to use a falling cadence for each line so that Stephen couldn't locate an immediacy with it). Caryl added to the end of the speech and then at the eleventh hour the rewrites were removed and the upshot was that I had stopped saying the last line – 'The water laps around your ankles in any case' – like it was the last line and we had a major breakthrough. The play just needed to be left hanging there, and the great heavy front cloth bashed into the stage with an amplified thud like the building was falling down and the theatre had been broken.

To get to grips with talking about killing cats and children under five and being mortally afraid of butterflies and deer takes some doing. It was a leap of faith and a tone that the play requires above all else. You mustn't flag up the preposterousness of this. It is deadly serious and terrifying that we were burning the grass that wouldn't serve. The pity of it still makes me well up. The black-and-white cows downstream having a drink still terrify me, and I was brought up on a dairy farm. Caryl remained calm and simple about this throughout. They were facts.

Everything about doing this play was odd really. It is the piece of work that I am still most proud of being involved with. It took me a while to recover from it. But why not when work is of this calibre? It is a gruelling play with a gruelling message and a terrifyingly light style of playing. Devastating really.

A Number (2002)

A Number *was directed by Stephen Daldry, part of whose interview on the play is given here (1); this is followed by comments from Sarah Wooley, who was assistant director (2). The last piece is an attempted telephone interview with Sam Shepard, who played Salter in New York (3).*

1. Stephen Daldry

As cloning is such a topical issue, both in the newspapers and in our general social conscience at the moment, it is inevitable that a lot of people will think that this play is about cloning. In fact I don't think that this play is an examination of the political and social issues regarding cloning, nor necessarily is it a play which explores the scientific or medical consequences and implications of cloning. The cloning which causes the play to occur is not really the subject of the play. I suppose the subject of the play is the nature of free will: what is free will, and in that sense is free will determined by your genetics or is free will determined by your environment? In simple terms it's a conflict between nature and nurture.

The main difficulties . . . I think Caryl always thought the production was probably going to be very simple, but simplicity is always the hardest thing to achieve. We had to go through quite a long process of deciding what exactly the world of the play was, how specific we needed to be and how non-specific. We have one actor playing three characters. We had to decide whether we needed to note the changes in character and how to note those changes, whether the actor needs to go off and do a full change of costume. Of course the issues about the full change would be that if you were going to do it, you can't just swap glasses or change hairstyle.

If you were going to do it rigidly and really properly you would need different wigs, you would need different make-up depending on what quality of skin they had at this point, as well as different behavioural characteristics.

In the end we decided not to do full changes, and found that it would be more powerful to allow the audience to realise that the character has changed in behaviour, rather than notating it through outward choices of costume, or indeed anything to do with the physical body that might be different because of their different upbringing. But that whole choice was obviously a complicated process to go through, and indeed the set that we've ended up with is certainly nothing like the set that we started off with . . .

Often the sentences that the characters say are half sentences and half thoughts. There is a large amount of repetition and jumping thoughts. The first thing you have to do is to examine the text as if everything was written, and you have to know exactly what the preceding thought is and what the subsequent thought is, and where the leaps are happening. So the first period of rehearsal is quite a close textual study to actually understand exactly what they would be saying. You just take one simple sentence and explain that sentence to understand exactly what Caryl has left in, but you can only really know what she's left in when you can understand what she's taken out.[20]

2. Sarah Wooley

Caryl came in quite a lot. She changed one word. The line in the last scene, which was 'We've got ninety per cent the same as a chimpanzee' became '. . . ninety-eight per cent . . .' Somebody had gone away and discovered that ninety per cent was incorrect . . . she was completely unobtrusive. She just lets you get on with it. You can always go and ask her, and she does have an answer . . . the actors [Michael Gambon and Daniel Craig] were fantastic. They both got on brilliantly. Daniel is understated; everything is so small and so intense. He was perfect for the part.

We started in Week 1 just going through the script. Caryl was there for that. We worked out the beats and where new thoughts began, and where a new chapter began. They got it on its feet fairly quickly, about the end of the first week. We'd work out what had happened before the scene started because they always start in the middle of an argument or the middle of a conversation.

Then Stephen just made them learn it. For the last two weeks, he just drove them hard, lines, lines, lines. When we did the first preview, we had this thing about how to distinguish between B1 and B2. We knew we were going to do it really simply, cutting back on everything. I remember at least two previews where Daniel changed his shoes. He would come up the steps at the back, and the last thing you would see were the shoes. Around the set was a kind of black oil, like a lake, really black. In the first previews people just used to laugh because Daniel would wear shoes as B1, and then return as B2 in bright red shoes or something. So the shoe change was cut. It was signalling too much. It was really a question of how much you wished to give away. We used to tell the box office not to tell people who rang up what the play was about. We finally distinguished between B1 and B2 via the accent. So in the first scene B2 was very received pronunciation (RP); in Scene 2, B1 was very cockney. Then back to RP as B2. Michael in the final scene was done in a Liverpool accent.

The play is so there. All there for you. It's exactly perfect.

3. Sam Shepard

You're appearing in Caryl Churchill's A Number. *What attracted you to her work?*
Well, it's kind of hard to say. I encountered the play in Australia, and I thought it was really fascinating, and I had no idea it would have a world premiere in New York.

Do you feel a kinship between her work and yours?
Not really. Only in the sense that I feel she's also inspired by Beckett.

Can you speak about your character, Salter?
No, I can't. Well, obviously he's a complicated . . . I can't do pocket reviews of this thing. This isn't going to work.

Um, do you think the play has something to say about cloning?
I can't describe the play. It's too complex. To me, the cloning
aspect is uninteresting. That's not what it's about. It has to do
with identity.

Can you elaborate on that, what it says about identity?
I have a feeling this really isn't going to work. I can't capsulize
it. I'd really rather not. I can't capsulize this. Thanks anyway.
[*Click*]²¹

A Dream Play (2005)

*Actors Angus Wright (1) and Sean Jackson (2) discuss the
rehearsals.*

1. Angus Wright

One of Katie and Caryl's instincts concerning the material was
that the language should not be anchored to Sweden in 1900
but be more attuned to a London audience in 2005. Perhaps
the most far-reaching decision, which I believe was forming in
Katie's mind at this time, and she certainly voiced by the second
or third week of rehearsal, was that we should attempt to create a dream on stage rather than a play. We began exploring
dreams, putting our own dreams 'on their feet' in the rehearsal
room and even some of those recorded by Freud and Jung.
What quickly became clear was that Strindberg's play (and
Caryl's version of it) was full of extended dialogue (obscure
and surreal though it was), whereas dreams rarely seem to have
much dialogue and indeed frequently feature no language at
all. What is important to remember is that none of us had any
idea in the first weeks of rehearsal where we were headed and
what the end result would be. We created material (i.e., scenar-
ios or dream sequences suggested by and directly influenced by
the text) and then began to shape these and order them. By
Christmas we had half an hour of material and Katie reckoned
we needed around ninety minutes by the opening night.

By this point our work had begun to diverge significantly from the text as written by Caryl, but she was always on hand or in close email contact to suggest the most accurate and appropriate choice of word or phrase.

2. Sean Jackson

Caryl was present at some discussions. She was in no way precious about the script, encouraged the exploratory process and certainly didn't mind if things weren't used or if we threw in a line of our own, e.g., some of the security supervisor's comments to the stage-door keeper were improvised lines. Because we were striving to recreate a dream on the stage, the text was only part of the process and not the whole (if you understand what I mean). I felt that Caryl understood that adding things and taking things away from the script were necessary and vital, and this attitude made the job much easier. She once even threw a couple of her own dreams into the 'pot', which we then enacted! On one occasion, after Caryl had been present at rehearsals, Katie said that Caryl had decided that a couple of my lines sounded wrong and had written something to replace them for the security man.

Some parts of Caryl's script never appeared in the final production:

Blind Man – improvised the scene but was cut eventually.
Officer – renamed Broker.
Bill Sticker – changed to security supervisor called Reg in Stock Exchange in Real world, became the same job in Broker's Dream World at Covent Garden.
Building Workers – cut.

We Turned on the Light (2006)

With a text by Churchill and music by Orlando Gough, this ten-minute work on the disaster of climate change was performed by Gough's vocal group, The Shout, and youth and

adult choirs across the UK, at the Proms on 29 July 2006.
Churchill's text is modelled on the medieval poem 'There Was
a Man of Double Deed'. Gough explains how the collaboration
came about (1); and this is followed by Churchill's text (2).

1. Orlando Gough

Caryl and I talked originally about a medieval poem we both
liked – 'There Was a Man of Double Deed' – in which an innocent
action leads eventually to disastrous consequences. This gave
Caryl the idea of writing a lyric about climate change, a potentially 'worthy' subject, but one that she treats of course with great
subtlety and power. There are three elements to the lyrics:

1. Actions and their consequences: 'We turned on the light /
   And flooded the city . . .'
2. Guilt towards one's descendants: 'My granddaughter's
   granddaughter says to my ghost . . .'
3. The immaculately sinister line: 'The flowers are growing
   higher up the mountain.'

I had already (rather dangerously) decided to flout the usual conventions of writing choral music for large forces by writing a piece
at an exclusively high tempo, really urgent, like a train approaching at speed; and of course the lyric idea worked very well with
this, the obvious urgency of the issue reflected in the music.

The music is scored for orchestra and 500 singers, divided
into three groups: The Shout; choral societies; volunteer amateur singers ('the rabble'). The three groups have different functions in the music which attempt to play to their strengths. The
choral societies carry the written lyrics, and lead the difficult
harmonic changes in the music; the rabble has an exuberant
answering part, singing mostly nonsense syllables of my own
invention, comment on what they have heard the choral societies sing, their role being rather like that of a brass section on
a big band; and The Shout has a slippery, slightly anarchic part,
including short solos for some of the singers, that glues the
piece together. The piece is, essentially, a musically sophisticat-

ed piece of agit-prop – a strange piece to find in the Proms (but none the worse for that I think).

2. Caryl Churchill

We turned on the light
And flooded the city

We drove the car faster
And saw the dust blowing

We bought a new t-shirt
And turned the grass yellow

We ate cherries in winter
And heard the gale howling

We wrapped food in plastic
And saw the bears starving

We chopped down a forest
And heard a child choking

We doubled our output
And killed to get water

We flew to the sunshine
And saw the ice falling

My granddaughter's granddaughter says to my ghost,
I hate you.

My ghost says, Sorry, I'm sorry now.

My granddaughter's granddaughter says to my ghost,
Didn't you love me?

My ghost says, Not enough.
It's hard to love people far away in time.

The flowers are growing higher up the mountain.

Drunk Enough to Say I Love You? (2006)

In two emails to Philip Roberts (8 Dec. 2006 and 6 Nov. 2007), Churchill explained an unwitting confusion about the play (1); and the play's director, James Macdonald, talks about rehearsals (2).

1. Caryl Churchill

People have taken the show to be: Sam = USA and Jack = Britain, which isn't what I meant. Sam is Uncle Sam all right, but Jack was supposed to be just a person. I shot myself in the foot by calling him Jack. He didn't have a name at all 'til long after the play was written, and I tried to think of a name that would just be an ordinary name, and Jack (as in Beanstalk, Giantkiller, I'm all right) seemed that, and I didn't, stupidly, think of Union Jack. I should have called him Jonathan or Fred. It doesn't work as Jack = Britain because it doesn't fit the actual politics – Britain didn't join in Vietnam, and in other ways too it would have to be different if it was meant to fit that relationship. What I wanted to write was about the way most people (in Britain, or other Western countries, or anywhere, almost) are a bit in love with America, whether it's movies, ice-cream or ideals, and are then implicated in all this stuff it does.

In productions in other languages, the Jack character can be someone from that country. In an American production, it could be even an American, a citizen patriotically in love with his country, though when we take it to New York it has to be an English person, since we're an English company. We will try to make what we mean a bit clearer. It may be as simple as giving Jack a surname in the programme, though I hate relying on anyone looking at a programme. It seems far more theatrically interesting that one character is a person, and the other a country, as well as assaying something slightly different. I wouldn't have bothered to write the play people assume I've written, which is annoying, and I blame myself for not getting it quite right.

The Bush/Blair thing – how people can take it to be about Bush or Blair I don't know, since it goes back over fifty years of events and is part of the point, of course – was to point out that America's been like this for a long time, not just under Bush. The Britain following America thing is so strong in people's minds that it overrides anything that's actually in the play, I think, and of course it was a factor in taking me in that direction, although it wasn't where I ended up. Still, the basic setup, love for America and bad stuff America does, is there either way.

... *Drunk* gets to New York at last in the spring [2008]. I'm thinking of calling Jack Guy to try and get away from the Union Jack thing and help steer people to seeing it's a play with one cartoon person and one real one. But it probably won't work. Heyho.

2. James Macdonald

We started from the same place as any play – you just have to listen to what the words are telling you, and gradually piece together the underlying architecture of the thing. To have so few instructions is a pleasure and a privilege. The lack of punctuation is in itself a kind of instruction. I love the fact that Caryl has moved such a long way stylistically, from the total precision of her earlier work, with its trademark pattern of interruptions, to the much freer shape of her more recent work, where it's really up to the director to excavate the right rhythm for the text.

To begin with we had to inform ourselves of the political background to the material – to know the argument as it were. Then to make sense of time in the piece, to find some kind of continuum, given that it doesn't sit in real time. And finally to investigate the emotional truth of the love story, and work out how to play that without losing sight of the underlying political argument.

It took a while and lots of experiment to find what seemed the right language for the production. When real time is as shredded as it is in this text it's hard to decide what to show. In the end it seemed to us we needed to show the love story that made the material complex and rich – the perversion of loving the person or thing you know is bad for you, or just plain wrong. So it felt more important to make a world for that than to show any reality to the political work, which is anyway skipping through time so fast it would be hard to capture. On the other hand, it felt consistent with the love story to show what one might call the drugs strand in the story – cups of coffee, class A chemicals, a cigarette. The combination of romance and politics eventually led us to a sofa in mid-air, both domestic and intimate, but also somehow removed from reality. And of course there's a scene set in space! This left the problem of how to make props appear and disappear instantly. Eugene [Lee, designer] suggested the language of nineteenth-century illusionism, and we chose a version where the characters simply dropped everything over the side of the sofa, which seemed to fit very well with both their isolation from the real world, and their complete carelessness about the planet. The frame of light bulbs around the pros arch stops the audience from seeing stage managers in ninja gear catching falling props . . .

The music between scenes felt necessary both as a rest from the density of the text, and as a way of rewinding or wiping the slate clean – in terms of political reference every scene seems to start at the beginning again, tracking through fifty years of American foreign policy. As the scenes are organised thematically, Matthew [Herbert] created the music by recording and sampling the sound of materials that related to those themes – from shell cases to election crowds to instruments of torture. But there was also a simple melody, the love theme if you want, which helped to carry forward the emotional arc of the story.

Caryl was always there – she loves being in rehearsal and is an impeccable contributor to the process, brilliant at standing back from her own writing. We made one or two small cuts and even added a line or two just to clarify certain arguments.

Notes

INTRODUCTION
 1. Email to Philip Roberts, Dec. 2006.
 2. *Doty and Harbin*, pp. 144–5.

1 *DOWNSTAIRS* TO *HENRY'S PAST*
 1. H. Carpenter, *OUDS: A Centenary History of the Oxford University Dramatic Society 1885–1985* (Oxford: Oxford University Press, 1985), p. 166.
 2. Unpublished interview with Colin Chambers, 18 Oct. 1991.
 3. *Chambers*, pp. 267–72.
 4. Ibid., p. 269.
 5. J. Thurman, 'Caryl Churchill the Playwright', *Ms*, May 1982.
 6. Unpublished interview with Colin Chambers, 18 Oct. 1991.
 7. *O'Malley*, p. 35.
 8. *Shorts*, Introduction.
 9. *O'Malley*, pp. 41–2.
10. Daniel Paul Schreber, *Memoirs of My Nervous Illness*. Introduction by R. Dinnage; trans. I. Macalpine and R. A. Hunter (New York: New York Review Book, 1955), pp. 74–7.
11. *Shorts*, Introduction.
12. F. Fanon, *The Wretched of the Earth* (Harmondsworth: Penguin, 1967), p. 222.
13. Ibid., p. 200.
14. Ibid., p. 203.
15. Ibid., p. 214.
16. Ibid., pp. 220–1.
17. Ibid., p. 221.

2 *OWNERS* TO *CLOUD NINE*
 1. *Chambers*, pp. 270–1.
 2. J. Heilpern, *John Osborne: A Patriot for Us* (Chatto and Windus, 2006), pp. 374–5.
 3. *Itzin*, p. 282.

4. The text is published in *Plays by Women*, vol. 4, selected and introduced by Michelene Wandor (Methuen, 1985).

5. Afterword by Churchill on *Objections to Sex and Violence*, in *Plays by Women*, vol. 4, selected and introduced by Michelene Wandor (Methuen, 1985).

6. Letter to Philip Roberts, n.d.

7. Introduction, *Plays: 1*.

8. *Ritchie,* part one; *Roberts/Stafford Clark*, pp. 21–9.

9. *Hanna*, p. xxxvii.

10. Introduction, *Plays: 1*.

11. *Doty and Harbin*, p. 155.

12. *Ritchie*, p. 118.

13. *Roberts/Stafford-Clark*, p. 24.

14. *Ritchie*, pp. 118–19.

15. Ibid., p. 119.

16. Ibid., pp. 103, 104.

17. *Plays and Players*, Feb. 1982.

18. The remarkable parallels between the play and contemporary politics was noted in press reactions to the 1997 revival at the National Theatre. See particularly Fiachra Gibbons, *Guardian*, 11 January 1997.

19. Introduction, *Plays: 1*.

20. Introduction, *Plays: 1*.

21. Production Note, *Plays: 1*.

22. *Fitzsimmons*, p. 34.

23. *Vinegar Tom* in *Plays by Women*, vol. 1, selected and edited by Michelene Wandor (Methuen, 1982), pp. 41–2.

24. *Hanna*, p. xxxix. See also *Hanna,* pp. xl–xli, and Michelene Wandor, *Carry on Understudies: Theatre and Sexual Politics* (Routledge, 1986), pp. 71, 187–8.

25. *Time Out*, 29 Oct.–3 Nov. 1977.

26. *Omnibus*, BBC 1, 4 Nov. 1988.

27. *Roberts/Stafford-Clark*, p. 72.

28. Ibid., p. 74.

29. Ibid., p. 82.

30. *Platform Papers*, no. 8, National Theatre, 30 April 1993.

31. *Omnibus*, BBC 1, 4 Nov. 1988.

32. The progress from workshop to performance is also chronicled by Tony Sher in *Ritchie*, pp. 138–42.

33. *Omnibus*, BBC 1, 4 Nov. 1988.
34. *Cousin*, pp. 38–9.

3 *THREE MORE SLEEPLESS NIGHTS* TO *ICECREAM* AND *HOT FUDGE*

1. Waters joined the Royal Court as an assistant director in 1979. He was Assistant Director to Stafford-Clark on *Cloud Nine*. When the play was revived at the Court in September 1980, he became Co-Director, but as he says, it was 'nonsense. How do you co-direct with your boss when he was director of the original production?' Email to Philip Roberts, 24 Mar. 2007
2. *New York Times*, 22 Nov. 1987.
3. *Hanna*, p. xlvii.
4. Email to Philip Roberts, 30 June 2006.
5. *Omnibus*, BBC 1, 4 Nov. 1988.
6. Ibid.
7. Ibid.
8. *Plays and Players*, Jan. 1984.
9. *Omnibus*, BBC 1, 4 Nov. 1988.
10. *Cousin*, p. 47.
11. *Plays: 3*.
12. Rob La Frenais, *Performance*, no. 30, June–July 1984.
13. Ros Asquith, *City Limits*, 18 May 1984.
14. Lynne Truss, *Plays and Players*, Jan. 1984.
15. Author's Note, *Plays: 2*.
16. Lynne Truss, *Plays and Players*, Jan. 1984.
17. *Plays: 2*.
18. Introduction, *Plays: 3*.
19. Interview with G. Cousin, *New Theatre Quarterly*, vol. 4, no. 13, 8. Lan's book is: *Guns and Rain: Guerrillas and Spirit Mediums in Zimbabwe* (Curry, 1985). His plays are published by Faber and Faber.
20. *Plays: 3*, p. vii.
21. *Cousin*, p. 56.
22. *Omnibus*, BBC 1, 4 Nov. 1988.
23. *New Statesman*, 23 March 1987.
24. *Roberts/Stafford-Clark*, p. 129.
25. *New Theatre Quarterly*, vol. 5, no. 19, Aug. 1989.
26. Quotations are from a script dated 2 Jan. 1988, lent to me by

Caryl Churchill. The critic for the *New York Times* describes
meeting Churchill in the summer of 1987: 'That day . . . she had
spent hours playing a single Bach fugue over and over on the
piano, trying to analyse and understand its structure. It was like
taking apart a clock or a car . . . to see how it works' (22 Nov.
1987).

27. *New Statesman,* 21 April 1989.
28. *New York Times,* 29 April 1990.
29. *Independent,* 12 April 1989.
30. *New Statesman,* 21 April 1989.
31. *New York Times,* 29 April 1990.
32. *Independent,* 12 April 1989.
33. Letter to the chairman of the English Stage Company, 3 Nov.
1989.

4 *MAD FOREST* TO *OUR LATE NIGHT*

1. *The Times,* 10 Oct. 1990.
2. 'To Romania with Love', *Guardian,* 13 Oct. 1990.
3. *Plays: 3.*
4. Production Note.
5. Mark Wing-Davey directed an American company in the play at
both the New York Theater Workshop and the Manhattan
Theater Club. Wing-Davey won an Obie for his direction.
6. *Plays: 3.*
7. The music is in *Lives of the Great Poisoners: A Production
Dossier* (Methuen, 1993). This volume also contains an
Introduction by the designer, Antony McDonald, and an
Introduction by the composer Orlando Gough, which is omitted
in *Plays: 3.* The *Dossier,* apart from the musical score, also
contains a breakdown of the performers' roles and some
illustrations.
8. Ibid., p. xii.
9. *Plays: 3.*
10. *Lives of the Great Poisoners: A Production Dossier* (Methuen,
1993), p. xiii.
11. *Platform Papers,* no. 8, National Theatre, 30 April 1993, p. 20.
12. *Independent,* 20 Jan. 1994.
13. *Plays: 3.*
14. Ibid.

15. Ian Spink, Introduction to *Hotel* (Nick Hern Books, 1997).
16. Introduction to *Hotel* (Nick Hern Books, 1997).
17. Minutes of Out of Joint board meeting, 14 July 1997.
18. Stafford-Clark, *The Times*, 24 Aug. 1997.
19. *Village Voice*, 27 Jan.–2 Feb. 1999.
20. *Guardian*, 25 Nov. 1998.
21. Email to Philip Roberts, 4 May 2007.
22. *Time Out*, 27 Oct. 1999.

5 FAR AWAY TO DRUNK ENOUGH TO SAY I LOVE YOU?

1. *Village Voice*, 16 Nov. 2004.
2. The play was given at the Crucible Theatre's Studio. It was played in the round with raked seating enclosing the playing area. Michael's line about the genetic make-up of a lettuce drew an incredulous gasp from the audience.
3. *Observer*, 21 Sept. 2003.
4. M. Shevtsova, 'On Directing: a Conversation with Katie Mitchell'. *New Theatre Quarterly*, vol. 22, Feb. 2006, p. 17.
5. Katie Mitchell, 'Director's Note', production programme.
6. Email to Philip Roberts, 7 April 2006.
7. Ibid., 20 Aug. 2006.
8. Ibid., 8 Dec. 2006.
9. Ibid., 24 July 2007.

PART 2

1. *Ritchie*, pp. 118–21.
2. *Time Out*, 24–30 Sept. 1976.
3. *Hanna*, p. xxxvii.
4. G. Hanna, 'Feminism and Theatre', *Theatre Papers*, second series, no. 8, Dartington, 1978.
5. *Itzin*, p. 276.
6. K. Betsko and R. Koenig (eds), *Interviews with Contemporary Women Playwrights* (New York: Beech Tree Books, 1987), p. 81.
7. *Itzin*, p. 280.
8. Ibid., p. 281.
9. *Hanna*, p. xxxix.
10. It is part published in *Fitzsimmons*, pp. 48–54.
11. *Ritchie*, p. 138.
12. Penelope Shuttle and Peter Redgrove, *The Wise Wound: Menstruation and Everywoman* (Marion Boyers, 1975).

13. *Fitzsimmons*, p. 62.
14. L. Goodman, 'Overlapping Dialogue in Overlapping Media: Behind the Scenes of Caryl Churchill's *Top Girls*, in S. Rabillard (ed.), *Essays on Caryl Churchill: Contemporary Representations* (Winnipeg: Blizzard Publishing, 1998).
15. *Ritchie,* pp. 150–2.
16. *Fitzsimmons*, p. 83.
17. *Theatre Craft,* Feb. 1988.
18. *Guardian*, 13 Oct. 1990.
19. *Lives of the Great Poisoners: A Production Dossier* (Methuen, 1993), pp.xvii–xviii.
20. Royal Court Education Resources – *A Number* (http//:www.royalcourttheatre.com).
21. *New York Magazine*, Fall 2004.

Select Bibliography

A – Primary Material

(Place of publication, unless otherwise stated, is London.)

Plays in Collections

Plays: 1   *Owners*; *Traps*; *Vinegar Tom*; *Light Shining in Buckinghamshire*; *Cloud Nine*. Introduced by the author (Methuen, 1996).

Plays: Two *Softcops*; *Top Girls*; *Fen*; *Serious Money*. Introduced by the author (Methuen, 1990).

Plays: 3   *Icecream*; *Mad Forest*; *Thyestes* (with Introduction); *The Skriker*; *Lives of the Great Poisoners* (co-authors: Orlando Gough and Ian Spink; with Introductions); *A Mouthful of Birds* (with David Lan) (Nick Hern Books, 1998).

Shorts: *Lovesick* (radio); *Abortive* (radio); *Not . . . Not . . . Not . . . Not . . . Not Enough Oxygen* (radio); *Schreber's Nervous Illness* (radio); *The Hospital at the Time of the Revolution* (stage, unperformed); *The Judge's Wife* (television); *The After-Dinner Joke* (television); *Seagulls* (stage, unperformed); *Three More Sleepless Nights* (stage); *Hot Fudge* (stage). Introduced by the author (Nick Hern Books, 1990).

Single Volumes/Other Collections

The Ants, in New English Dramatists, vol. 12 (Harmondsworth: Penguin, 1968).

Vinegar Tom, in *Plays by Women*, vol. 1, selected and intro-

duced by Michelene Wandor (Methuen, 1982). With an
Afterword by Churchill.

Objections to Sex and Violence, in *Plays by Women*, vol. 4,
selected and introduced by Michelene Wandor (Methuen,
1985). With an Afterword by Churchill.

Top Girls, with Commentary and Notes by Bill Naismith,
Methuen Student Edition (Methuen, 1991).

Mad Forest: A Play from Romania (Nick Hern Books, rev.
edn 1991). Contains a chronology and other details.

Lives of the Great Poisoners: A Production Dossier (Methuen,
1993). Introductions by the three collaborators, illustrations and the musical score.

Hotel (Nick Hern Books, 1997). Introductions by Churchill,
Gough and Spink.

Blue Heart (Nick Hern Books, 1997).

This Is a Chair (Nick Hern Books, 1999).

Far Away (Nick Hern Books, 2000).

A Number (Nick Hern Books, 2002).

A Dream Play (Nick Hern Books, 2005).

Drunk Enough to Say I Love You? (Nick Hern Books, 2006).

Other Original Pieces

ARTICLES

'Not Ordinary, Not Safe: A Direction for Drama?', *The
Twentieth Century*, Nov. 1960, pp. 443–51.

'Driven by Greed and Fear', *New Statesman*, 17 July 1987
(*Serious Money*).

'To Romania with Love', *Guardian*, 13 Oct. 1990 (*Mad
Forest*).

'Theatre, West Bank Style', *Guardian*, 21 Feb. 2001.

LETTERS

To *Plays and Players*, Oct. 1975 (about the closure of the
Theatre Upstairs).

To the *Guardian*, 27 July 1979 (Women's Theatre); 25 Nov.
1998 (Royal Court sponsorship); 10 April 1999 (the former

Yugoslavia); 21 Feb. 2001 (West Bank Theatre); 23 June 2001 (on *Top Girls* in Israel); 23 Feb. 2002 (Julie Burchill and *Top Girls*); 6 March 2002 (America and Britain); 25 March 2004 (carnage in Gaza); 16 April 2004 (Bush and Israel); 12 July 2006 (Israel's oppression of Palestine).

Letter to Richard Seyd, *Fitzsimmons*, pp. 48–54 (*Cloud Nine*).

Letter to Tony Garnett, *New Statesman*, 27 March 1987 (*Perdition*).

Letter resigning from the Council of the English Stage Company, 3 Nov. 1989.

INTERVIEWS

Churchill has declined all requests for interviews since 1997. In an interview with Linda Fitzsimmons (*Fitzsimmons*, 91), she explained why:

> I dislike the feeling of being pinned down as being one thing or another, a feeling that that definition is perhaps limiting what people expect of you.
>
> I don't think things you say in interviews necessarily reflect your work . . . I think I tend to respond to the questions asked as if I believed there was a correct answer which I don't quite know, and will I be able to come up with it. And another thing: whenever I read them, they're nearly always misquotes anyway . . .

Given that the interviews are already in the public domain, they are listed below, but they should be treated with caution and with both due regard to the context and to the misgivings of the writer.

Armistead, C., *Guardian*, 12 Jan. 1994.
Barber, J., *Daily Telegraph*, 21 Feb. 1983.
Benedict, D., *Independent*, 19 April 1997.
Betsko, K. and R. Koenig (eds), *Interviews with Contemporary Women Playwrights* (New York: Beech Tree

Books, 1987).

Billington, M., *Third Ear*, Radio 3, 17 April 1989.

Clayton, P., *Round Midnight*, Radio 2, 7 July 1987.

Cousin, G., *New Theatre Quarterly*, vol. 4, no. 13, 1988.

Crowley, J., *Radio Times*, 10–16 April 1982.

Fitzsimmons, L., in *Fitzsimmons, 1989 (passim)*.

Gooch, S., *Plays and Players*, Jan. 1973.

Gussow, M., *New York Times*, 22 Nov. 1987.

Hall, J., *Guardian*, 12 Dec. 1972.

Hayman, R., *Sunday Times Magazine*, 2 March 1980.

Hiley, J., *The Times*, 10 Oct. 1990.

Jackson, K., *Independent*, 12 April 1989.

Kay, J., *New Statesman*, 21 April 1989.

'Late Theatre', BBC2, Jan. 1994.

McFerran, A., *Time Out*, 28 Oct.–3 Nov. 1974.

Mackrell, J., *Independent*, 20 Jan. 1994.

Marcus, F., *Sunday Telegraph*, 17 Dec. 1972.

Omnibus on Caryl Churchill, BBC1, 4 Nov. 1988.

Platform Papers, Royal National Theatre, no. 8, April 1993.

Radin, V., *Observer*, 15 Aug. 1988.

Rose, M., *Sipario*, Nov.–Dec. 1987.

Simon, J., *Vogue*, Aug. 1983.

Stone, L., *Village Voice*, 1 March 1980.

Thurman, J., *Ms*, May 1982.

Truss, L., *Plays and Players*, Jan. 1984.

Vidal, J. *Guardian*, 21 Nov. 1986.

Winer, L., *New York Times*, 29 April 1990.

B – Secondary Sources

The Churchill critical industry is huge. Below is given a selection of material which has been useful.

Ashley, J., 'Thatcher's exit means that women can be themselves', *Guardian*, 27 March 2002.

Asquith, R., *City Limits*, 18 May 1984. (*Midday Sun*)

Aston, E., *Caryl Churchill*, 'Writers and Their Work' (Tavistock: Northcote House, 2nd edn 2001).

Briggs, M., *The Fairies in Tradition and Literature* (Routledge, 1967). (*The Skriker*)
'British Theatre in Crisis', *New Theatre Quarterly*, vol. 5, no. 9, Aug. 1989.

Carpenter, H., *OUDS: A Centenary History of the Oxford University Dramatic Society 1885–1985* (Oxford: Oxford University Press, 1985).
Chamberlain, M., *Fenwomen: A Portrait of Women in an English Village* (Virago, 1975).
Chambers, C., *Peggy: The Life of Margaret Ramsay, Play Agent* (Nick Hern Books, 1997).
——, and M. Prior, *Playwrights' Progress: Patterns of Post-War British Drama* (Oxford: Amber Lane, 1987).
Cohn, N., *The Pursuit of the Millennium: Revolutionary Millenarians and Mystical Anarchists of the Middle Ages* (Pimlico, 1970). (*Light Shining in Buckinghamshire*)
Cousin, G., *Churchill the Playwright* (Methuen, 1989). First attempt at an account of the plays up to 1987.
——, 'Owning the Disowned: *The Skriker* in the Context of Earlier Plays by Caryl Churchill', in S. Rabillard (ed.), *Essays on Caryl Churchill: Contemporary Representations* (Winnipeg: Blizzard Publishing, 1998).

Davies, Siobhan, *Observer*, 21 Sept. 2003. (*Plants and Ghosts*)
De Angelis, April, 'Riddle of the Sphinx', *Guardian*, 10 Sept. 2005.
Doty, G. A. and B. J. Harbin (eds), *Inside the Royal Court, 1956–1981: Artists Talk* (Louisiana: Louisiana State University, 1990).
Dymkowski, C., 'Caryl Churchill: Far Away . . . but Close to Home', *European Journal of English Studies*, vol. 7, no. 1, 2003, pp. 55–68.

Edgar, D., 'Ripe for a Dramatic Change', *Sunday Times*, 9 Oct. 1994.

Ehrenreich, B. and D. English, *Witches, Midwives and Nurses: A History of Women Healers* (New York: Feminist Press, 1973). (*Vinegar Tom*)

Fanon, F., *The Wretched of the Earth* (Harmondsworth: Penguin, 1967). Preface by Jean-Paul Sartre. Translated by C. Farrington. (*The Hospital at the Time of the Revolution*)

——, Black Skin, White Masks (New York: Grove Press, 1967).

Figes, E., *Patriarchal Attitudes* (Basingstoke: Macmillan, 1986). With a new introduction by the author. (*Owners*)

Fitzsimmons, L., 'I Won't Turn Back for You or Anyone: Caryl Churchill's Socialist- Feminist Theatre', *Essays in Theatre*, vol. 6, no. 1, 1987, pp. 19–29 (*Top Girls* and *Fen*).

——, *File on Churchill* (Methuen, 1989). Detailed documentary account of the plays up to 1988.

Flaherty, K., 'Feminist Drama: Railing and Redress: A Brief Study of Sarah Daniels' *Byrthrite* and Caryl Churchill's *Top Girls*, *Philament*, no. 2, Jan. 2004.

Foucault, M., *Discipline and Punish* (Harmondsworth: Penguin, 1977). Translated by A. Sheridan. (*Softcops*)

——, *This Is Not a Pipe* (Berkeley: University of California Press, 1983). Translated and edited by J. Harkness. (*This Is a Chair*)

Gardner, J., 'Caryl Churchill's *Top Girls*: Defining and Reclaiming Feminism in Thatcher's Britain', *New England Theatre Journal*, vol. 10, 1999, pp. 89–110.

Gardner, L., 'Material Girls', *Guardian*, 2 Jan. 2002. (*Top Girls*)

Gibbons, F., 'In the 1660s, They Cut the Tongues from Levellers' Mouths. Now They Just Arrest Them', *Guardian*, 11 Jan. 1997. (*Light Shining in Buckinghamshire*)

Goodman, L., 'Overlapping Dialogue in Overlapping Media:

Behind the Scenes of Caryl Churchill's *Top Girls*', in S. Rabillard (ed.), *Essays on Caryl Churchill: Contemporary Representations* (Winnipeg: Blizzard Publishing, 1998).

Gottlieb, V., 'Theatre Today – The "New Realities" ', *Contemporary Theatre Review*, vol. 13, no. 2, May 2003.

Gray, F., 'Mirrors of Utopia: Caryl Churchill and Joint Stock', in J. Acheson (ed.), *British and Irish Drama Since 1960* (Basingstoke: Macmillan, 1993). (*Light Shining in Buckinghamshire*)

Hanna, G., (Selected and Compiled), *Monstrous Regiment: A Collective Celebration* (Nick Hern Books, 1991). (*Vinegar Tom*; *Floorshow*)

Harding, J., 'Cloud Cover: (Re)Dressing Desire and Comfortable Subversions in Caryl Churchill's *Cloud Nine*', *PMLA*, vol. 113, no. 2, 1998, pp. 258–72.

'Hartwell Mints Money In a Hurry', *Theatre Craft*, Feb. 1988. (*Serious Money*)

Heilpern, J., *John Osborne: A Patriot for Us* (Chatto & Windus, 2006).

Hill, C., *The World Turned Upside Down: Radical Ideas During the English Revolution* (Temple Smith, 1972). (*Light Shining in Buckinghamshire*)

Itzin, C., *Stages in the Revolution* (Eyre Methuen, 1980).

Jernigan, D., '*Traps*, *Softcops*, *Blue Heart* and *This Is a Chair*: Tracking Epistemological Upheaval in Caryl Churchill's shorter plays', *Modern Drama*, vol. 47, no. 1, 2004, pp. 21–43.

Keyssar, H., 'The Dramas of Caryl Churchill: The Politics of Possibility', in H. Keyssar, *Feminist Theatre* (Basingstoke: Macmillan, 1984), pp. 77–101.

Kilpatrick, D., 'Same Difference: On Caryl Churchill's *A Number*. James Macdonald in Conversation', *The Brooklyn*

Rail, Nov. 2004.

Kintz, L., 'Performing Capital in Caryl Churchill's *Serious Money*', *Theatre Journal*, vol. 51, no. 3, 1999, pp. 251–65.

Kritzer, A., *The Plays of Caryl Churchill: Theatre of Empowerment* (Basingstoke: Macmillan, 1991).

La Frenais, R., *Performance*, no. 30, June–July 1984. (*Midday Sun*)

Laing, R. D., *The Divided Self* (Harmondsworth: Penguin, 1965). (*The Hospital at the Time of the Revolution*)

Lan, D., *Guns and Rain: Guerrillas and Spirit Mediums in Zimbabwe* (Curry, 1985). (*A Mouthful of Birds*)

Lavell, I., 'Caryl Churchill's *The Hospital at the Time of the Revolution*', *Modern Drama*, vol. 45, no. 1, Spring 2002, pp. 76–94.

Lavender, A. (ed.), 'Theatre in Thatcher's Britain: Organising the Opposition', *New Theatre Quarterly*, vol. 5, no. 18, May 1989.

Lawson, M., 'Mrs. Thatcher and Her Theatricals', *Guardian*, 12 Jan. 2002.

Lott, T., 'Could Thatcher Really Be the Most Important Feminist Role Model of the Past 20 Years?' *Guardian*, 5 Feb. 2002.

McFerran, A., *Time Out*, 24–30 Sept. 1976. (*Light Shining in Buckinghamshire*)

Marohl, J., 'De-realised Women: Performance and Identity in *Top Girls*', *Modern Drama*, vol. 30, no. 3, 1987, pp. 376–88.

Millett, K., *Sexual Politics* (Virago, 1977). (*Cloud Nine*)

Mitchell, T., 'Caryl Churchill's *Mad Forest*: Polyphonic Representations of Southeastern Europe', *Modern Drama*, vol. 36, no. 4, Dec. 1993, pp. 499–511.

Morton, A., *The World of the Ranters: Religious Radicalism in the English Revolution* (Lawrence and Wishart, 1970). (*Light Shining in Buckinghamshire*)

Neblett, R., ' "Nobody Sings About It": In Defense of the Songs in Caryl Churchill's *Vinegar Tom*', *New England Theatre Journal*, vol. 14, 2003, pp. 101–122.

Nightingale, B., 'Chairwoman of the Boards', *The Times*, 13 Nov. 2006.

O'Malley, J. F., 'Caryl Churchill, David Mercer and Tom Stoppard: A Study of Contemporary British Dramatists who have written for Radio, Television and Stage' (unpublished Ph.D, Florida State University, 1974).

Patterson, M., *Strategies of Political Theatre: Post-War British Playwrights* (Cambridge: Cambridge University Press, 2003). (*Cloud Nine*)

Rabillard, S. (ed.), *Essays on Caryl Churchill: Contemporary Representations* (Winnipeg: Blizzard Publishing, 1998). Assorted essays, including ones on *Top Girls* and *Cloud Nine*.

Randall, P. (ed.), *Caryl Churchill: A Casebook* (Garland, 1988).

Reinelt, J., 'Caryl Churchill: Socialist Feminism and Brechtian Dramaturgy', in J. Reinelt's *After Brecht: British Epic Theater* (Michigan: University of Michigan Press, 1994).

——, 'Caryl Churchill and the Politics of Style', in E. Aston and J. Reinelt (eds), *The Cambridge Companion to Modern British Women Playwrights* (Cambridge: Cambridge Unversity Press, 2000), pp. 174–93.

——, 'Navigating Postfeminism: Writing Out of the Box', in E. Aston and G. Harris (eds), *Feminist Futures? Theatre, Performance, Theory* (Basingstoke: Macmillan, 2006).

Ritchie, R., *The Joint Stock Book: The Making of a Theatre Collective* (Methuen, 1987).

Roberts, P., *The Royal Court Theatre and the Modern Stage* (Cambridge: Cambridge University Press, 1999).

——, and M. Stafford-Clark, *Taking Stock: The Theatre of*

Max Stafford-Clark (Nick Hern Books, 2007).

'Sam Shepard, The Silent Type', *New York Magazine*, Sept. 2002. (*A Number*)

Schreber, D. P., *Memoirs of My Nervous Illness* (New York: New York Review Book, 1955). Introduction by R. Dinnage. Translated by I. Macalpine and R. A. Hunter. (*Schreber's Nervous Illness*)

Shadwell, T., *The Volunteers, or the Stock-Jobbers, 1693* (Printed for James Knapton, 1693). (*Serious Money*).

Shepard, S., *Village Voice*, 16 Nov. 2004. (*A Number*)

Sher, A., in R. Ritchie, *The Joint Stock Book: The Making of a Theatre Collective* (Methuen, 1987), pp. 138–42. (*Cloud Nine*)

Shevtsova, M., 'On Directing: A Conversation with Katie Mitchell', *New Theatre Quarterly*, vol. 22, Feb. 2006. (*A Dream Play*)

Solomon, A., 'Witches, Ranters and the Middle Class: The Plays of Caryl Churchill', *Theater*, vol. 12, no. 2, 1981, pp. 49–55. (*Owners, Vinegar Tom* and *Light Shining in Buckinghamshire*)

Soto-Morettini, D., 'Revolution and the Fatally Clever Smile: Caryl Churchill's *Mad Forest*', *Journal of Dramatic Theory and Criticism*, vol. 9, no. 1, 1994, pp. 105–18.

Spare Rib, Jan. 1978. (*Floorshow*)

Stafford-Clark, M., 'A Programme for the Progressive Conscience: the Royal Court in the Eighties', *New Theatre Quarterly*, vol. 1, no. 2, May 1986.

——, *The Times*, 24 Aug. 1997. (*Blue Heart*)

——, *Village Voice*, 27 Jan–2 Feb. 1999. (*Blue Heart*)

Stoller, J., in R. Ritchie, *The Joint Stock Book: The Making of a Theatre Collective* (Methuen, 1987), pp. 150–4. (*Fen*)

Swanson, M., 'Mother/Daughter Relationships in Three Plays by Caryl Churchill', *Theatre Studies*, 31, 1986, pp. 49–66. (*Cloud Nine, Top Girls* and *Fen*)

Time Out, 27 Oct.–3 Nov. 1977. (*Floorshow*)
Time Out, 27 Oct. 1999. (*Our Late Night*)

Wandor, M., *Carry On Understudies: Theatre and Sexual Politics* (Routledge, 1986).
——, *Look Back in Gender: Sexuality and the Family in Post-War British Drama* (Methuen, 1987). (*Owners* and *Top Girls*)
Waters, Les, *New York Times*, 29 April 1990. (*Ice Cream with Hot Fudge*)

Acknowledgements

A huge number of theatre workers responded to my questions, by letter, by email and in interviews. That not one turned me down is a measure of the respect and affection in which the subject of this book is held. My respect for them is not diminished by their being listed alphabetically, together with helpful colleagues.

John Ashford [Director, *Traps, Midday Sun*]; Marion Bailey [*This Is a Chair; Cloud Nine* revival]; Sarah Ball [*Mad Forest*]; Desmond Barrit [*This Is a Chair*]; Linda Bassett [*Fen, Serious Money, Far Away*]; Richard Boon; Chris Bowler [*Vinegar Tom, Floorshow*]; Amelda Brown [*Fen, A Mouthful of Birds*]; Colin Chambers; Penelope Cherns; Steve Cosson [The Civilians Theater Company, New York]; Tony Coult; Ken Cranham [*Owners*]; Jonathan Cullen [*Our Late Night*]; Josefina Cupido [*Floorshow*]; Lee Dalley; John Dobson (Questors Theatre); Katrina Duncan; Karina Fernandez [*Blue Heart*]; Deborah Findlay [*Top Girls*]; Hugh Fraser [*Traps, Cloud Nine* revival]; Bernard Gallagher [*Blue Heart*]; Michael Gambon [*A Number*]; Philippe Giraudeau [*A Mouthful of Birds, The Skriker*]; Orlando Gough [Composer, *Lives of the Great Poisoners, Hotel, We Turned on The Light*]; Gillian Hanna [*Vinegar Tom, Floorshow*]; Peter Hartwell [Designer, *Cloud Nine, Top Girls, Icecream*]; Carole Hayman [*Light Shining . . ., Cloud Nine, Top Girls, Icecream, Hot Fudge*]; Jim Hooper [*Cloud Nine*]; Bill Hoyland [*Cloud Nine*]; Seeta Indrani (*Midday Sun*); Philip Jackson [*Icecream, Hot Fudge*]; Sean Jackson [*A Dream Play*]; Tricia Kelly [*Fen, A Mouthful of Birds*]; Ingrid Lacey [*Our Late Night*]; David Lan [Co-writer,

A *Mouthful of Birds*]; David MacCreedy [*Mad Forest*]; Mary McCusker [*Vinegar Tom, Floorshow*]; James Macdonald [Director, *Lives of the Great Poisoners, Thyestes, A Number*, New York, *Drunk Enough to Say I Love You?*]; Ann McFerran; Kevin McMonagle [*Thyestes*]; Rosemary McHale [*Objections to Sex and Violence*]; Ian MacNeil [Designer, *This Is a Chair, Far Away, A Number*]; Lesley Manville [*Top Girls, Serious Money*]; Joan Mills, [Director, Royal Court Young People's Theatre Scheme, 1975; *Strange Days*]; Mick O'Connor [*Lives of the Great Poisoners*]; Mary O'Malley [*Save It for the Minister*]; Eve Pearce [*Blue Heart*]; Saskia Reeves [*Icecream, Hot Fudge*]; Rob Ritchie [Former Literary Manager and Associate Director of the Royal Court]; Lottie Roach [*A Dream Play*]; Linus Roache [*This Is a Chair*]; Prunella Scales [*Abortive*]; Richard Seyd [Director, *Cloud Nine*, San Francisco]; Bijan Sheibani (*A Dream Play*); Annie Smart [Designer, *Fen, A Mouthful of Birds, The Skriker*]; Ian Spink [Director and Choreographer, *A Mouthful of Birds, Fugue, Lives of the Great Poisoners, The Skriker, Hotel*]; Max Stafford-Clark [Director, *Light Shining . . ., Cloud Nine, Top Girls, Serious Money, Icecream, Hot Fudge, Blue Heart*]; Janine Stanford (National Theatre); Ewan Stewart [*Our Late Night, Thyestes*]; Jennie Stoller [*Fen, Moving Clocks Go Slow, Perfect Happiness*]; Gwen Taylor [*Top Girls*]; Katherine Tozer [*Far Away, Top Girls* revival]; Michelene Wandor [*Floorshow*]; Julian Warren [the Arnolfini Bristol]; Les Waters [Assistant Director, *Cloud Nine*, Director, *Three More Sleepless Nights, Fen, A Mouthful Of Birds, The Skriker, Ice Cream With Hot Fudge*, New York, Maeterlinck pieces, UC, San Diego]; Jason Watkins [*Blue Heart*]; Sam West [*A Number*, Crucible, 2006]; Nicholas Wright [Director, *Owners*]; Mark Wing-Davey [Director, *Mad Forest, Mad Forest* and *Owners*, New York, *The Skriker*, New York, *Top Girls, Serious Money, Hotel*]; Sarah Wooley [Assistant Director, *A Number*, Director, *Three More Sleepless Nights*]; Angus Wright [*A Dream Play*].

A particular thank you to Margaret Flower, who typed it all.

My principal obligation is to Caryl Churchill herself, who lent me unpublished scripts, sent email addresses of colleagues to me, allowed me to visit her, sent me emails about the plays, and who, like those before her, embodies the spirit of the Royal Court Theatre.

For permission to reprint copyright material the publishers gratefully acknowledge the following:

A&C Black for quotations from those of Caryl Churchill's plays it publishes, and selected material from: L. Fitzsimmons, *File on Churchill*, 1989; C.Itzin, *Stages in the Revolution*, 1980; *Lives of the Great Poisoners: A Production Dossier*, 1993.

Professor Lizbeth Goodman for parts of her article, 'Overlapping Dialogue in Overlapping Media: Behind The Scenes of Caryl Churchill's *Top Girls*', in S. Rabillard (ed.), *Essays on Caryl Churchill: Contemporary Representations* (Winnipeg: Blizzard Publishing, 1998).

The Peggy Ramsay Foundation for extracts from three letters sent to Caryl Churchill.

Nick Hern Books for quotations from those of Churchill's plays it publishes, and selected material from: G. Hanna (Selected and Compiled), *Monstrous Regiment: Four Plays and a Collective Celebration*, 1991; P. Roberts and Max Stafford-Clark, *Taking Stock: The Theatre of Max Stafford-Clark*, 2007.

Index